Operation Banner

Also by Nick van der Bijl

Pen and Sword
Nine Battles to Stanley
5th Infantry Brigade in the Falklands
Victory in the Falklands
Confrontation – The War with Indonesia
Commandos in Exile: No 10 (Inter Allied) Commando 1942-45

Osprey
Argentine Forces on the Falklands
Royal Marines 1939-1993
No 10 (Inter Allied) Commando 1942-45

HawkEditions
Brean Down Fort and the Defence of the Bristol Channel

Operation Banner

The British Army in Northern Ireland 1969 to 2007

Nick van der Bijl BEM

Pen & Sword
MILITARY

First published in Great Britain in 2009 by
Pen & Sword Military
an imprint of
Pen & Sword Books Ltd
47 Church Street
Barnsley
South Yorkshire
S70 2AS

Copyright © Nick van der Bijl, 2009
ISBN 978184415 956 7
The right of Nick van der Bijl to be identified as Author of this Work
has been asserted by him in accordance with the
Copyright, Designs and Patents Act 1988.

Typeset in Sabon by Lamorna Publishing Services.

Printed and bound in England by CPI UK.

Pen & Sword Books Ltd. incorporates the imprints of
Pen & Sword Aviation, Pen & Sword Maritime, Pen & Sword Military,
Wharncliffe Local History, Remember When Publications,
Pen & Sword Select, Pen & Sword Military Classics and Leo Cooper.

For a complete list of Pen & Sword titles please contact
PEN & SWORD BOOKS LIMITED
47 Church Street, Barnsley, South Yorkshire, S70 2AS, England
E-mail: enquiries@pen-and-sword.co.uk
Website: www.pen-and-sword.co.uk

Contents

THIS BOOK IS DEDICATED TO THE WIVES, PARENTS, BROTHERS AND SISTERS AND FAMILIES OF THE MEN AND WOMEN OF THE ARMED FORCES WHO SERVED IN NORTHERN IRELAND. THEY ARE A VERY SPECIAL GROUP OF PEOPLE. SOME LIVED IN NORTHERN IRELAND UNDER DIFFICULT CONDITIONS.

ALL WERE BRAVE, DIGNIFIED AND VERY SPECIAL.

Acknowledgements

Northern Ireland is still a sensitive subject for those associated with the campaign 'across the water'. When I set out to write this snapshot of Operation Banner, I decided to research as far as possible public sources; however histories relating to the security forces are few. There were several acquaintances, friends and colleagues who also contributed and to them I am most grateful. Some did not wish for their identities to be divulged. I am most grateful to Jonathan Lee, Harry Long, Shaun Metcalfe, Roy Millard, Rob Millington, Jeff Niblett, Brigadier Andrew Parker-Bowles, Tom Priestley, Stuart Small and Major Gerry Webb for their contributions and to John Triggs of D Squadron The Household Cavalry Association and the Royal Signals Archives.

The CAIN Web Service (Conflict Archive on the Internet) listing details of the conflict and politics in Northern Ireland was invaluable. As to military material, David Barzilay's volumes on *The British Army in Ulster* and Michael Dewar's *The British Army in Northern Ireland* set the military scene. *Operation Banner; An Analysis of Military Operations in Northern Ireland* ordered by General Mike Jackson, when he was Chief of the General Staff, was invaluable although I am not convinced the authors realized just how difficult the campaign was in the early years. Ken Wharton's *A Long, Long War* is essential reading for anyone studying Operation Banner. Northern Ireland is part of our modern military history and I hope that the regiments and corps that fought 'over the water' now begin to include it in some detail in military histories. They have nothing to fear. My principle source in describing the IRA and its factions is Ed Molloy's excellent *History of the IRA* and Tony Geraghty's *The Irish War*. At last, someone has exposed the culture and ideology of the Provisional IRA, as opposed to that wrapped up in folk songs and poems.

This can only be a brief account of the longest operation that the Armed Forces have undertaken in modern times – the defence of Great Britain in Northern Ireland. It is not a history; never really in the public mindset after 1970 and less so today, except for those soldiers, sailors and airmen and their families who live with the consequences of frequent tours, death and destruction and days of uncertainty. In the early years, it was a difficult campaign and then, after 1990, a sideshow to events in the former Yugoslavia, Sierra Leone, the Middle East and Afghanistan. Sent to support Stormont, the Armed Forces found themselves engaging Irish Nationalist insurgency and forced them into a ceasefire in 1974. When the extremists then embarked on a terrorist campaign to create a Marxist state in Great Britain's back door, the Armed Forces contained them until a political solution was first engineered by Prime Minister Major. A problem for the Armed Forces was that although they had successfully dealt with similar campaigns since 1945, Northern Ireland was within easy reach of politicians, judges, policemen and editors in London. The fact is that the IRA badly miscalculated their military abilities and then persisted in terrorism that achieved very little except an invitation to negotiate; an invitation that had first existed in 1970. One wonders whether the current tranquillity in Ulster is merely an interval.

Photographs listed as 'author's collection' are mostly briefing and training aids used in Northern Ireland, their origins not known. I am grateful, as always, to Peter Wood, a former Royal Engineer, for compiling the maps and to John Noble for preparing the index and asking searching questions. I must also thank Brigadier Henry Wilson, the Commissioning Editor.

There is one other person who must be mentioned – my wife, Penny. She also spent two long tours in Northern Ireland. She read the draft and asked searching questions.

The stresses and strains of Service families are frequently forgotten when their men and women go into action and it is therefore to them that I dedicate this book.

Nick van der Bijl
Somerset

Glossary

14 Int	14th Intelligence Company
AAC	Army Air Corps
ADO	Ammunition Disposal Officer
ANFO	Ammonium Nitrate and Fuel Oil
APC	Armoured Personnel Carriers
ASU	Active Service Unit
AVRE	Armoured Vehicles Royal Engineers
CLF	Commander Land Forces
Co-op	Co-operative
CS	Ortho-Chlorobenzal-Malone-Nitrile irritant gas
CWIED	Command Wire IED
ECM	Electronic Counter Measure
EOD	Explosive Ordnance Disposal
FRU	Force Research Unit
GC	George Cross
GHQ	General Headquarters
GOC	General Officer Commanding
HF	High Frequency
HMAV	Her Majesty's Army Vessel
HME	homemade explosive
HMP	Her Majesty's Prison (Service)
ICO	Interim Custody Order
IED	Improvised Explosive Device
INLA	Irish National Liberation Army
Int	Intelligence
IRA	Irish Republican Army
IRSP	Irish Republican Socialist Party
King's	King's Regiment
KOSB	King's Own Scottish Borderers

LI	The Light Infantry
LS	(Helicopter) Landing Site
MRF	Mobile Reconnaissance Force
NICRA	Northern Ireland Civil Rights Association
NORAID	Northern Ireland Aid – Irish-American US based fund-raising group
Para	The Parachute Regiment
PLO	Palestine Liberation Organisation
PVCP	Permanent Vehicle Check Point
PWO	The Prince of Wales Yorkshire Light Infantry Regiment
QC	Queen's Counsel
QLR	Queen's Lancashire Regiment
Queen's	Queen's Regiment
R Anglians	Royal Anglian Regiment
RAF	Royal Air Force
RAOC	Royal Army Ordnance Corps
RAVC	Royal Army Veterinary Corps
RCIED	Radio Controlled IED
RE	Royal Engineers
REST	Royal Engineer Search Teams
RGJ	Royal Green Jackets
RHA	Royal Horse Artillery
RIC	Royal Irish Constabulary
RLC	Royal Logistic Corps
RPG	Rocket Propelled Grenade
RRF	Royal Regiment of Fusiliers
RRW	Royal Regiment of Wales
RTR	Royal Tank Regiment
RUC	Royal Ulster Constabulary
SAS	Special Air Service
SDLP	Social Democratic and Labour Party
Sioux	A light helicopter with a distinctive glass bubble cockpit
SLR	L2A1 FN 7.62mm Self Loading Rifle
SMG	9mm Sterling Sub Machine Gun
SRU	Special Reconnaissance Unit
TD	Teachta Dála – an Irish MP
UDA	Ulster Defence Association
UDR	Ulster Defence Regiment

UFF	Ulster Freedom Fighters – the military wing of the UDA
USC	Ulster Special Constables
UVF	Ulster Volunteer Force
VCP	Vehicle Check Point
VHF	Very High Frequency
VOIED	Victim Operated IED
WRAC	Women's Royal Army Corps

NORTHERN IRELAND

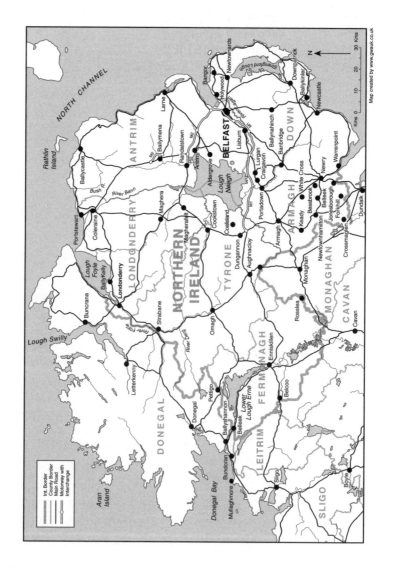

Chapter 1

Background to Irish Nationalism
1169 to 1969

The struggle of the Irish for independence can be traced to 1169 when three longships, with an advance guard of Normans, Welshmen and Flemings sailing from Milford Haven, crunched onto a beach at Bannow Bay, Co. Wexford. A century after the Battle of Hastings and the systematic colonization of England, the conquest of Ireland had begun.

The landings sprang after King Dermot MacMurrough of Leinster had abducted the wife of Tiernan O'Rourke of Breifne. With Tiernan bent on revenge, Dermot travelled to English-occupied Aquitaine in France and gained the support of Henry II. When Dermot returned to Bristol, he persuaded the out-of-favour Earl of Pembroke, who was also known as Strongbow, to restore his standing with the king by raising an Anglo-Welsh army. Dermot's first landing in 1167 resulted in defeat. However two years later near Waterford, he routed a strong Irish and Norse army. In October 1171, Henry II landed and encouraged his barons to govern Ireland with formidable castles and, although occasional parliaments were summoned, it was Irish resistance that laid the foundations for 800 years of Anglo-Irish conflict.

The Normans settling in Ireland became more Irish than the Irish and eventually whittled English influence to a small area around Dublin known as The Pale. During the sixteenth century, successive Tudor monarchs tried to extend their authority against strong resistance from the northern province of Ulster.

After the Protestant break with Rome, Catholicism became a factor in the struggle and soon after Elizabeth I came to the English throne in 1558, an Irish Parliament passed an Act of Supremacy requiring office holders in Church and State to swear allegiance to her, but the Gaelic earls and their 'Old English' allies remained staunchly Roman Catholic.

In 1588, when the refusal by the Earl of Tyrone in Ulster to execute Spanish Armada survivors washed up in Ireland led to doubts about his loyalty, Elizabeth tightened her grip by giving English settlers confiscated land. There were no English settlements or garrisons west of Lough Neagh and Tyrone found a willing ally in Red Hugh O'Donnell of Tyrconnell to exploit the difficult terrain to harry English patrols.

In 1601, when O'Donnell marched to Kinsale to support an invading Spanish army and was routed, Tyrone submitted to the Queen but found English rule unacceptable and fled. The Flight of the Earls stripped Ulster of its Gaelic aristocracy and, in 1609, the government planted English and Scottish settlers into Ulster and laid the foundation of Ireland as a divided island, the intermingling of faiths proving a dangerous cocktail of nationalism. The 'plantation' introduced three classes of landowner. The English and Scottish 'undertakers' were required to import their tenants but, as few were attracted to Ireland, they were forced to accept Irish tenants. 'Servitors' who had served the Crown in Ireland were permitted to take Irish tenants and newcomers. Finally some Irish, deemed to be loyal, owned land, provided they adopted English farming practices.

During the English Civil War, in October 1641 Catholic uprisings in Ulster spread fear among the Protestant settlers and those not massacred fled to defendable towns, where plague and starvation soon took their toll and led to deep sectarian distrust.

After 1642, when a Catholic government was formed in Kilkenny, Oliver Cromwell landed near Dublin in August 1649 and, giving no quarter to the rebels, confiscated their land to pay his troops and the 'adventurers' who had financed the parliamentary cause. In Drogheda, every man in the garrison was executed, as were the townspeople and garrison at Wexford. Leaving his son-in-law, Henry Ireton, to destroy Irish resistance, Catholic landowners were dispossessed and the population was reduced by two-thirds with many sent to the plantations on Caribbean islands as slaves. 'The curse of Cromwell on you' became an Irish oath.

There is no more iconic Irish battle than the one fought on the picturesque banks of the River Boyne in March 1689 when the Catholic James II was defeated by the Protestant William of Orange. The previous year the Earl of Tyrconnell had summoned a parliament to repeal the legislation in which Protestants were stripped of their influence, except in Ulster where, in September 1688, the Derry apprentice boys had closed the city's gates to a Catholic regiment and signalled the call to arms with big deep bass drums. The city survived a three-month siege before relief arrived by sea. The Battle of the Boyne is celebrated annually on 12 July by the Orange Order with sombre Orangemen in bowler hats and orange sashes escorting 'King Billy' on horseback, escorted by uniformed pipes and drums and rowdy 'aggro' bands of young Protestants. The eleven days were lost during the change from the Julian to the Gregorian calendar in 1752. The most publicized march is that to Drumcree Church in Portadown in which the parade passed through the Catholic enclave centred on Obins Street.

By the end of July, James had returned to France and Irish resistance finally crumbled after the Dutch General Ginkel's victory at Aughrim in 1691. The subsequent Treaty of Limerick was not ungenerous to the Catholics but they soon suffered from the 1695 Anti-Catholic Penal Laws, which were designed to reinforce Protestant ascendancy throughout Irish life. By the early 1700s, Catholics owned just 7 per cent of the land.

As the French Revolution tore France apart, for the British the nine years from 1796 were as dangerous as the dark days of 1940. When French agents reported that England and Wales were ripe for insurrection, the Directory examined stretching British resources by landing in Cornwall and on the east coast and attacking her colonial and trading interests in India, which France had lost twenty years earlier. However, the agents were mistaken. The unrest was consequent to the social upheaval induced by the Industrial Revolution, indeed the British had watched, with horror, as the Revolution developed into the vengeful bloodbath of the Terror.

In October 1791 in London was a Protestant barrister with liberal views, Theobold Wolfe Tone. He was a founder of the Society of the United Irishmen, whose intention was to promote political union between Catholics and Protestants and obtain parliamentary reform in a country in which faction fighting was common. When the Irish Brehon legal system was replaced by English legislation, the colonizers kept the Irish divided by encouraging the resolution of internecine issues with violence. Since the sword was outlawed, the favourite weapon was the shillelagh herdsman stick. By the 1880s,

3

the faction fighting had become so violent and politically orientated that the authorities banned the practice.

Faction fighting undermined the United Irishmen and, by 1794, they realized that universal suffrage and equality was unlikely and suggested to Napoleon Bonaparte that Great Britain could be threatened by landing in Ireland. When Tone penned a memorandum that Ireland was ripe for revolution, its betrayal to the Directory led to Tone agreeing to inform on United Irishmen activities until he was warned that the counterintelligence net was closing in and so he fled to the United States in May 1795, where again he associated with United Irishmen exiles. Still believing that France held the key to his ambitions, in February 1796, he persuaded the Directory to invade Ireland and, in December, after being commissioned into the French Army to give him protection if captured, Tone joined a naval expedition commanded by General Lazar Hoche. However on arriving in Lough Swilly, Bantry Bay, the troops were prevented from landing by gales. The following year Tone joined Dutch plans to land in Ireland. However when their fleet was crushed at the Battle of Camperdown, Tone returned to Paris to find Hoche had died and Napoleon was ambivalent about landing in Ireland; indeed in 1798, he left for Egypt. The 1798 United Irishmen rebellion was crushed with violence and cruelty hitherto not seen in Ireland and, even though the Directory supported the insurrection, 30,000 rebels cornered at Vinegar Hill were smashed by General Gerald Lake. Fear of further French landings culminated on 23 August when General Joseph Humbert landed near Killala, Co. Mayo. After inflicting an ignominious defeat on Lake at the Battle of 'The Races at Castlebar', he surrendered after being trapped by Lake and Lord Cornwallis at Ballinamuck on 8 September. Tone's brother, Matthew, also commissioned into the French Army, had established a revolutionary government in Castlebar and was captured and hanged. Reinforcements accompanied by General Napper Tandy, the senior United Irishmen in the French Army, arrived to take over from Humbert but left when he heard of the surrender at Ballinamuck. Tone sailed with a third fleet carrying 3,000 men commanded by General Hardy that arrived at Lough Swilly. But, two days later, it was intercepted by an English squadron and, after being captured, Tone was court-martialled and sentenced to hang, as opposed to being shot, as he requested. In his final statement, he lamented the outbreak of mass violence and then, trying to cut his throat with a penknife, he died several days later. The grave of this Protestant lawyer at Bodenstown, Co. Kildare, became a focal point for the various strands of Irish republicanism. Gaelic Athletic Association clubs are named in his honour and the Society of Wolfe Tone keeps his politics alive, in particular the term Physical Force Irish Republicanism. The term is used by Irish historians to describe the twinning of non-parliamentary armed insurrection with passive democracy to achieve an Irish republic by guaranteeing the Irish people the ownership of Ireland and breaking Irish links with the United Kingdom.

The United Irishmen ideology was adopted by Young Ireland but its failure to address the social and economic upheaval then blighting Ireland during the 1848 Great Famine, saw its demise, particularly as many Irish were emigrating to America where they promoted nationalism. The 1867 Irish Republican Brotherhood (IRB) rebellion by the secretive Fenians, intending to establish an Irish Republic by subverting radicalized Irish units of the British Army, was under-mined by informers and subverted units transferred from Ireland. Although launched against the judgement of the leadership, its failure became a focus of Irish folklore. The term 'Irish Republican Army' (IRA) was used by the IRB in America to describe several paramilitary 'regiments'. For the first time, England was targeted with several bombings to free imprisoned colleagues.

Throughout the evolution of Irish Republicanism, the dominant political issue was Home Rule, in which a democratically elected parliament in Dublin managed domestic Irish affairs within the United Kingdom. This differed from the views of the republican Daniel O'Connell in the first half of the nineteenth century for an independent Irish state separated from the United Kingdom but sharing a monarch. Four Home Rule Bills were drafted, of which those in 1914 and 1920 were enacted but a complicating issue was the desire of the Protestant majority in the North to remain with the United Kingdom and the close alliance of the Unionists with the British Conservative Party. Delays led to the Ulster Volunteers being formed in January 1913 by the Ulster Unionist Council (UUC) preparing to set up a provisional government should Ulster be included in any settlement. The force was limited to 100,000 men and was armed with 30,000 rifles supplied by Germany in April 1914, distributed from Larne with the pursuing authorities blockaded by the Ulster Volunteers. To deal with the threat of violence from the Ulster Volunteers, when the Army commander at Curragh Barracks, General Sir Arthur Paget, was instructed by the

War Office in March 1914 to prepare plans to march to Ulster, he misinterpreted the orders and gave his officers the choice – march or resign. Fifty resigned. When the British Government sent 800 soldiers to Ulster to enforce the Bill and to guard depots in the province, which was thought necessary after the illegal importation of the rifles, the Government backed down after the War Office could not guarantee that the Army could enforce Home Rule legislation.

The Irish Republican movement was not convinced of the impartiality of the Army and this led to the formation of the Irish Volunteers by southern Nationalists to ensure enactment of the Home Rule Act. From its inception, the leadership was heavily influenced by the radical Irish Republican Brotherhood which resulted in a split between hardliners and moderates. Shortly after the formation of the Volunteers, parliament banned the importation of weapons into Ireland. However Sir Roger Casement organized the landing of 1,000 rifles near Dublin but, as the Volunteers returned to Dublin, they encountered a force from the Dublin Metropolitan Police and the Army. Most escaped largely unscathed but when troops returning to Dublin fired on a group of unarmed Irish Volunteers heckling them, enlistment into the Volunteers soared. The remainder of the weapons were landed at Kilcoole a week later.

Although the September 1914 Government of Ireland Act, or more generally the Third Home Rule Act, gave Ireland regional self-government, its implementation was interrupted by the outbreak of the First World War and a split among Irish Nationalists with 100,000 National Volunteers led by the Irish Parliamentary Party leader, John Redmond, accepting British promises to deliver Home Rule while 12,000 Irish Volunteers, led by Eoin MacNeill, refused to join the war effort. A ship carrying weapons supplied by Germany was intercepted in early April. Although 20,000 Irishmen were serving in the British Army, the Fenians, the Irish Volunteers and the Irish Citizen Army, impatient at the granting of Home Rule, launched the Easter Rising on 24 April 1916 with simultaneous attacks. The Fenians seized the Dublin General Post Office proclaiming independence, however support for the uprising was limited. MacNeill discovered the plan almost at the last minute and instructed the Irish Volunteers not to become involved, nevertheless about 2,000 turned out. The British Army, fully engaged on the Western Front, were robust in restoring order that led to parts of Dublin being destroyed, 500 civilians killed and captured rebels being stoned while being escorted to ships that would ferry them to Welsh internment camps. The public demand for the death sentence of the ringleaders shifted over the next two years, largely at the revulsion of the executions of sixteen leaders, some of whom were too ill to stand, and then moved to sympathy with the Republicans in 1917 when conscription was imposed on Ireland to replace the heavy casualties on the Western Front. Rubble from the Easter Rising was used to construct a grassy hill on the railway end of the sports pitch at Croke Park and was known as Hill 16.

The Easter Rising had a dramatic impact on the drive for Irish independence. The small nationalist party Sinn Fein was blamed for orchestrating the Rising and its leader, Arthur Griffith, who had advocated Irish self government under a monarchy, was replaced in 1917 by Éamon de Valera, who was committed to founding the Republic of Ireland. In October, the remnants of the Irish Volunteers were assembled into the Irish Republican Army (IRA) at the Sinn Fein annual convention.

From 1916 to 1918, Sinn Fein and the Irish Parliamentary Party fought a series of by-elections but it was not until 1918 that the balance tipped in favour of the Nationalists. However, its MPs refused to take their seats in Westminster and instead established an independent 'Assembly of Ireland', known in Irish as Dáil Éireann. On 21 January 1919, when this unofficial parliament assembled in the Mansion House in Dublin, it led to conflict with the British and, as the internal security situation deteriorated, the IRA fought its first campaign against the British Army from 1919 to July 1921.

The Royal Irish Constabulary (RIC) estimated that 162 IRA companies were active, many with veterans of the Easter Rising. Given that the Irish Volunteer constitution insisted on obedience to its executive, the Nationalist politicians' fear that the IRA would not accept their authority emerged on the day the Dáil first met when the South Tipperary IRA seized a quantity of gelignite and shot two RIC constables on their own initiative and were held up to be an example of rejuvenated militarism. The IRA published a list of principles including that 'the armed forces of the enemy – whether soldiers or policemen – be treated exactly as a national army would treat the members of an invading army'. In August, the Dáil insisted that the Volunteers swear the same oath of allegiance as the membership to the Dáil, although it would be a full year before the IRA enacted their promise. In practice, the IRA was commanded by the charismatic Michael Collins, who was a member of the Dáil and Director of Organization, from his powerbase as a member of the Supreme Council of the Irish Republican Brotherhood. Although he issued directives to the IRA, the irregular nature of the organization meant that his control over local commanders, such as Tom Barry, was limited. De Valera resented Collins's influence, which he saw as coming from the secretive Brotherhood rather than from his position as a minister of the Irish Parliament. When he urged the IRA to undertake conventional military actions for propaganda purposes, Collins proposed instead that the British Cabinet be assassinated. Some members of the Dáil preferred a campaign of passive resistance and thus it was not until 1921 that the Dáil accepted responsibility for IRA actions, three months before the end of the Irish War of Independence.

The war was a brutal affair with most of the fighting taking place in and around Dublin and Munster. Collins, now IRA Director of Intelligence, established 'The Squad' specifically to assassinate RIC intelligence officers, killing six in the first year. In the rural areas, flying columns ambushed Army patrols and attacked remote police barracks. When, in April 1920, 400 police stations were attacked in a coordinated operation, the RIC was forced to consolidate in the larger towns, thereby effectively surrendering rural areas to the IRA. The British responded with martial law, internment and reinforced the Army with the paramilitary Black and Tans and the RIC with the Auxiliary Division. Most were veterans brutalized by their experiences on the Western Front and had very little training in internal security or guerrilla warfare. The military veterans wore black police trousers and khaki army jackets, thus the 'Black and Tans' and although they gained a reputation for brutality, the Auxiliaries were probably more robust. By August, the fighting had escalated into reprisals on both sides including the burning of houses and businesses and the execution of prisoners and informants, the IRA sometimes taking the opportunity to murder those against whom they had grudges – particularly if they were Protestants. Several stately homes in Munster, most owned by prominent loyalists accused of aiding the British, were burnt to discourage the government policy of destroying Republican homes. In September British officials, predicting the administrative needs of a future loyalist Northern Ireland, established the armed Ulster Special Constables. Broken into three categories, the 3,500 fulltime officers of A Division served in the police division in which they were recruited; the 16,000 B-Specials were trained, unpaid, part-time volunteers mobilized in emergencies;

and the 1,000 C-Specials were a reserve to be called out only in an emergency.

The third phase of the war involved the IRA taking on the Army by moving away from attacking well defended barracks to the greater use of flying columns. In Dublin on 21 November, in a coordinated operation, The Squad murdered fourteen of eighteen experienced British military intelligence officers in the city, some in front of their families. Trained by MI5 and known as the Cairo Gang, most had served in Egypt and Palestine during the First World War. Reprisal was swift. During the afternoon, an Auxiliary Division unit interrupted a Gaelic football match at Croke Park and shot thirteen spectators and a player in an incident that became known as Bloody Sunday. Collins then amalgamated The Squad and parts of the Dublin Brigade into Active Service Units (ASU) with instructions to carry out at least three shooting or grenade attacks on British patrols every day. In Munster, the IRA was successful in several actions against British troops. Tom Barry's Flying Column, ambushed at Crossbarry in March 1921, avoided encirclement by 1,200 soldiers. In Belfast, the Northern Division was forced into defending Catholic enclaves.

In April, although the Dáil endorsed the IRA by forming it into regional divisions and brigades with responsibility for geographical areas, in practice this had little effect on the localized nature of the guerrilla warfare. In May, against Collins's recommendation, de Valera authorized an ill-timed attack on Dublin Custom House that led to five Dublin IRA killed and eighty captured. In some respect, it was the pinnacle of IRA operations because the Army had developed counterinsurgency tactics and, deploying into the most active areas, their searches led to chronic shortages of IRA arms and ammunition. A plan to buy arms from Italy collapsed when the money failed to reach the dealers and, of a consignment of Thompson sub machine guns purchased in the US, 450 were intercepted by the American authorities. A few reached Ireland shortly before the truce. With almost 5,000 IRA imprisoned or interned, over 500 killed and the estimated number of effective guerrillas down to about 2,500, Collins believed the IRA was near to collapse. However, the IRA had made Ireland almost ungovernable and the political, military and economic costs were higher than the British Government was prepared to pay, particularly after the First World War. When Prime Minister David Lloyd George came under increasing international and domestic pressure to end the fighting, it was George V who persuaded the British and the Irish Republican government to agree to the Anglo-Irish Treaty, which led to Ireland being partitioned on 6 December 1922 into the twenty-six counties of the Irish Free State, and the six counties of Ulster becoming a province of the United Kingdom. The IRA was deeply divided about the Treaty and the discontent expressed by many led to defiance of the elected Provisional government, the dissidents arguing that while the IRA's allegiance was to the Dáil, its decision to sign the Treaty meant that the IRA no longer owed that body its allegiance. Most IRA commanders had interpreted the truce as temporary and had set about recruiting volunteers so that by 1922, the organization numbered 72,000 men. Michael Collins planned a clandestine campaign against the North by sending IRA units to the border and equipping the Northern Division. In March, the IRA declared that it would no longer obey the Dáil as it had violated its oath to uphold an all-Ireland Republic and that 'We will set up an Executive which will issue orders to the IRA all over the country'. A week later, that Executive announced that the Minister of Defence no longer exercised control over the IRA and, ordering an end to enlistment into the Irish National Army and police force, instructed its members to reaffirm their allegiance to the Irish Republic. Tensions in the IRA led to a bloody civil war that resulted in the defeat of the anti-Treaty faction, the ceasefire in May seeing many quit political activity, the hardliners insisting that the Irish Free State was illegitimate and that the 'IRA Army Executive' was the real government of the all-Ireland Republic.

Physical force republicanism remained a potent force and although Republicans saw the Irish Free State and Ulster as being imperialist proxies, by the 1930s most anti-Treaty Republicans had accepted the Irish Free State and entered political activity as Fianna Fail. The IRA still saw itself as the army of the all-Ireland Republic temporarily forced into a ceasefire.

When Sean Russell was elected to the Army Council, he planned a bombing campaign against England – The Sabotage Plan (The S-Plan). Designed to destroy armament factories, disrupt civil infrastructure and attack specific industrial plants, commercial premises and large newspaper organizations, propaganda and military operations were to be confined to English population centres where IRA cells could operate without drawing attention and be financially independent and self-supporting using material cached in dumps. The strategy was supported by elements within the Irish Free State. Even though some IRA officials assessed that the

10

structure of their organization was uncoordinated and militarily inexperienced, the IRA Army Council authorized force to be used against the British units of the Northern Ireland District garrison.

S-Plan opened with several attacks on customs posts in Northern Ireland on 28/29 November 1938, the only casualties being three IRA men killed in a premature explosion at Castlefin, Co. Donegal. Premature explosions were later known as 'own goals'. On 12 January 1939 the Army Council issued the British with an ultimatum to signal its intent, within four days, of withdrawing from Northern Ireland. The timing, with Europe hurtling to war, led to British suspicions that Germany had influenced its development. Not surprisingly, the British did not respond and three days later, the IRA declared war on Great Britain and, citing the Easter Rising, sought the support of Irishmen at home and abroad, in particular those in the US, to support the proclamation. Between January and June, the IRA launched fifty-seven attacks in London and seventy in the provinces, that resulted in one person killed and fifty-five injured. The British responded by introducing the Prevention of Violence Act limiting Irish immigration, extending deportation and for Irish considered to be hostile to register with the police. Sixty-six sympathizers were convicted. The Germans considered the plan to be an annoyance because it was not damaging British capability to wage war and, by mid-1940, with the Battle of Britain frustrating invasion plans, they had lost confidence in using the IRA to infiltrate Great Britain. After the IRA announced on 3 August that S-Plan would continue for another two-and-a-half years, a bomb, placed in the basket of a bicycle leant against a wall in Coventry, killed five and wounded fifty people and caused outrage in Britain and Ireland. One hundred and nineteen Irish, who were quickly deported, bit into the IRA recruitment. In December, the conviction of three men and two women for the bomb and the sentencing of two to hang, triggered reprisals against post offices, post boxes and mail trains. While thousands of Irishmen and women were fighting with the British Armed Forces, demonstrations in America proclaimed that it was Partition that had forced young Irish to perpetrate such outrages. S-Plan statistics are cited as 300 explosions, seven deaths and ninety-six injuries. In Ulster, there was a gun battle in the Lower Falls in April 1942, otherwise the B-Specials and their intimate knowledge of their local areas largely kept the IRA deflated. Coupled with the immediate deportations, the 1939 Treason Act, the Prevention of

Violence Act and the Irish Free State Offences Against the State Act led to 1,100 IRA members being interned during the Second World War, effectively reducing its capability as a military organization.

In 1948, the IRA leadership accepted the existence of the Republic of Ireland and issued a General Order focusing on removing the British from Northern Ireland. Raids on military and cadet force armouries launched from the sanctuary of Ireland gained support. For instance in June 1954 Gough Barracks, Armagh, lost 290 rifles, thirty-seven Sten guns and nine Bren light machine guns. In December 1955, when the extremist splinter group Saor Uladh attacked six border Customs posts and the election in November 1956 of two Sinn Fein to the Irish Parliament suggested increased republican support, Chief of Staff Sean Cronin devised Operation Harvest. The plan was for four Flying Columns of fifty men each to attack pre-determined military and infrastructure targets in Northern Ireland. Belfast was not to be attacked because it was thought the Royal Ulster Constabulary (RUC) had penetrated the IRA. There was recognition that attacks would provoke Loyalist retaliation against the Catholics. The aim was to:

> Break down the enemy's administration in the occupied area until he is forced to withdraw his forces. Our method of doing this is guerrilla warfare within the occupied area and propaganda directed at its inhabitants. In time as we build up our forces, we hope to be in a position to liberate large areas and tie these in with other liberated areas – that is areas where the enemy's writ no longer runs.

The strategy was based on revolutionary principles developed by Mao Tse Tung and was the very strategy being successfully undermined by the British in Malaya. Under command of HQ Northern Ireland District at Thiepval Barracks, Lisburn, was 39 Airportable Brigade and several Territorial Army units. Raised in September with three Midlands battalions, the Brigade joined 13th (Western) Division and in July 1915 relieved the 29th Division at Gallipoli, staying until the evacuation in January 1916. It then took part in the Mesopotamian campaign in Iraq and was disbanded in 1919. In March 1951, it was reformed as 39 Independent Infantry Brigade in Dover as part of the UK-based 3rd Division. The following year, it deployed to the Suez Canal Zone and a year later was sent to Kenya during the Mau Mau Campaign before being sent to Lisburn in

Northern Ireland in April 1956. In addition to the armoured car Lisanelly Barracks and 26 Squadron RCT at Lisburn, which had been formed at the Curragh in 1888, Ballykinler, on the Co. Down coast, housed an infantry battalion, some ranges and the Command Ammunition Dump. 33 Field Squadron RE was at Antrim. In leaky huts and muddy roads at Kinnegar was the RAOC central stores depot and 46 Command Workshops REME. In Londonderry was HM Naval Base *Sea Eagle* near the Waterside and near Aldergrove Airport, a RAF base.

Claiming that an independent, united, democratic thirty-two county Irish Republic and national liberation would emerge when the English were driven from Irish soil, during the night of 11 December 1956, three Flying Columns crossed the border and launched simultaneous attacks by bombing the Londonderry television transmitter, attacking the Army barracks under construction in Enniskillen, burning Magherafelt Courthouse and the Newry B-Special post. The raid on Gough Barracks was beaten off. Although traditionally a rural guerrilla force, the IRA was no match for the B-Specials on their own turf. Three days later, another column damaged RUC Lisnaskea with explosives but attacks on RUC Rosslea and Derrylin were defeated. When on 21 December, the Northern Ireland Parliament in Stormont introduced internment under the 1922 Emergency Powers Act, these again limited IRA operations. The second attack on RUC Derrylin on New Year's Day resulted in the first Security Forces' casualty when Constable John Scally was killed. Next day, when two IRA were killed in a bungled raid on RUC Brookborough when a Flying Column attacked the wrong building, the two became Republican martyrs, their funerals provoking a strong reaction in Ireland and inducing support for Sinn Fein in the general election that year. In January 1957, Dublin, fearing a British military response, interned most of the IRA leadership and undermined Operation Harvest with incidents dropping from seventy-seven to twenty-six in 1960. The British military contribution was largely confined to 213 Independent Signal Troop supporting police communications. During 1957, the IRA carried out 341 incidents but in November suffered their biggest loss when four men died in an 'own goal' in a farmhouse in Co. Louth. An 'own goal' is when a homemade bomb explodes during preparation. By 1960, those interned in Ireland were being released, even though in November 1961, after a second RUC officer was killed in a gun battle in South Armagh, the Irish Minister for Justice, Charles Haughey, introduced military courts to try IRA men.

The IRA terminated Operation Harvest on 26 February 1962 when a statement widely thought to have been written by Rory O'Brady, of the Army Council, blamed inactive public support and, pledging eternal hostility to the British Army in Ireland, called on Irish people to help. It would prove an ominous summons. Fatalities in this Border War amounted to eight IRA, four Republican supporters and six RUC. Of the 256 interned in Northern Ireland, eighty-nine pledged to renounce violence in return for their releases, which began in late April 1961. The IRA leadership considered the operation a disaster and, when Republican failures since 1798 were examined, while there had been plans to achieve the freedom of Ireland as an independent state, there was no overall strategy. There was also a realization that secrecy resulted in lost contact with sympathizers. When, in 1966, Stormont fears emerged that the IRA would commemorate the fiftieth anniversary of the Easter Rising, the British Government rejected reinforcing the Northern Ireland Command.

For decades, the Roman Catholics in Ulster had faced widespread discrimination from Protestants determined to remain within the United Kingdom. Gerrymandering ensured that the 20,000 voters living in Londonderry managed to elect twelve Unionist and eight Nationalist councillors. Twice as many Catholics were unemployed and they were underrepresented among doctors, lawyers, artisans and tradesmen and throughout the Civil Service. Of the approximate 1,000 houses built in Co. Fermanagh, Protestants were allocated 80 per cent. The discrimination became the catalyst for the Nationalist leadership to develop a strategy of agitation by exploiting Catholics as 'second class citizens'. On 29 January 1967, the Northern Ireland Civil Rights Association (NICRA) was founded at the Belfast International Hotel by several disparate organizations including the Communist Party, trade unions, Republican clubs and student activists demanding basic freedoms and rights and the dismantling of abuses of official power, in particular the Emergency Powers Act and the emergence of the B-Specials during the Border War as the principal counterinsurgency force. NICRA formally entered the political scene on 9 April and, imitating the American civil rights movement, protested noisily, picketed industrial relation disputes and organized sit-ins. Funding, support and sourcing of equipment emerged from Irish families in the US. In August, the IRA leadership agreed to follow the Marxist-Leninist philosophy of the Irish Marxist James Connolly of working to a thirty-two county socialist Irish Republic governed through committees of workers. This broke with electing Members of Parliament to Westminster who would then not take their seats – the so-called abstentionism. Connolly had been executed after the Easter Rebellion. In spite of local suspicions of links between NICRA and the IRA, to what extent MI5 recognized the internal security of the United Kingdom was at risk is unclear, nevertheless the fact is that Stormont and London were ill-prepared.

The first major NICRA demonstration was held on 24 August 1968 when protesters marched between Coalisland and Dungannon and then when NICRA and the Derry Housing Action Committee announced a march for 5 October, in an attempt to get it banned, the Apprentice Boys of Londonderry announced that they intended to parade on the same route on the same day and time. Northern Ireland Home Affairs Minister, William Craig, duly obliged and banned the march, however NICRA defied the order and marched through the city centre. Images of RUC baton charges shocked television viewers. On 22 November, when Northern Ireland Prime Minister Captain Terence O'Neill announced several reforms, including abolishing the Special Powers Acts and changes in local government and allocation of public housing, NICRA leaders declared a month-long halt to demonstrations. However, in a period of widespread civil disturbances throughout Europe, the left wing People's Democracy committee at Queen's University, Belfast, ignored the declaration and organized a march to Londonderry. Leaving Belfast on 1 January 1969, the students had repeated skirmishes with Protestants until it reached Burntollet where 200 Loyalists attacked with iron bars, bottles and stones. There was little intervention from the RUC. The march arrived in Londonderry on 5 January and again rioting broke out between the protesters and the RUC and then, that night, police officers assaulted several residents when they searched homes in the Catholic Bogside area. The Republican leaders responded by establishing the Derry Citizens Defence Association to protect the Bogside and erected barricades guarded by men controlling access. The famous slogan 'You are now entering Free Derry' was painted on a gable wall in Columbs Street by a local activist named John Casey.

When a bomb badly damaged an electricity substation at Castlereagh on 30 March and was followed the next month by several attacks on water pipelines to Belfast and the Silent Valley Reservoir in Co. Down, the IRA were blamed until it emerged that they were the work of the UVF aiming to discredit Stormont and end the reforms.

The UVF had been reformed in 1966 by Gusty Spence, a former Royal Military Policemen who had served in Cyprus, with the express purpose of 'upholding the constitution of Ulster by force or arms, if necesssary'. Spence was jailed for life for murder in 1967. Since the attacks were on national key points, on 24 April, the 2nd Battalion, The Queen's Regiment (2 Queen's), which was stationed in Palace Barracks, Holywood as part of 39 Airportable Brigade, was deployed to guard key points and was the first battalion to patrol the streets of Belfast. Patrols also visited the dams, pumps and pipes in the Mountains of Mourne. A fifth bomb on 26 April threatening the water supply to Belfast led to the 1st Prince of Wales Yorkshire Light Infantry (1 PWO), which was the Spearhead Battalion, being flown from Colchester to Ballykinler where they joined 1st Battalion, the Light Infantry (1 LI), which was also part of 39 Airportable Brigade. Every six months an infantry battalion in England, placed on immediate notice to move, was known as the Spearhead Battalion. The 1 LI Band spent several weeks escorting trucks ferrying obsolete .303-inch ammunition from the ammunition dump to Londonderry for shipment to UK and then men were recalled from summer leave to patrol Belfast. Most detected tension in the narrow streets.

Chapter 2

Phase One: Military Aid to the Civil Power 1969

Serious rioting broke out on 12 July in Belfast and Londonderry with some Catholic families abandoning their homes on the day that the Orange Order traditionally marched to celebrate the Battle of the Boyne. Those who served in Northern Ireland knew that if there was one period that would persistently cause trouble, it was the Loyalist marching season in July and August. Two days later, Francis McCloskey, aged 67, died after being clubbed with a baton by an RUC officer in Dungiven. Next day, when Prime Minister Chichester-Clark mobilized the B-Specials, Ulster dived to chaos as Samuel Devenny died from injuries received when the RUC broke into his Bogside house after a clash with Catholics on 19 April. In spite of the tension, Stormont refused to ban the Apprentice Boys' March scheduled for 12 August because it would invite trouble from the Loyalists and therefore it should go ahead. But the politicians failed to consult with Nationalist representatives, such as the diminutive Bernadette Devlin, largely because they had not entered the Creggan or Bogside for several months.

On 8 August, Home Secretary Callaghan advised Chichester-Clark that if he wanted troops to support the RUC, they were available. Next day Lieutenant General Ian Freeland arrived as General Officer Commanding (GOC) Northern Ireland Command. Under command, he had 39 Airportable Brigade and 1st Royal Regiment of Wales (1 RRW), which had been formed in Metford Camp, Lydd on 11 June from the 1st Royal Welch Fusiliers and 1st South Wales Borderers. Over the next two months, the Battalion carried out several 'Keep the Army in the Public Eye' public relations and ceremonial duties in south Wales before being deployed to Belfast from Lydd on 28 July.

As the 15,000-strong Apprentice Boys' March passed provocatively close to the junction of Waterloo Place and Williams Street on 12 August, taunts from several thousand Bogsiders developed into exchanges of bricks and stones. Several hundred RUC were deployed to Londonderry and, as they shepherded the Catholics back into the Bogside, they were followed by about 100 Protestants escalating the unrest with hails of stones, bricks, missiles and Molotov cocktails in an event that became known as the Battle of the Bogside. Ill-prepared, the RUC was overwhelmed but attempted to compensate for its failures by firing about 1,000 gas canisters into the densely populated narrow streets. But police resources were stretched further when the rioting spread to other parts of Londonderry. Private Cliff Sweeting was a member of the 1 PWO Intelligence Section and was in the Battalion Operations Room listening to the police radio net:

> The RUC weren't prepared for the barrage of petrol bombs. If they ventured down side streets, they would find barricades moved into place, trapping them in the alleys, as petrol bombs and lumps of concrete rained down on them from the rooftops. Attempts to use teargas to disperse crowds was utterly futile as well. Quite often, they failed to gauge wind strength and direction, and the gas came back at them. Horrific injuries were sustained as the rioters used sharpened iron fence pickets as spears, smashing through the thin sides of the Land Rovers and wounding the occupants. It became clear that the police were being tactically outmanoeuvred and outfought by a determined and well-prepared enemy. (*Across the Sea To Ireland* – www.britains-smallwars.com)

With no relief system in place, exhausted RUC officers, at their limits of endurance and alienated from the Nationalist estates, snatched short periods of rest wherever they could. During the evening, Minister for Home Affairs, Robert Porter, asked Brigadier Tony Dyball, Freeland's Chief of Staff, to deploy a military detachment to HMS *Sea Eagle* in Londonderry, as a contingency. 1 PWO were at Magilligan Point Camp on low profile ready to return to Londonderry at a moment's notice.

On 13 August, media reporting inflamed the rioting and when it spread and the B-Specials were deployed, NICRA's call for diversionary disturbances to take the pressure off events in Londonderry was a rallying call to Catholic working classes to defend their homes against Protestant working classes, a theme that remained constant

18

throughout the next thirty-eight years. The middle classes were hardly involved except as victims. Taoiseach Jack Lynch in Dublin observed that Ireland 'could not stand by and watch innocent people injured and perhaps worse' and, when Irish Army units, including a field hospital, moved close to the border, the announcement was interpreted in the Bogside to be the imminent arrival of Irish troops. The Protestants perceived it as an invasion.

Northern Ireland was in crisis. In the Bogside, almost the entire community had mobilized, many galvanized by false rumours that St Eugene's Cathedral had been attacked by the police. When the B-Specials opened fire with their Shoreland .30-inch Brownings, there were fears of a massacre and at about 1.30 p.m., after RUC Inspector General Peacocke had requested military assistance from Robert Porter, Prime Minister Chichester-Clark telephoned Prime Minister Wilson during mid-afternoon. So far the unrest had cost ten civilians killed and 368 RUC and 521 people injured and homes and factories gutted and damaged. When the Cabinet assembled to debate the implications of military assistance to Stormont, Wilson prophetically suggested that, 'If we go in, it will take many years to get out'. After going around the table twice seeking the views of his ministers, at about 4.30 p.m., the Ministry of Defence was ordered to send troops to Northern Ireland to aid the civil community. Within thirty minutes, 1 PWO, reinforced by a 1 RRW company, was committed to the Bogside. Private Sweeting:

At 1700 hours on the 14th, the RUC requested that the military be sent in. Three companies went in immediately, to be greeted with tears of joy by the Catholics. Not that they particularly liked us, we understood that much, but they did not hate us with anything like the venom they reserved for the RUC and USC. As the realisation dawned that they had won this mammoth struggle, they emerged from behind the barricades. A new era had dawned. For the time being, peace had been restored. We knew that it would not last. It was only a honeymoon period like so many others before it in the turbulent history of this place. But I take pride in reflecting that we played our part in this story effectively, with professional efficiency and with honour. (*Across the Sea To Ireland* – www.britains-smallwars.com)

After Brigadier Peter Hudson, who commanded 39 Airportable Brigade, saw the devastation and columns of refugees abandoning wrecked houses, he calculated he was short of troops and sought reinforcements. 3 Division in the United Kingdom was then ordered to reinforce Northern Ireland District and the next evening, 3 LI, which was also based at Plymouth and was now the Spearhead Battalion, landed at Aldergrove. HQ 24 Airportable Brigade and its 210 Signal Squadron were recalled from exercise in France and deployed to Ballykelly from Plymouth on 17 August to take command of an area of operations covering Cos. Londonderry, Fermanagh, Tyrone and Armagh. With the Movements Branch struggling to organize the reinforcements, 60 Squadron RCT, also from Plymouth with 24 Airportable Brigade, arrived with some elements moving direct from France. 63 Parachute Squadron RCT from 16 Parachute Brigade also arrived with a Troop from 42 Squadron. The 1st Hampshires arrived on the 19th immediately after returning from a United Nations tour in Cyprus, and was followed next day by 1st Royal Green Jackets (1 RGJ), both units deploying to Belfast. HQ 39 Airportable Brigade deployed a Tactical HQ to Belfast. Most of the reinforcements expected to be home by Christmas.

With soldiers planted between the opposing communities, the rioting de-escalated into periods of 'aggro'. 'Aggro' was the military nickname for the aggravation of stone throwing and insults. They had averted civil war and although their arrival had been viewed with some suspicion by Catholics, who saw them as replicating the Easter Rebellion, and yet also as protectors. On 19 August, Wilson circulated The Downing Street Declaration in which London undertook to support Stormont provided that Stormont addressed the social causes of the unrest, energetically. By the beginning of September, troop levels had risen to 4,000 with most units based in vacant factories, empty schools because of the summer holidays and hangars at RAF Aldergrove. Many had been recalled by notices on radio and television, announcements in cinemas and Automobile Association signs on roads and expected the deployment to be short. Some were veterans of the Second World War and of fighting communists in Korea and Africans in Kenya and, more recently, Greek-Cypriot nationalists in Cyprus, fanatical Arabs in the messy withdrawal from Aden and Indonesians in the spectacular, but little known, confrontation in the jungles of Borneo. In West Germany, although most units were preparing for the annual autumn NATO exercises, some introduced internal security into the training schedule. In Detmold, the Blues and Royals cheerfully threw stones and abused their rivals in Hobart Barracks, the 3rd Royal Horse Artillery (3 RHA).

When the barricaded Catholic No Go areas were deemed acceptable by Stormont, Protestant leaders, not appreciating that it was their discrimination that was the cause, accused the Army of not defending their streets. General Freeland convinced Wilson that the solution to removing the barricades was by negotiation and when, on 5 September, Major General Dyball persuaded the Lower Falls residents to dismantle their barricades, it was one of several agreements between Catholic leaders and Army that lasted for several months. When the *Sunday Times* reported the talks as negotiations with the IRA, the Protestants protested. Generally, that the IRA was rarely seen led to it being nicknamed 'I Ran Away', seems to have escaped the investigative expertise of the newspaper. A week later, after several Catholic community leaders visited 10 Downing Street, the Turf Lodge residents replaced the barricades with a peace line separating the Loyalist Shankill and the Nationalist Falls Road. Nevertheless, some Catholics moved to the new town at Craigavon.

Within four hours of being notified during the morning of Sunday 27 September, when 41 Commando flew to Aldergrove from RAF Lyneham as the Spearhead Battalion, elements moved into the requisitioned King's Hall, Balmoral and its ice rink. Tactical HQ was at RUC Hastings Street. With rifle companies based at the Corporation Cleansing Station and in a small warehouse alongside McClelland's Brewery, over the next week, the Commando took over from 1 Hampshires patrolling the labyrinth of narrow streets of houses, alleys and gutted buildings bordering the peace line. The brewery was draughty and chilly and the nearest washroom was at Hastings Street. The Protestant owner donated sufficient Guinness for the Royal Marines to have two bottles per day – a small price to pay for its protection. When the weather later turned cold, the troops sheltered in a derelict fish shop, which stank strongly of its previous products. Second hand US M1952 'flak jackets', some covered with Vietnam logos, were issued to patrols and the fitting of `Starlight Image Intensifiers' to rifles improved night operations. Visors fitted to helmets were unpopular because they scratched easily, produced glare and reduced visibility at night.

The platoons were on thirty minutes' standby with their 4-ton Bedford RL lorries loaded with timber triangular road block barriers covered in Dannert barbed wire. There were not enough riot control batons and the few shields protected only the upper body. Dustbins helped to make up the shortfall. The practice was that once the RUC accepted they had lost control of a disturbance, notification for the troops to take over was formalized on a piece of paper. When a Loyalist crowd crossed the peace line and fire-bombed several Catholic houses, leaving more residents homeless, and 1 LI reported another mob forming up in the darkness of the night, 41 Commando, smartly dressed in green combat kit, '44 pattern helmets and their 7.62mm Self Loading Rifles (SLR) with fixed bayonets at the slope, formed up behind the soldiers in the standard 'box formation'. From their experiences since 1945, British riot control had developed into a disciplined affair designed to maintain the psychological advantage over untidy, ill-disciplined mobs, but with the withdrawal from the Empire, it was near the bottom of training priorities. Generally, riots consisted of youths shouting abuse, throwing chunks of paving slabs, petrol and acid bombs, discharging air rifles and crossbows and using catapults to launch spiked golf balls and lumps of lead, accompanied by burning vehicles and looting shops. Arrows were sometimes fitted with firework gunpowder. Objects were often dropped from upstairs rooms and roofs. Since much of the rioting had been taking place on Saturday nights, after the pubs closed, Stormont later announced closing time would be at 7 p.m. at weekends, which had some success. When the mob spilled out of the pubs, the Royal Marines were subjected to a barrage of bricks and bottles, but as they had done in Aden, Cyprus and elsewhere, two men unfurled a banner on 10-foot poles which read, 'This is an unlawful assembly and you must disperse immediately.' Elsewhere, banners displayed Arabic words, which caused some much needed amusement. When the warning failed to impress, as it usually did, the two soldiers crossed to display on the rear 'If you do not disperse now, we will fire tear gas'. When this failed, the box advanced under a hail of missiles intending to get behind the mob – and then a gunman fired two shots. The mob quickly vanished leaving the commandos exposed.

The troops adapted to the inadequacies of the standard drills quicker than most observers expected into the Derry Cohort in which the box formation was discarded in favour of soldiers massing behind Pig and Saracen Armoured Personnel Carriers (APC) and covered in depth by snipers watching for gunmen. In front was a thin line of soldiers and on the flanks were small lightly armed 'snatch squads' of big men, often from the rugby team, who rushed into the mob and wrestled selected rioters back to the APCs to be handed over to the RUC. Military vehicles, parked across streets, controlled the routes of mobs, and water cannons filled up from fire hydrants usually produced rapid mob dispersal. On occasion, Loyalist rioters claimed the soldiers were being too rough. By 1974, soldiers were taught the basics of Tae Kwan Do to enable struggling rioters to be more effectively immobilized. When CS irritant gas was used, the soldiers learnt to lob the canisters into the centre of a mob where they were difficult to be kicked out. CS was fired from a 38mm (1.5-inch) riot gun or pistol or could be thrown but it was two edged because if the wind shifted, the troops were forced to wear respirators, thereby reducing visibility and having to ensure that the crowd did not get close enough to rip them from their heads.

41 Commando spent most of its first six week tour dealing with riots usually started by a Loyalist mob abusing the RUC and Catholics. On one occasion, when the RUC arrested a man with a pronounced limp and produced a three foot brass Victorian poker from a trouser leg, he claimed, 'My poor old Granny is sick in bed and I was on my way round to stoke her fire!' After the police failed to persuade a crowd, egged on by the booming figure of the Reverend Ian Paisley, to disperse the Royal Marines gassed the lot and watched as the loudly cursing Paisley emerged from the mist, clutching his streaming eyes. In another Paisley-inspired riot, families watching from the pavements encouraged a large mob to stream into the street occupied by a 41 Commando Troop. When the warnings to disperse were ignored, as usual, with V-signs, missiles and a band belting out Loyalist songs, a Royal Marines sergeant used a loud hailer, 'Knock! Knock!' Jokers shouted back, 'Who's there?' As was customary, the sergeant replied, 'It's the gasman!' accompanied by a volley of CS gas canisters lazily somersaulting into the crowd. The coughing mob dissolved, the accordion section of the band trailing off in a ghastly wail, choking flute players staggering down a side street and a small bass drummer still trying to beat the time.

Since 1922, the B-Specials had been a symbolic and practical representation of the ability of Northern Ireland to defend itself against internal and external threats. When Lord Cameron examined the August unrest, he concluded in his report on 12 September that Stormont had discriminated against the Catholics and, suggesting that the B-Specials were partisan, also accused that 'a number of policemen were guilty of misconduct, which involved assault and battery, malicious damage to property...and the use of provocative sectarian and political slogans' and should be disarmed. The Hunt Report on 10 October recommending that the B-Specials should be disbanded and that a RUC Reserve and part-time volunteer military force be formed, led to Loyalist fury igniting into a riot known as the Battle of the Shankill. For about ninety minutes, 3 LI in Hopeton Street remained steady, in spite of an estimated 1,000 rounds being fired at them and two casualties. After being given permission, the troops returned fire resulting in a gunman claimed and others wounded and then the battalion hammered the streets, rifle butts replacing banners and arrests rigorous. Sixty-six rounds were actually reported fired, however the correct figure was sixty-eight because a private in Support Company had found two rounds that he had not handed in. From the start of Operation Banner, the troops were expected to account for every round fired and those that could not, resulted in a military police investigation. Even though for the first time, the Loyalists felt the raw power of the Army, the battle was a demonstration of even-handedness to the Catholics, a culture that was generally evident throughout the entire campaign, in spite of the efforts of the IRA, editors and the liberal elite to undermine the strategy.

The disturbances continued, the orange fires from burning vehicles glowing in the smoky, autumn night sky. At 2.40 a.m., a gunman with a .22 rifle opened fire on anything that moved and forced the Royal Marines to take cover in between directing traffic away from the immediate area. When several more gunmen opened fire, in the belief that the shots were coming from the upper floors of the Divis Flats, the Royal Marines swung a powerful searchlight onto their firing positions until its crew came under fire. The battle raged all night with the gunmen wounding two officers and nineteen soldiers, of whom fourteen were hospitalized. Next day, a major cordon and search of the Shankill turned up petrol bombs; arms and ammunition was protected by strong foot patrols reinforced by Ferret Scout Cars dominating the streets. Even so several shots were fired.

Sporadic rioting continued and then at about 10 p.m. on 11 October, as the RUC broke up a big crowd near St Peter's Hill Road in the Shankill, three police officers were wounded by gunshots and Constable Victor Arbuckle was fatally shot in the head, the first RUC officer to be killed in Operation Banner – shot by a Loyalist. The RUC signed over to the military. When 41 Commando used CS to corral a mob near Percy Street and a commando shot a petrol bomber near Boundary Street, the crowd realized the Royal Marines meant business and dispersed. Two armed men arrested near Grosvenor Road turned out to be off-duty B-Specials.

By 21 October, the internal security situation had calmed sufficiently for the RUC to patrol the Falls Road and Shankill, nevertheless Royal Engineers began erecting sandbagged sangars on street corners, a task that would keep them fully occupied for the next thirty-eight years. On 14 November, 41 Commando handed over to 1st Parachute Battalion (1 Para) and sailed for Liverpool, with very few predicting that by 2007, the Royal Marines would complete forty tours at a cost of twenty-four killed.

Chapter 3

Phase Two: Republican Insurgency 1969 to 1971

By the New Year, HQ 24 Airportable Brigade had handed the west of Northern Ireland over to HQ 8 Infantry Brigade from its role of supporting the Army Strategic Command in Chester. On 1 March, Brigade HQ moved into HMS *Sea Eagle*, which was renamed Ebrington Barracks.

The soldiers found patrolling streets, that in England would be regarded as slums, and standing on street corners with a loaded rifle, steel helmet and gas mask, watching people go about their daily business, to be surreal. Many sympathized with Catholics when told, over cups of tea, cakes and biscuits, about the discrimination and were confused about the politics; but at least learning a foreign language was not necessary although they soon became schooled in distinguishing dialects. For the Catholics, with the imminent disbandment of the B-Specials and new civil rights legislation being discussed at Stormont, there was hope, however, the failure of the Labour Government to order the No Go areas to be dismantled gave hardline Republicans the opportunity to convert the civil rights campaign into a struggle for Irish nationalism. A new word then circulated from behind the barriers – Provisionals, 'Provos'; to the Army, PIRA – the Provisional IRA.

At a Special Convention on 28 December 1969 in Dublin, the IRA leadership debated whether to be represented in, or abstain from, the Dáil and discussed their response to the vulnerability of Catholics in Northern Ireland. Citing the failure of Operation Harvest, the moderate traditionalists had little desire to be involved in sectarian violence and no stomach to launch another campaign against

Northern Ireland. They favoured exploiting social issues by developing a political base among Catholics and Protestants throughout Ireland in order to dismantle partition and allow the democratic process to raise the profile of the working class. When the Convention voted to recognize Stormont, Dublin and Westminster, an aggressive revolutionary faction, headed by Sean MacStiofain the Director of Intelligence, accused the leadership of not representing Republican goals. MacStiofain then contacted two IRA leaders in Belfast, Billy McKee and Joe Cahill, both of whom had been refusing to take orders since September in protest at the failure of the leadership to defend Catholic areas. When he learnt that nine of the thirteen IRA units, numbering about 120 activists and 500 supporters, were dissatisfied with the IRA Council, he and several hardliners formed the 'Provisional Army Council'. The original IRA regarded itself as the Official IRA. The leaders of the breakaway group denounced the conciliatory politics of the Officials and advocated a robust defence of Catholics by provoking the retaliatory nature of armed forces and shift the focus of the Army to be seen as the enemy. Their political aim was still a thirty-two county Ireland but to be Marxist. Their determination to escalate sectarian violence and risk reprisal became a major disagreement between the two factions and would lead to lethal faction fighting between Republican and Republican, Loyalist and Loyalist and Republican and Loyalist. In the middle stood the Army and the law abiding and generally middle class Protestants and Catholics. The political wing, Provisional Sinn Fein, was founded on 11 January 1970 by Rory O'Brady after a third of Sinn Fein delegates abandoned Official Sinn Fein in protest at the leadership's attempt to force through ending their abstentionism from Irish politics.

Since the IRA drew its support from working class Catholic estates and rural areas with strong Nationalist traditions, in advocating armed struggle, the Provisional leadership was an attractive recruiting sergeant among young Catholics lacking prospects. Few had long-standing Republican aspirations and were easy targets for their embittered leaders ambitious for a Marxist republic echoing the 1916 Rebellion, rejecting British rule in Northern Ireland and claiming that the IRA Army Council was the legitimate government of the Irish Republic. Willing to flex their muscles with their new found popularity in Nationalist enclaves, the recruits were often known as the '69ers'. The strategy developed by MacStiofain in this 'War of Independence' was 'escalation, escalation and escalation' and taking every opportunity to eject the 'Brits' by causing sufficient military casualties that the British public demands for the withdrawal of the Army would lead to the collapse of Stormont. The term 'Brits' was used by the Republican movement to describe the Crown, Parliament and the Army, which the Provisionals saw to be English. It was England that was the enemy because the IRA identified an affinity with the Celts of Scotland and Wales.

The IRA was divided into units in Ireland and five largely independent brigades in the 'war zones' of Belfast, Londonderry, East Tyrone and Armagh and the three counties bordering Northern Ireland. By 1972, the Belfast Brigade had grown to about 1,200 activists divided into the 1st (Andersonstown/Upper Falls) Battalion, 2nd (Ballymurphy/Lower Falls) Battalion, whose legendary D Company covered the Falls Road, and the 3rd Battalion covering the rest of Belfast, including the Ardoyne. The South Armagh Brigade with its 1st (Newry/Forkhill) and 2nd (Crossmaglen) Battalions and the iconic East Tyrone Brigade retained significant independence. The latter and its predecessors had a long history of activity in Northern Ireland, most recently in the Border War. Small units also existed in South Down and North Antrim. The titles 'brigade', 'battalion' and 'company' are merely nomenclatures and do not reflect the size of the units. Total strength is hard to gauge because membership was rarely admitted, except in court. However by the 1970s, the Provisionals are thought to have numbered about 8,000.

In his enlightening *A Secret History of the IRA*, the Irish journalist Ed Moloney traces the rise of the young Republican firebrand, Gerry Adams, from activist in the Ballymurphy to Provisional Sinn Fein politician. Born in 1948 to a fervent Nationalist family steeped by the influence of the conservative Redemptionist faction of the Catholic Church that preached in the Catholic estates, Adams worked as a barman before becoming involved in 'defence work' in Catholic areas of Belfast in 1969. While he has never admitted to being in the IRA and is alleged never to have engaged the Security Forces, that he was later interned largely from the intelligence gathered about him from informers, documents and observations, suggests that he had a significant influence throughout Operation Banner.

As with nearly every militant organization, there were disagreements. Dissidents in the Officials in December 1974 led to the establishment of the Irish Republican Socialist Party (IRSP). Trotskyite in ideology, the IRSP promoted an independent Irish

29

Republic divorced from the European Union. A founder was Bernadette Devlin who was the Mid Ulster MP in Westminster from 1969 to 1974. Its military wing was the Irish National Liberation Army (INLA), which attracted dissident Provisionals and managed to destroy itself through internal squabbling during the 1980s. Its most high profile action was the murder of the Conservative Party Northern Ireland spokesman and Colditz prison camp escaper, Airey Neave, within the confines of the House of Commons.

Libya became the biggest single supplier of arms to the Provisionals and influential American-Irish interests gave financial, political and logistic support, particularly through the Northern Ireland Aid (NORAID) pressure group. US Courts regarded the IRA as a political organization and used this in mitigation. After years of contributing to British difficulties in Northern Ireland, how the worm turned on 9/11. The Official IRA was generally supported by the Soviet Union. Irish nationalism has deep historical connections in Europe and it was not long before the determination displayed by the Provisionals led to alliances with international terrorists and radicals with links established to the Palestine Liberation Organization, the Sandinistas in Nicaragua and the Basque separatists. Ireland was in an invidious position.

In 1970, Captain James Kelly, an Irish Army intelligence officer, was later tried, along with two senior politicians, Charles Haughey and Minister for Defence, Neil Blaney, of conspiracy to buy arms for Republican paramilitaries to defend Nationalist areas in 1969. In dramatic trials, all three were found not guilty with Kelly insisting that the ministers were aware of the plan. In 2001, it emerged that the statement of his superior, Colonel Michael Hefferon, had been doctored to imply that Blaney knew nothing of Kelly's activities.

On 31 March, the B-Specials were disbanded and with them went an important intelligence resource. They were replaced, in part, by the Ulster Defence Regiment (UDR), as recommended in the 1969 Hunt Report, to protect the state from attack and sabotage by guarding key points and patrolling the border and areas not in civil disturbance. They were an early component of Ulsterization, the process of handing responsibility for Northern Ireland to the provincial government. The need to raise and train a RUC Reserve meant that the police were generally operationally ineffective.

The UDR was a major infantry component. Its establishment was similar to the raising of the Home Guard in 1940. On 1 January 1970 men of good character aged between 18 and 55 were invited to enlist for a minimum of three years as part-time soldiers by completing applications available from RUC stations and Army Careers Offices and later in libraries and post offices. Former B-Specials were permitted to enlist. Applicants were vetted by military security. On 18 February 1970 James McAree, a Catholic bookmaker's clerk aged 19 years, and Albert Richmond, a Protestant aged 47 years, were the first two sworn in. On the day that the UDR became operational, it was the largest regiment in the British Army with a strength of 2,440, including 946 Catholics, about half with military experience. It was divided into seven units – 1st and 2nd (Co. Armagh), 3rd (Down), 4th (Fermanagh), 5th (Co. Londonderry), 6th (Tyrone) and 7th (City of Belfast) Battalions. 3 UDR was noted for having the highest percentage of Catholics. A small number of full time UDR guarded UDR bases and carried out administrative tasks, supporting about 200 fulltime British officers and Other Ranks filling command and training appointments.

The first Commanding Officer was Brigadier Logan Scott-Bowden DSO OBE, a Royal Engineer. He was followed by the Catholic Colonel Kevin Hall. The depot was at Ballykinler. Shortage of equipment led to early patrols deploying in private cars and using public telephones and commercial radios to communicate. In 1972, the raising of 8th (Tyrone), 9th (Antrim), 10th (City of Belfast) and 11th (Craigavon) Battalions took UDR strength to 9,200, the equivalent of an infantry division. In 1973, the UDR was the first unit in the Army to admit UDR-badged women, largely as searchers and filling vital operational duties, such as signallers. A high percentage were executive professionals and were known as 'Greenfinches' from their nickname on the radio. Private Eva Martin was the first of four Greenfinches killed when RUC Clogher in May 1974 was attacked. Her husband was also wounded.

By 1972 intimidation, including the daubing of homes with graffiti, threatening letters and telephone calls, arson, children being bullied and sent to Coventry, was affecting the recruitment of Catholics. The first Catholic UDR soldier to be murdered was 7 UDR Private Sean Russell, shot in front of his wife in the Nationalist area of New Barnsley. After internment, about 75 per cent of the Catholics had resigned, one factor given was that no Protestants were rounded up. This led to the UDR becoming almost entirely Protestant and it was inevitable that some would be subverted. By 1973, military intelligence assessed that between 5 per cent and 15 per cent were associated with Loyalist paramilitary organizations.

31

An investigation into fourteen rifles missing from the HQ 10 UDR armoury in October 1972 found that the guard commander had nine convictions for deception, had spent time in jail and had been arrested in September outside RUC Tennant Street following the shooting of two men by Security Forces in the Shankill and the arrest of an UDA leader, who was also in the UDR. Of 106 weapons stolen from the 11 UDR armoury in Lurgan in October 1973, sixty-three rifles and eight Sterling sub machine guns were found in an abandoned Land Rover. A purge of subversives in 1972 saw about 1,000 UDR forced to retire.

A month after being formed, 400 UDR deployed with 1,600 Regulars on Operation Mulberry, a night search for arms by installing Vehicle Check Points (VCP) on roads from the border throughout Armagh, Tyrone and Fermanagh. Throughout the campaign, serving, off duty and former UDR were prime targets for assassination at home and at work, forcing some, particularly those living near the Fermanagh border, to sell their properties. By 1982, the attacks had become so serious that 120 Security Section in Lisburn was tasked by HQ UDR to analyse the murders and develop a survival training programme, the main issue being to contest the fatalistic idea that, 'If my number is up, it's up'. A member of the team, Corporal Nigel Gibson, was instrumental in making a training film at Fort Halstead, near Sevenoaks.

Sectarian squabbling again developed in Belfast when Nationalists from Ballymurphy stoned Junior Orangemen at Loyalist Easter parades in the Shankill. It was an Orange parade that had caused violence in August 1969 and, perhaps, it should have been banned, however the columns of Orange Orders, led by 'officers' in bowler hats, dark suits and Orange sashes following routes of historical significance, were statements of historical ascendancy over the Catholics and of such deep seated importance that few Protestant politicians dared challenge. For nearly three days, the 1st Royal Scots, with five Saracens supported by Royal Engineers ordered to dismantle barricades, separated the factions and suffered thirty-five soldiers wounded. Lieutenant General Freeland warned that petrol bombers would be shot after a warning.

As the summer months of 1970 wore on and the Loyalists prepared for their antagonistic marching season, celebrating the Battle of the Boyne, tension increased. In Belfast and Londonderry, encouraged by the Provisionals, friction between young Catholics and the Army developed, some accusing the soldiers of being foreigners. On 26 June, when 45 Commando, the 1st King's Own Scottish Borderers (KOSB) and the Royal Scots were tasked to prevent Nationalist mobs from interfering with marching Loyalists, the Royal Marines Support Company placed in the middle of two opposing howling mobs from the Ardoyne and the Shankill Road had every man in 11 Troop injured. A brick was smashed into the mouth of the troop commander from a range of about five yards. The same day, two young girls were the first children to die in the troubles when their IRA father experienced an 'own goal'. Throughout the day and night, the soldiers prevented 2,000 Catholics getting at 3,000 Protestants being corralled by the RUC and then at dawn, the mobs cheerfully dispersed, the Protestants waving Union Jacks and the Catholics their Irish tricolours.

BELFAST

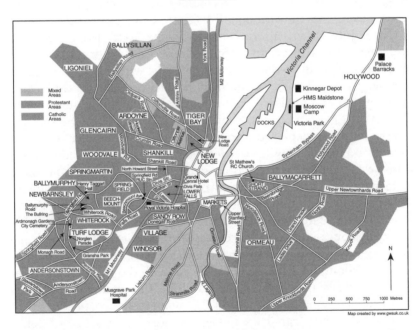

Map created by www.gwauk.co.uk

Next night, after the IRA killed three Loyalist gunmen in East Belfast, an Orange parade entering Mayo Street sparked another riot, which cost six gunmen shot dead, and three soldiers and about 300 people injured. Army estimates indicate that about 1,600 rounds had been fired from Catholic estates and 264 from Protestant ones. Killed armed terrorists were frequently referred to as civilians, which helped to stigmatize troops as murderers. The emergence of gunmen

33

in No Go areas introduced a new dimension to military tactics, in particular those who used disturbances as shields. Stormont, which was refusing to hand direct rule powers to Westminster, placed Lieutenant General Freeland under intense pressure to remove the barricades in the Lower Falls and impose sufficient law and order for the RUC to patrol without military assistance. On 1 July, troop levels reached 11, 250 all ranks when HQ 24 Airportable Brigade returned to the Province for a month, specifically to cover the Orange Order marches and was committed to North Belfast from the Firmount Territorial Army Centre with 45 Commando and 1 KOSB under command. The arrival and rotation of an increasing number of troops set the pattern for the next four years and when the Infantry sources began to dry up, Royal Armoured, Royal Artillery and Royal Engineers units became boots on the ground. HQ 5 Airportable Brigade also arrived and was accommodated in tents at Long Kesh until it took over the Firmount TA Centre from 24 Brigade.

On 3 July, when information from the RUC led 39 Brigade ordering 1 Royal Scots to search a house used by an Official IRA member in Balkan Street in the Lower Falls, within twenty minutes, twelve pistols, a rifle, a German Schmeisser sub machine gun, ammunition and explosives were found. Hostile mobs, furious that Protestant estates were not being searched, surrounded the soldiers. As the Battalion deployed to relieve them, in a helicopter overhead, Brigadier Hudson saw barricades being erected around the estate. Minute by minute, the situation deteriorated. And then, at about 6.45 p.m., two grenades were thrown at the Royal Scots, followed by three more ten minutes later as the Officials took on the Army. The 1 RRF, in Northumberland Street, had five soldiers wounded in an explosion and a big crowd, gathered in Grosvenor Road and refusing to disperse, was subjected to CS gas. A 2 Queen's company deployed along the Falls Road to link up with the Royal Scots at the junction with the Falls Road. Within the sealed-off area, 9 Independent Parachute Squadron RE removed the barricades in the Lower Falls and cleared the immediate area under a hail of petrol bombs and homemade grenades and ferocious rioting. By 10 p.m., the unrest was relentless and shortly after three soldiers were wounded in Omar Street, Lieutenant General Freeland ordered the area be placed under curfew and the troops to search for weapons, if the opportunity arose. During a search in Leeson Street, 2 Queen's found several automatic pistols, a printing press and arrested eleven people in a back room using a homemade radio to transmit instructions. The soldiers then came under heavy fire while removing barriers in the street and soon after RUC Springfield was attacked, heavy accurate gunfire developed from Plevna Street. 1 Devon and Dorsets, in positions on Grosvenor Road, arrested two bombers. The violence flooded into the city centre and continued through the night with the troops frequently coming under small arms fire and grenades as they struggled to dismantle barricades of buses, cars and other heavy objects. By 9.45 a.m. next day, the Lower Falls barricades had been removed and the curfew was briefly lifted soon after 2 p.m. to allow the residents to shop for the weekend. It was finally removed at 9 a.m. on 5 July.

The Balkan Street Search, or the Rape of the Falls in Nationalist circles, resulted in the seizure of twenty-eight rifles, two carbines, fifty-two handguns, fourteen shotguns, 100 incendiaries, 250lbs of gelignite, a grenade and nearly 21,000 rounds of ammunition. Four gunmen were shot by the Army, twelve people were treated in hospital and 337 were arrested. Military casualties amounted to thirteen from gunshot wounds and five injured by grenades. Military ammunition expenditure was 1,427 x 7.62mm rounds fired and 1,385 CS cartridges and 218 canisters discharged. Although the operation was intended to show military resolve, the robust manner in which searches were conducted and the failure to demonstrate impartiality by searching Protestant estates, who, after all, had first shot at the troops, led to Nationalist psychological warfare accusing the Army of being pro-Loyalist and RUC patrols unable to enter the Falls Road for years.

But was the incident entirely the fault of the Army? Special Branch still had overall responsibility for the collection of intelligence, however the information exchange with the Army was complicated and was unbalanced against the Catholic community, and therefore the IRA. The Army, although answerable to Westminster, was in support of Stormont, and carried out this and several other operations often against its better judgment.

In August, the Army introduced the 1.5-inch (38mm) rubber baton round. Capable of being fired from the same riot gun and pistol used to fire CS, the Rules of Engagement for PVC Baton Rounds stated that they could be used to disperse a crowd at ranges of not less than 20 yards when it was reasonable to minimum force. The rounds were to be fired at individuals and bounced onto the ground. There were occasions when rounds were fired directly at people resulting in fatalities and injury. By 1975 when the plastic baton rounds were issued, over 55,000 rubber bullets had been fired, many ending up on shelves as souvenirs or farewell presents. Later the 1.5mm Federal Riot Gun was introduced until it was replaced by the 37mm (1.5 in.) L 48 Riot Gun.

Military patrols besieging the No Go areas were challenged in gun battles that lasted for hours and led to the situation developing from public disorder into insurgency. Briefly, insurgency is armed insurrection by paramilitary bodies against an established civil or political authority. A paramilitary force can be defined as a military organization that has no allegiance to a particular country but is organized on military lines either in support of, or in opposition to, the constitutional force. The establishment of No Go areas policed by hooded armed gunmen and women banging dustbin lids when Army patrols approached, and a large Irish tricolour flying in the centre followed the revolutionary theory of 'liberated zones', indeed the Bogside was declared to be 'Free Derry'. Inside, the IRA exercised their brand of law enforcement. Punishment was usually summary and ranged from threatening caution for first offences to beatings varying in severity but included breaking bones in sustained attacks by groups of men, often armed with staves or metal bars. Shooting hands and crippling by 'kneecapping' and tying tarred and bird feathered 'offenders' to lamp posts in public places became common. Interrogations, often brutal involving torture, remained unchallenged by editors and civil liberty organizations. At best, offenders were exiled within hours with the threat to fear the worst if they returned. At worst, execution was a bullet in the back of the head and burial in an unmarked grave or left, sometimes booby-trapped, in a public place. To be fair, Loyalist paramilitaries were equally brutal, with the Shankill Butchers achieving an infamous reputation. In 1974, a mother was beaten to death with a brick while her small daughter hammered on the door.

When parades and marches were banned until the New Year, the 11,000 troops in theatre during the summer had been reduced to 7,000 by the New Year. But the next storm broke on 15 January 1971 with riots and shootings in Catholic estates. During the morning of 3 February, after several searches in Clonard, barricades were erected in several enclaves and serious unrest broke out, resulting in baton rounds fired and CS lobbed. In New Lodge three days later, a foot patrol from a Troop of 94 (Locating) Regiment deployed from the pretty town of Celle in West Germany and attached to 32nd Light Regiment, came under fire in Lepper Street from the Templer House Flats and Gunner Robert Curtis, aged 20, had the doubtful honour of being the first British soldier to be killed in action on Operation Banner. Four gunners were wounded in the same incident with Lance Bombardier John Laurie dying five days later. Their deaths led to Prime Minister Chichester-Clark declaring that Stormont was at war with the IRA. Curtis was the first soldier to be killed in action. Trooper Hugh McCabe, of the Queen's Royal Irish Hussars, was on leave, watching rioting below his parent's Divis Flat on 13 August 1969, when he was shot, probably by the B-Specials. Allegations that he was firing at them seem unfounded. On 13 September 1969, Lance Corporal Michael Spurway, of 24 Airportable HQ and Signal Squadron, was killed in an accidental discharge by a colleague while he was on the telephone to his wife, shortly after returning to his base after manning a rebroadcast station supporting 3 LI rear link communications. Other soldiers lost their lives in drowning and road traffic accidents and natural causes. The escalation in violence saw HQ 16 Parachute Brigade and its 216 Signal Squadron arrive at the former hosiery factory in Lurgan nicknamed The Knicker Factory and take responsibility for the southern part of Northern Ireland.

When the troops found that their VHF and HF Larkspur range of military radios were ineffective in the narrow streets, and incompatible with RUC and UDR communications, the Royal Signals set about resolving the issue with 233 Signal Squadron developing a network of commercial Pye Westminster personal radios that grew to 10,000 sets. Royal Military Police and sentries were issued with Pye Bantams while HQs had Cougars. Radio relay detachments were established on high ground throughout the Province to facilitate communications between the Brigade HQs and battalions. Typical was the Mount Divis site overlooking Belfast. With accommodation in 160lbs tents and the tracks muddy, resupply was by helicopter or Land Rovers in good weather. Nissen huts flown in two years later were replaced by Portakabins in 1979 and the site was nicknamed the Divis Hilton. UDR platoons provided the guard force. In January 1971, the IRA tried to disrupt BBC and Pye communications by attacking hill top sites. A 48lb bomb left at the Fathom Mountain site was defused but, during the mid-morning of 6 February, two BBC technicians and three contractors were killed when their Land Rover was blown up by a mine triggered by a nylon fishing line stretched across the road leading to the Brougher Mountain transmitter site. The device was intended for a 17/21st Lancers patrol visiting the site. E Troop, or British Army Signals Unit, Northern Ireland from 1972, provided electronic warfare intercepting and jamming illegal broadcasts and was instrumental in directing search teams to radios. It took as their mascots two grey and one red squirrel collected from England.

Lieutenant General Harry Tuzo took over as GOC on 2 March from Lieutenant General Vernon Erskine, who had suffered a heart attack a month after arriving. When, on the 20th, Major Chichester-Clark received just 1,500 troops of the 3,000 he believed that he needed, he resigned in favour of Brian Faulkner. The upsurge in the popularity of the Provisionals emerged during the Easter Rebellion parades when its Belfast march attracted far more support than the Officials. Faulkner faced a major crisis at the end of March when the Provisionals began a murderous campaign of 134 explosions between April and June, mostly car bombs. Sergeant Michael Willets, of 3 Para, was on duty in RUC Springfield Road when, during the evening of 25 May, a suitcase with a fizzing fuse was dumped inside reception, where there were several police officers, a man, a woman and two children. While one police officer raised the alarm and organized the evacuation through reception, Willets sent an NCO to evacuate the first floor and then went to reception himself where he held the door open until he was mortally wounded when the bomb exploded. For this act of selfless courage, Sergeant Willets was posthumously awarded the first George Cross of Operation Banner.

Riots intensified in the Bogside when two civilians were shot dead on 8 July in disputed circumstances, the Army and the RUC refusing to contribute to an unofficial investigation that then concluded Seamus Cusack was not armed with a rifle and Desmond Beattie was not about to throw a nail bomb. Three days later, the day before the Orange parades, the Provisionals, in a brutal attempt to increase tension between the Protestants and Catholics, exploded twenty bombs in Belfast over a twelve hour period. Although Tuzo deduced that a military solution could not be achieved, it was clear that the Provisionals intended to make Northern Ireland ungovernable and force Westminster to withdraw the troops. Since the New Year, thirteen soldiers, two policemen and sixteen civilians, mainly gunmen, had been killed and the bombing was causing economic damage and personal disruption to those who suddenly found them-selves unemployed. Unionist politicians believed the only way to defuse the situation was to introduce internment. As Faulkner commented, 'Is internment more of an evil than to allow the perpetrators of these outrages to remain at liberty?' It had, after all, previously been a successful and traditional method used by Dublin and Westminster to undermine the IRA. On 5 August, Faulkner persuaded Prime Minister Edward Heath that internment was the only option, a decision that would pitch Westminster into controversy that rumbles today. As always, the aim was to remove from circulation those believed to be involved in insurgency but impossible to place in the courts. While Faulkner was seeking to lock up 500 suspects, Lieutenant General Tuzo had serious doubts about the strategy and believed that the IRA could be defeated with reliable intelligence gained from about fifty suspects. Intelligence is the conversion of information from a variety of sources into knowledge about an enemy in time for commanders, at any level, to use it. However, the Army had no alternative but to follow the political lead of Stormont and Operation Demetrius was planned to lift 450 IRA suspects identified by the RUC. Faulkner insisted that no Loyalists, who had provoked the unrest in 1969 which had led to the troops being sent, be interned. Few would have believed that internment would be so controversial, in particularly the interrogation of suspects.

Reinforcements arrived from the United Kingdom and the UDR was placed on full alert. HQ 19 Airportable Brigade took over from HQ 16 Parachute Brigade in Lurgan in June. The training camps at Magilligan and Ballykinler were selected as holding centres, as was Girdwood Barracks and Palace Barracks. The former RAF station and Army vehicle depot at Long Kesh (translated as 'long bog crossing') near Lisburn was converted into a prison camp. In Belfast Harbour, the submarine-depot ship HMS *Maidstone*, which had been recommissioned as an accommodation ship for 2,000 troops in October 1969, was converted into Her Majesty's Prison Maidstone (HMP Maidstone) and run by the Northern Ireland Prison Service, supported by a military force and naval party.

Information is the soul of intelligence and since the Army was reliant upon unreliable RUC intelligence, a small team was sent from the Joint Service Interrogation Wing to debrief suspects of an Irish Republican organization that included 'Army' in its title and was known to practise resistance. While not suggesting that interrogation is a pleasant experience, naval and military prisoners understand that it is an extension of the battlefield and is permitted under the Geneva Conventions. When, in May 1972, the former Ministry of Defence official Cyril Cunningham, apparently an authority on brainwashing, described the reinforcements from the Wing as a 'bunch of roughs ... belonging to field interrogation teams', he clearly did not understand they were there to add to the intelligence picture by debriefing suspects from an organization that posed a subversive threat to national security. British military interrogation first came to public note in 1946 when parliamentary questions inquired about the Bad Nenndorf centre in occupied West Germany. Concerns were also raised in Kenya, Cyprus and Aden but not in the confrontation with Indonesia in Borneo, probably because there were not enough hotels for journalists, or during the Falklands Campaign where the battlefield debriefing of prisoners became crucial and correspondents were diverted from witnessing activities involving prisoners. Unfortunately for the Army, Belfast was a short flight from London and there was a comfortable watering hole at the Europa Hotel. The 'roughs', who were all trained at the Wing, knew that most prisoners are prepared to talk, that humanity gets the best results and torture and brutality is counter-productive and nowhere is this more important than in counterinsurgency where human intelligence is critical. They used techniques developed during the 1950s, which had been updated after lessons learnt during confrontation in the 1967 'Joint Directive on Military Interrogation in Internal Security Operations Overseas'. Among the techniques available to undermine resisting prisoners were five techniques, used in holding centres, of rationing food, water and sleep; isolating prisoners gathered in a room by the wearing of hoods and use of 'white noise' and reducing physical resistance by stressful postures against the wall. These were known as the Five Techniques and were also used to train Allied personnel to resist interrogation. Although interrogation is a legitimate form of warfare, it is too often equated with the torture and brutality used as political tools by organizations such as by the KGB and individuals such as Pol Pot in Cambodia, Saddam Hussein in Iraq and President Mugabe in Zimbabwe. The 2003 BBC documentary *We Have Ways of Making You Talk* examined Northern Ireland in 2003 and, in following the well-trodden route of accusing the Army of brutality, it failed to expose the brutality of Provisional interrogation. Although the Army trained a few RUC in military interrogation methods, many Army officers had considerable reservations that it would be misused. Their global experience was that a chat after a good night's sleep was just as effective.

As dawn broke on Monday 9 August, Operation Demetrius saw a total of 342 suspects bundled into lorries and APCs and ferried to one of the screening centres. Although many soldiers were distinctly uncomfortable about breaking into bedrooms and arresting suspects amid frightened, protective women and screaming, weeping children, they had moved into estates that were known to be dangerous and where soldiers had been killed and wounded. The raids sparked considerable civil unrest and banging dustbin lids led to mobs throwing anything to hand at the soldiers, including nail bombs, and also sniping. The Ballymacarret and Ardoyne residents threw up barricades. Londonderry was quieter. When Private Winston Donnell of 6 UDR, was shot dead at a VCP near Claudy, Co. Tyrone, he was the first UDR soldier to be killed in Operation Banner. By nightfall, it became clear to Army commanders that mistakes in identification had been made. Most of the arrest lists concentrated on the Official IRA because Stormont believed it presented more of a threat to national security than the embryonic Provisionals. Others were political opponents of the Unionists and some were elderly IRA veterans. Joe Cahill, the Provisional Chief of Staff, admitting to thirty IRA being arrested, claimed on 16 August that he had expected internment to be introduced at some time. Several hardliners had avoided arrest by going 'on the run' across the border in Ireland. Nevertheless, enough information was gathered to damage the Londonderry Brigade with arrests, arms caches found, safe houses identified and about eighty crimes solved. The unrest over the next two days was the worst since 1969 with seventeen people killed, including ten IRA shot by the Army and a priest caught in crossfire giving last rites to a dying gunman.

Within forty-eight hours, 116 suspects had been released. The remaining 226 (eighty-six in Belfast, sixty in Armagh, twenty each from South and Mid Armagh and forty in Fermanagh and Tyrone) were detained under Interim Custody Orders (ICO) with 124 being detained in C Wing, Crumlin Road Prison with the remainder boarding HMS *Maidstone*. Of the 882 arrests made over the next three months, 416 were released within forty-eight hours and the remainder either interned or detained. The first Protestant to be interned was on 2 February 1973. By the end of January, 2,357 people had been arrested of which 598 were interned and 159 detained. Throughout, Prime Minister Faulkner claimed all those lifted were terrorists or members of the IRA. On the direct orders of Stormont, eleven suspects were transferred from HMS *Maidstone* to the Ballykinler interrogation centre. Not surprisingly, the eleven found the process intimidating and frightening and they were released and told their stories. The IRA realized that they had a significant propaganda weapon that could be exploited to disrupt intelligence gathering and cried 'Foul'.

With Operation Demetrius showing clear discrimination against opponents of Unionist politicians, Stormont, which had insisted on internment, remained unusually silent as the Army, which had thought the idea unwise, faced political and editorial onslaught with the *Sunday Times*' Insight Team in the van. The Government accused the BBC of political bias, the first sign of several disagreements between the public broadcaster and government about Northern Ireland. The new Social Democratic and Labour Party (SDLP) protested at internment and organized a campaign of civil disobedience and strikes. When its leader, Gerry Fitt, complained to the United Nations on 25 August about interrogation techniques, Home Secretary Reginald Maudling commissioned Sir Edmond Compton, the Northern Ireland Ombudsman, to investigate. His 'Report of Enquiry into Allegations Against the Security Forces of Physical Brutality in Northern Ireland Arising out of Events on 9th August 1971' dated 16 November, acknowledged that, while the Army had exercised restraint under adverse conditions, the Five Techniques constituted physical mistreatment. To some extent, the Compton Report was discredited because most of those interviewed were employed in the interrogation centres.

With Westminster and the Army reeling from the international criticism of internment, and Stormont strangely uncommunicative, recruitment into the IRA swelled. Civilians employed by, and contracted to, the Security Forces were intimidated, Customs posts attacked and, at the end of September, a 3.5-inch rocket launcher used for the first time. In the four months after internment, thirty soldiers, eleven RUC and seventy-three civilians, which included terrorists, were killed. On 15 October for two hours, thirty gunmen from the safety of Ireland engaged a British patrol not allowed to deploy or fire mortars across the border. Eight days later, the Army shot two female members of the Lower Falls IRA giving warnings of raids on addresses. Ten days later, when HQ 19 Airportable Brigade at Kitchen Hill was relieved by HQ 5 Airportable Brigade, its 205

Signal Squadron had Signalman Paul Genge, one of three brothers serving with the Royal Signals, killed on 7 November while he was off-duty in Lurgan. For years afterwards, patrols noted, on the anniversary, a floral posy left at the spot. Another signaller was badly wounded in the same attack. In the last months, off-duty UDR soldiers were attacked for the first time and fifteen people died when a Loyalist bomb destroyed McGurk's Bar in Belfast. It was originally thought to have been an IRA 'own goal'.

Chapter 4

Over The Water: The Provisional Offensive 1971 to 1972

By the end of 1971, insurgency was on the increase and the Army was in a position that it was neither trained for, nor wanted. Compared with the knowledge of the ideology, personalities and methods of the Official IRA, little was known about the Provisionals except that its members were dangerous, clever, highly politicized with revolutionary fervour and were challenging Army patrols that entered No Go areas. The Army had been welcomed by the Catholics as the constitutional armed force to protect them from Protestant mobs, but the Provisionals had chipped at this belief and it was now the enemy. Troop levels had increased to 13,600 from 12,300 in August 1971. So far, 43 soldiers had been killed as had five UDR, eleven RUC and 150 civilians. Corporal Ian Armstrong, of the 14/20th Hussars had been killed when two Ferrets that accidentally crossed the border near Crossmaglen were attacked by a mob and his was set on fire. Sixty-four IRA and two Loyalists had been killed in gun battles or 'own goals' and there had been 1,515 bombs.

While Westminster and Stormont squabbled as to who should govern the Province, investment was drying up and emigration was increasing with about 7,000 Catholics leaving, many never to return. With the RUC re-organizing, the unified police/military command structure was weak and consequently the vital coordinated internal security strategy was virtually non-existent. 'Hearts and minds', so important to counterinsurgency, was practised only at low level and NICRA was testing the authorities by announcing illegal marches and forcing the Security Forces to prevent marches from reaching trouble spots and then arrest the leaders. Intimidation in the courts was rife and offenders were walking away from justice with a grin.

In October, HQ 3 Infantry Brigade took over from HQ 5 Airportable Brigade at 'The Knicker Factory' in Lurgan. Part of the 1st Infantry Division, the Brigade was evacuated from Dunkirk in 1940, had landed in North Africa with 1st Army in 1943 and then fought through Tunisia and Italy until 1945. Deploying to Palestine and Egypt, it returned to UK after Suez and then took part in operations against Greek-Cypriot Nationalists in Cyprus until disbanded in 1963. It arrived to control the border from Carlingford Lough to Fermanagh and straddle IRA supply routes to Belfast through the hardline South Armagh and East Tyrone. Its population centres included Bangor, Downpatrick, Newry, Banbridge, Armagh, Dungannon, Omagh and Enniskillen. South of the picturesque, fresh water Lough Neagh, the new town of Craigavon, stretching between Lurgan and the Protestant stronghold at Portadown, had several derelict estates in which patrolling was a nightmare. The families that had moved brought endemic sectarianism that led to the estates nearest Lurgan being Catholic and those nearest Portadown being Protestant. At the height of Operation Banner, the Brigade had resident battalions on two year tours in Ballykinler and Omagh and rotating roulement HQs at Bessbrook, Armagh, Dungannon and Long Kesh prison. The Knicker Factory was near the Northern Bank where some soldiers had accounts and the nearby British Legion welcomed the soldiers but at high risk of retaliation. The base was surrounded by a green corrugated iron fence overlooked by sangars manned by a roulement infantry company. Inside on the ground floor was the transport compound, the Sergeants' Mess, armoury, stores and offices and a small gym with a folding squash court and a basketball court that doubled as a parade ground and chapel. Wide spaces, such as the cookhouse, were sub-divided by mortar shelter walls. Kitchen Hill was often sniped at, was hit by RPG-7 rockets and, in November 1972, was mortared from a convent used by military families to christen their babies. A helicopter landing site (LS) outside the perimeter was at risk from gunmen. Brigade HQ was on the fourth floor and, on the upper floors, the soldiers squeezed into rooms with rows of double bunks. Other Ranks on long tours were accommodated at Westacres, a small estate between Mandeville and Brownlow guarded by a Royal Pioneer Corps section. The popular Private Phillip Drake, aged 18, was killed in an Officials ambush en route to Kitchen Hill on 26 August 1974; however by the end of the day, the gunman had been arrested. Service children went to local schools. Employment opportunities for wives were non-existent and most shopping focused on the Protestant centres at Portadown and Banbridge. One wife found the driving test in Armagh easy because the city centre was barricaded. Officers lived in Bacombra, a small estate near Portadown. Unlike Cyprus and Aden where several Service wives and children were murdered, the only direct attack occurred on 9 August 1973 when the Provisionals exploded a 400lbs bomb outside the Alexandra Road married quarters at Lisanelly Barracks, injuring three women. Such was the outcry that there were no further attacks. A problem for those serving at Kitchen Hill was that the route passed through two hardline Catholic estates. Cycling was out of the question and for those who did not use cars, a small blue removals van ferried the soldiers, who always expected the worst – an ambush – and hoped for the best. Varying routes was limited.

In Londonderry, Chief Superintendent Frank Lagan, the Catholic Divisional Commander, had kept reasonable tranquillity for several years by regular contact with Catholic community leaders through intermediaries. After the first NICRA march on 5 October 1968 had ended in widespread violence, when on 16 November, a protest crossed the Craigavon Bridge and headed toward the city centre, he negotiated that as it approached the police cordon, the leaders could symbolically breach the barricades and would then be diverted along an agreed route. The strategy was confined to Londonderry but always at risk of disruption and violence. On 22 January 1972, several thousand people approaching Magilligan Point to protest at the internment camp, ignored hot refreshments being offered by 1 RGJ and headed for a line of barriers manned by 1 Para. Commanded by Lieutenant Colonel Derek Wilford, it was on its second tour and usually based at Holywood Barracks as the 39 Infantry Brigade Resident Battalion and Reserve. Soon after arriving in Northern Ireland in September 1970 and after becoming involved in gun battles in the cauldron of Belfast in which it was not unknown for IRA gunmen to use mobs as shields, the Battalion had developed tactics to intercept escaping gunman by outflanking the crowd in pincer movements. When the protesters filtered around the barricades and the paras fired rubber bullets and CS, not for the first time would they be singled out when SDLP member John Hume described them 'beating, brutalizing and terrorizing the demonstrators'. With its reputation for resolute action, units wearing the Red Beret of the Airborne Forces soon became a red rag to the Nationalist bull. After NICRA announced it intended to hold a non-violent demonstration at Foxes Corner in Londonderry during the afternoon of Sunday 30 January, tension rose throughout Northern Ireland. Colloquially known as 'Free Derry Corner', the venue was symbolic because it was the scene of the first civil rights demonstration three years earlier.

Brigadier Andrew MacLellan had arrived as Commander, 8 Infantry Brigade in October 1971 and, after witnessing Lagan divert the NICRA march on 16 November, he saw no good reason to change the strategy. By early 1972, HQ Northern Ireland had become concerned that compared with the robust tactics used by 39 Infantry Brigade in Belfast, which then was commanded by Brigadier Frank Kitson, this 'softly, softly' approach and the copious use of CS in crowd dispersal was not taking the initiative to defeat the IRA. Kitson was an incisive thinker fresh from a defence fellowship, who had published *Low Intensity Operations: Subversion, Insurgency and Peacekeeping* in which he concluded that the coordination of intelligence and counter-revolutionary measures were critical in defeating insurgency. Advocating that, 'We beat terrorists before we negotiate with them', he predicted that the disorder in Ulster would threaten civil stability in UK. On 24 January, Brigadier MacLellan took Lagan's recommendation to Major General Robert Ford, Commander Land Forces, that the march be allowed without military intervention because of the sensitivity of gathering at Foxes Corner. However Ford told him to plan an arrest operation and to use 1 Para. This induced concern at HQ 8 Infantry Brigade because of the criticism of the Battalion after Magilligan and that it was unfamiliar with Londonderry. Even after two RUC officers were shot dead in the Creggan on 27 January, Brigade HQ and Superintendent Lagan still favoured conciliation, nevertheless MacLellan planned to chaperone the march and protect the city centre and its commercial heart with manned barriers.

At about 2.50 p.m. on 30 January, the 800 protesters that had assembled in Central Drive in the Creggan left Bishop's Field and headed toward the Bogside to join the agreed route at the junction of Eastway and Lone Moor Road. Half an hour later, the march, now some 4,000 strong, passed the Bogside Inn, ambled along William Street, turned into Rossville Street and headed toward the Rossville Flats behind a lorry prepared as a speaker platform. Major General Ford was on the ground near William Street. At Brigade HQ, MacLellan was listening to reports being beamed down from a

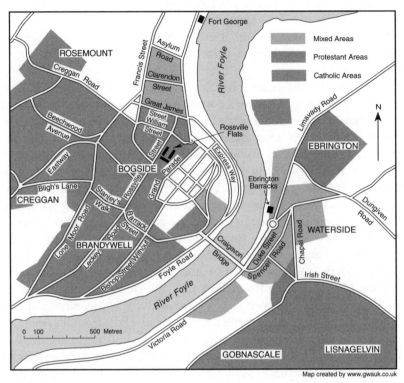

ROSEMOUNT

Francis Street
Asylum Road
Clarendon Street
Great James Street
William Street

Creggan Road

Beechwood Avenue

Eastway

BOGSIDE

Bligh's Lane

CREGGAN

Stanley's Walk

Barrack Street

Lone Moor Road

Leckey Road

BRANDYWELL

Bishop Street Without

Foyle Road

Rossville Street

Grand Parade

Fort George

River Foyle

Rossville Flats

Express Way

Ebrington Barracks

EBRINGTON

Limavady Road

Dungiven Road

WATERSIDE

Chapel Road

Craigavon Bridge

Spencer Road

Duke Street

Irish Street

River Foyle

Victoria Road

GOBNASCALE

LISNAGELVIN

Mixed Areas
Protestant Areas
Catholic Areas

N

0   100   500 Metres

Map created by www.gwauk.co.uk

circling helicopter. As the march turned into Rossville Street, some protesters approached Barrier 14 from 'Aggro Corner' and pelted soldiers manning it with a hail of missiles, including fire grates and metal rods used as javelins. 'Aggro Corner' was the scene of regular confrontations after school and at weekends between groups of Catholic youths known as the 'Derry Fusiliers' and the Army. Supported by the soldiers firing controlled volleys of rubber bullets, a water cannon doused the 'Fusiliers' sheltering under corrugated iron 'tortoises' with liquid dye. By about 4 p.m., the pressure on Barrier 14 was beginning to lessen, with reports that the rioting was no more intense than usual. Since the arrest operation was determined by the location and strength of the protest, it was up to 1 Para when to launch it. At 3.55 p.m., Wilford asked Brigade HQ for permission to deploy a company to arrest the Derry Fusiliers. What happened next is controversial. At 4.09 p.m., Major Steele, the

Brigade Major, agreed with the request and instructed 'Not to conduct running battles down Rossville Street'. By now, protesters were assembling at Free Derry Corner.

Meanwhile, Major Ted Loden, who commanded Support Company, had sent Mortar Platoon to find a route so that Aggro Corner could be approached from William Street. When the Platoon reached the Presbyterian Church on Great James Street and was clearing wire from a perimeter wall, a bullet fired from the area of the Rossville Flats punctured the gutter at the side of the church. When Loden then sent Machine Gun Platoon to cover Mortar Platoon from a derelict house on William Street and lingering rioters at Aggro Corner saw the soldiers and attacked them with a hail of missiles, including two nail bombs, the paras opened fire and wounded two men in the belief that they were throwing grenades. When Loden was ordered to initiate the arrest plan, Mortar Platoon, crammed into two Pigs followed by Company HQ, Anti Tank Platoon in empty Pigs and Composite Company in two 4-ton Bedford lorries, advanced down Little James Street. As they breached Barrier 12 and entered Rossville Street, the Derry Fusiliers scattered and joined people in front of C Company, which was advancing on foot down Chamberlain Street toward the Flats from Barrier 14. When the Mortar Platoon commander stopped his Pig at the derelict Eden Place and his Platoon Sergeant parked in front of a barrier of rubble in front of the Rossville Flats Block 1, it caused some panic among the crowd endeavouring to avoid arrest. It was now that the paras believed they came under small arms fire and nail bombs and returned fire. Major Loden later reported coming under automatic fire when he dismounted from his Ferret Scout Car. In Rossville Street, Anti Tanks and half Composite Platoon deployed onto Kells Walk and opened fire at gunmen reported to be in Glenfada Park North. After C Company had linked up with Support Company at Eden Road, by about 5.30 p.m., the area had quietened and 1 Para had withdrawn.

The event was witnessed by camera crews and journalists, and global indignation grew when it emerged that thirteen people, most in the Glenfada Park area and six of them minors, had been shot and four injured by 1 Para. The first fatality, Jackie Duddy, aged 17, carried through the para lines accompanied by Father Edward Daly waving his white handkerchief, is possibly the iconic image of the day. One of the two shot at William Street, an elderly man, died four and half months later. When Brendan Duddy, a Catholic businessman with close links to the Officials and a strong believer in political negotiation, heard about the events, he told his friend, Chief Superintendent Lagan, that the incident was 'absolutely catastrophic. We're going to have a war on our hands'. Duddy ran a fish and chip shop in Londonderry and was supplied with beefburgers brought by a van driver named Martin McGuiness. Controversy grew. While Ivan Cooper, an SDLP MP, claimed that he had been assured that no armed IRA men would be near the march, Father Daly and others alleged they had seen an Official haphazardly firing a revolver in the direction of the paras and that he had been photographed in the act of drawing his weapon. As had happened at Croke Park in 1916, Nationalist historians dubbed the event Bloody Sunday. Next day, Home Secretary Reginald Maudling reported in Westminster the Army version that the troops had 'returned fire directed at them with aimed shots and inflicted a number of casualties on those who were attacking them with firearms and bombs'. However this was challenged by eyewitness claims that the paras had fired into an unarmed crowd.

The IRA immediately issued orders to shoot as many British soldiers as possible, an order that remained in force until 1994. Some were shot while on patrol, others were victims of mines and bombs and some while on leave. By 2007, over 1,000 members of the Security Forces had been killed on active service in defence of the country from subversion just 200 miles from London, a fact that is largely forgotten. Private Gary Barlow, aged 19 years, of 1st Queens Lancashire Regiment (QLR) was separated from his patrol during a disturbance in Albert Street, Lower Falls on 5 March 1973 and surrounded by a crowd who wrestled his SLR from him. Some women tried to hustle Barlow to safety by jostling him to a garage in McDonnell Street but an IRA gunman pushed his way through the crowd into the garage and executed Barlow with two shots.

On 1 February, Prime Minister Heath announced that Lord Chief Justice Widgery would conduct an investigation into Bloody Sunday. However some witnesses, suspicious of Widgery's impartiality, boycotted the hearings. Next day, a few hours after the funerals in the Creggan of eleven of the dead, Anglo-Irish relations hit a low ebb when mobs burnt the British Embassy in Ireland and Dublin demanded UN intervention in Northern Ireland. When Sir Peter Rawlinson mentioned that Dublin was contributing to the unrest by failing to arrest IRA using Ireland as sanctuary, the Irish Attorney-General Colm Condon accused him of being emotive. Condon had been Attorney-General during the Kelly trial and had IRA connections through his father. When the retired British Army Major Hubert O'Neill, the Londonderry coroner, issued a statement on 21 August that, 'It strikes me that the Army ran amok that day and shot without thinking what they were doing...I would say without hesitation that it was sheer, unadulterated murder. It was murder,' there were calls for his resignation from Stormont. The day after Widgery began his inquiry on 21 February, the Officials exploded a bomb at HQ Parachute Regiment in Aldershot in direct retaliation for Bloody Sunday. In April, Widgery concluded in his 'Report of the Tribunal Appointed to Enquire into the Events on Sunday, 30th January 1972, Which Led to Loss of Life in Connection with the Procession in Londonderry on That Day' that there was no evidence that any of those shot had handled firearms or bombs but there were suspicions that others had handled weapons. While acknowledging that, had 8 Brigade persisted with its low key attitude, the march would probably have passed off without incident, he criticized Brigade HQ for underestimating the hazards to civilians when the troops believed they came under fire. Widgery acknowledged that 1 Para had showed a high degree of responsibility, however opening fire had bordered on reckless, nevertheless he did not believe that there had been a breakdown in discipline and those soldiers who had fired had done so in accordance with the rules listed in the Yellow Card governing the rules of engagement. Nationalists labelled the findings the Widgery Whitewash and induced controversy that has lasted years. In 1992, Prime Minister John Major wrote to SDLP MP John Hume reminding him that the Government in 1974 had admitted that:

> Those who were killed on 'Bloody Sunday' should be regarded as innocent of any allegation that they were shot whilst handling firearms or explosives. I hope that the families of those who died will accept that assurance.

When the Peace Process gathered pace in the early 1990s, in spite of Provisional atrocities remaining largely unaddressed, Bloody Sunday had become so embedded in Republican mythology with songs, dramas and books that the new Prime Minister, Tony Blair, not only apologized but was persuaded by Republican negotiators to order a second inquiry. Chaired by Lord Saville and more comprehensive than the Widgery Inquiry, some witnesses, including soldiers, refuted earlier statements. McGuiness, Sinn Fein deputy leader in 1998 and second-in-command of the Londonderry Provisionals on Bloody Sunday, admitted that he was present but refused to answer questions because, he claimed, it would compromise the safety of the individuals involved. At first, Saville insisted that the soldiers should be identified. At the end of six years, 432 days of oral testimony from over 900 witnesses and the 42-day opening speech by Counsel to the Inquiry, the second longest inquiry in English legal history and costing £180 million and rising, Saville has yet to publish his findings. There has been some suggestion that future inquiries in Northern Ireland should adopt truth and reconciliation committees.

Matters worsened for the reputation of the Army when Lord Chief Justice Hubert Parker published his 'Report of the Committee of Privy Councillors Appointed to Consider Authorized Procedures for the Interrogation of Suspects of Terrorism'. Although the Committee Report concluded that interrogation was a vital intelligence resource and that there had been no brutality, Lord Gerald Gardiner of Kittisford published a Minority Report criticizing the interrogations and claimed that crucial intelligence had not been gained. Emphasizing the rising profile of human rights and that psychological abuse was as inhumane as physical brutality, he pinned the blame on:

> Those, who, many years ago, decided that in emergency conditions in Colonial-type situations that we should abandon our legal, well-tried and highly successful wartime interrogation methods and replace them by secret, illegal, not morally justifiable and alien to the traditional methods by the greatest democracy in the world.

Gardiner, was a reformer who had served with the Friends Ambulance during the Second World War. Presented with opportunities to express moral indignation and interrogation, the Provisionals and liberty pressure groups forced the Army onto the ropes for the second time within months. Such was the international political pressure on Prime Minister Heath that, on 2 March, he had little option but accept the Minority Report and told the House of Commons that the Five Techniques 'will not be used in the future as an aid to interrogation', although debriefing would continue. But the matter did not rest and the IRA watched British liberal opinion undermine military operations in Northern Ireland. The respected

British political analyst Alistair Cooke mobilized official, public and private American opinion, particularly among families with Catholic Irish antecedents, in the US by commenting that torture in the guise of interrogation had been used in Northern Ireland. One result was that in US Courts, Irish terrorism was seen to be political and a defence. Nationalists were still in full cry two years later and at the European Court of Human Rights, Great Britain was convicted on a charge brought by Ireland of 'inhumane and degrading treatment' and instructed to pay compensation to the detainees. Arguably, the Minority Report and the editors who undermined interrogation, and still do, lengthened Operation Banner by several years because intelligence had to be reorganized.

In the meantime the Provisionals escalated their murderous campaign of bombings and shootings and still Stormont, in spite of the deteriorating internal security situation, refused to hand over Direct Rule to Westminster.

On 4 March, the bombing of the Abercorn Restaurant in Belfast, without warning, that killed two young women and injured 130 was followed a week later, after a three day truce, with bombings in Belfast and Londonderry. During the month, the Army was involved in 399 gun battles that rose to 724 in April and 2,718 in July. British soldiers, in particular, now had to be vigilant on operations, in barracks and at home and abroad. Orders were issued that uniform was not to be worn in public places and no longer could they hitchhike. Armed patrols patrolled barracks and training facilities wherever the Armed Forces were deployed. The pressures of this 24 hour, 365 day vigilance over thirty-eight years are rarely recognized today.

The history of ordnance disposal can be traced to the Boer War when the Army Ordnance Corps and, after the First World War when the RAOC assumed responsibility for the disposal of land ordnance until, on its disbandment, the role was taken over by the Royal Logistic Corps. In June 1969, 321 Explosive Ordnance Detachment (EOD) was formed to support overseas operations and took the grinning cat Felix as its insignia, alluding to the feline nine lives. The radio message 'Fetch Felix' summoning an Ammunition Technical Officer (ATO), probably became the second most used radio message throughout Operation Banner. The Pink Card Guidelines for 'Dealing with Terrorist Ambush, Bombs and Booby Traps in Northern Ireland' established the procedures to be adopted with suspicious objects. A warning was given to search and secure all vantage points and reliability of information checked. A cordon and an Incident Control Point were to be sited, a plan developed and intelligence collected before, during and after the incident, in particular deploying observers to look out for suspects watching Security Force activity.

Bombs, or more accurately, Improvised Explosive Device (IED) require two fundamental components – explosive and a trigger. At first, the explosive was often gelignite stolen from agricultural stores and quarries. Triggers were initially rudimentary, such as the pressure on the jaws of a clothes peg forcing solder wire to stretch and form an electrical circuit to a battery, but grew in sophistication with the increased availability of electronic components. While there is no doubt that most IEDs were supported by code warnings, they were designed to disrupt economic and commercial life. Collateral damage led to loss of life, physical and psychological injury and hardship, as employees suddenly lost their jobs. Incidents always tied up sizeable Security Force operations evacuating the public and cordoning areas until the all clear was given. The collection of evidence by Royal Military Police bomb intelligence teams and its examination by scientists at HQ Northern Ireland, led to the identification of bomb makers. One East Tyrone bomber was regularly identified by a pile of faeces deposited at the bomb site. By 1973, most towns were surrounded by a network of oil drums and barriers filled with concrete, 'sleeping policemen' across roads, parking restrictions and warnings that empty cars were liable to be blown up.

In the early days, marksmen sometimes sniped at parts of the bomb and 84mm Carl Gustav anti-tank projectiles broke up the solidity of explosive. Initially, ATOs, making the lonely walk, wore an armoured vest that covered the front of the body down to knee level and a helmet with a visor until the Stores and Clothing Research Development Establishment, Colchester and Galt Glass then developed the first of several variants of the fireproof Kevlar Suit Explosive Ordnance Disposal to allow ATOs to examine devices and decide how they should be tackled. Initially bulky, heavy, restrictive with a radio slotted in a pocket on the back, the glass reinforced plastic Kevlar plates protected the chest and abdomen from blast. The helmet was fitted with an armoured visor and a ventilation/demisting system.

The 170 IEDs defused in 1970 rose sharply in 1971 to 1,515. Captain David Stewardson was the first ATO killed when he disturbed an anti-tampering micro switch at the Castle Robin Orange Hall on the road between Belfast and Aldergrove on 9 September 1971. When controls were placed on gelignite in 1972, the bomb makers resorted to deadly homemade explosive (HME) cocktails, usually by boiling NET fertilizer to make ammonium nitrate and mixing it with fuel oil (Anfo). NET was legally available in the thousands of farms throughout the island of Ireland. The process was seriously flawed – miscalculating the percentage mix in the manufacturing process was sometimes fatal. About 120 IRA scored 'own goals' either while manufacturing, ferrying or placing devices. A veteran of the 1940s campaign suffered a lingering death in December 1971 when he generated sparks while mixing HME with a metal shovel on a concrete floor. The relative ineffective power of HME was countered by packing several hundred pounds into a gas cylinder in a car or a series of milk churns placed in a culvert under a road and detonated from firing points across the border. Corporal David Powell of the 16/5th Lancers, was killed on 22 October 1971 when his Ferret was mined near Kinawley a few hours after his squadron had taken over from the 17/21st Lancers.

As patrols gained more experience, the buried cables of Command Wire IEDs (CWIED) were detectable by sharp observation, supported by air photography. When a 2 Para patrol in South Armagh noted buried wires leading from the border and found a 160lbs bomb in a culvert, a helicopter with a scanner located eight devices laid in a horseshoe pattern. Victim Operated (VOIED) could be defeated by awareness, in particular checking underneath cars. The most loathsome device was the 'proxy' bomb in which a driver would be blackmailed to deliver it. On 21 April 1974, four men packed a hijacked car with about 650lbs HME bomb and instructed the driver to park in the centre of Newtownbutler. When it exploded, a RUC officer and a farmer both lost a leg and twelve families abandoned badly damaged homes. Initially, proxy bombs were difficult to counter because of the understandable determination of drivers to complete the instruction. Incendiary devices frequently deposited in clothing shops by Republican women were countered by searchers and electronic searching. When radio controlled IEDs (RCIED) first appeared in 1972, some were defeated by portable, vehicle and airborne Electronic Counter Measures (ECM) operated by Romeo Troop, 233 Signals Squadron, which had been formed in October. When, at the end of 1972, 321 EOD requested urgent technical support from HQ Northern Ireland to improve bomb disposal technology, within days a Royal Artillery lieutenant colonel at the Fighting Vehicle Research and Development Establishment had developed a prototype wheeled robot, invented by Foreman of Signals Jackson, then at Kitchen Hill. This consisted of a system of universal mechanical arms controlled by a long cable connected to a console. Morfax Ltd of Mitcham took the idea and manufactured the tracked Wheelbarrow with several fittings, including a boom for other devices, such as a grab and tow hook, a camera linked to a monitor, an automatic shotgun to blow open packages and fracture doors and windows locks and a device that fired nails into floors to prevent doors closing. 'Pigstick' provided an explosively-propelled jet of water. Wheelbarrow teams consisted of the No 1 – ATO/team leader, No 2 – robot operator, No 3 – 321 EOD Signals Troop radio operator and No 4 – an infantry soldier for close protection. With over 400 Wheelbarrows damaged or destroyed between 1972 and 1978, the REME had a critical role in repairing and maintaining the equipment. ATOs first transported their equipment in APCs and then in Ford Transit vans until the arrival of the Pinzgauer 718 all terrain EOD Variant in the 1990s, itself replaced by Leyland DAF lorries. In the UK, fast saloon cars driven by police-trained military drivers and equipped with sophisticated computers allowed bomb intelligence to be shared.

Early on 14 March 1972, Staff Sergeant Christopher Cracknell and Sergeant Anthony Butcher defused several HME devices in the York Street Belfast Co-Op and left others to be soaked by the Fire Brigade, a not uncommon practice. The HME mix of sodium chlorate and nitro benzene became known as Co-Op. Butcher had defused 100 devices and Cracknell forty-four since December 1971. At about 5 p.m. next day, when a 1 Glosters patrol became suspicious of a Ford Corsair near the Ormeau Road and radioed 'Fetch Felix' at about 7.30 p.m., both ATOs blew open its boot in a controlled explosion using Cordtex. When they noted a box on the back seat, they used a hook and line to open the rear door and returned to the car where Butcher radioed the patrol that he thought the device to be sophisticated and that he would bring it out. But as Cracknell reached into the car, there was a massive explosion, which killed both ATOs, and then gunmen opened fire on the cordon. Because ATOs were so valuable, 321 EOD decided that from henceforth one ATO would deal with one device – the long, lonely walk. When a bomb exploded six days later in Lower Donegal Street killing six people, including two RUC officers evacuating people and a UDR soldier, and injured

100 others, an iconic image is of Private Wayne Evans of 1st Parachute Battalion cradling a woman who had just lost both legs while another para administered treatment. Cracknell and Butcher and Major Bernard Calledene, on 30 March, were the only ATOs killed defusing car bombs throughout Operation Banner and are included in the eighteen killed between 1971 and 1985.

A simple tactic of ambushing military vehicles was to use two parallel roads. On 10 September 1972, a 1st Argyll and Sutherland Highlanders patrol in a Saracen was on the road between Dungannon and Benburb when a 500lbs RCIED mine hurled the APC onto its side 20 yards across the road. Five civilians who arrived at the scene left without calling for an ambulance, but a Mini, on its way from Benburb, drove into the 20 foot crater, injuring its woman driver. Privates Douglas Richmond and Duncan McPhee were killed instantly and Lance Corporal William Macintyre, who had just returned from a fortnight's leave, died of his wounds. Richmond's deaf parents were told that he would not be going on leave within days, as they expected.

In 1975, an analysis of border incidents at HQ 3 Infantry Brigade attributed all to paramilitary activity except for three men stabbed with pitchforks in Fermanagh in late October 1972. There the matter rested until 1978 when a man implicated four Argylls to Glasgow detectives. In 1981, a sergeant and a private were sentenced to life for the murder of two of the men, neither of whom was involved in the insurgency. An officer resigned his commission. Their motivation appears to have been revenge for the killing of the Argylls. The murder of the third man, a well known terrorist, remains a mystery.

The Royal Engineers have a long history of dealing with conventional unexploded bombs and searching for mines and booby traps. Throughout Operation Banner, speculative rummaging and intelligence searching was a major component of daily operations although, at first, the poor reliability of RUC information and the robust manner in which searches were sometimes conducted alienated the Army in Catholic estates. Nevertheless by 1971, planned and opportunity searches were disrupting the IRA supply chain and the caching of arms, ammunition and equipment. In 1977, the thirteen infantry battalions in the Province carried out about 130 searches each week. All resident and roulement battalions trained in 'rummaging' vehicles at VCPs. When patrols were seen to shelter in abandoned houses in poor weather and took cover in particular places, they were careful to check for booby traps. Dogs trained by the Royal Army Veterinary Corps (RAVC) proved invaluable in sniffing out explosive material and documents with traces of explosive. Several were killed. When Corporal Derek Hayes was killed on 21 May 1988 by a booby trap in Crossmaglen, the ashes of his Labrador, Ben, were buried with him. Each infantry company had a specialist search adviser, usually the Company Sergeant Major, supported by the battalion specialist advisor, often the Regimental Sergeant Major (RSM). The next level up was Royal Engineer Search Teams (REST) who usually dealt with IEDs before 'Fetch Felix'. Lieutenant Winthrop, of the Royal Green Jackets, introduced an innovative technique of patrols asking, 'What is an obvious marker for a cache?' – perhaps a distinctive headstone in a cemetery – and then searching the immediate area. Naval boarding parties searched vessels ranging from yachts to merchantmen.

The shape of the Loyalist response to the escalation of Republican insurgency had emerged in September 1970 when several Loyalist Defence Associations in Belfast amalgamated. A year later, the Ulster Defence Association (UDA) emerged as the most influential of the Loyalist paramilitary organizations and, at its peak in the mid-1970s, numbered about 40,000 members. A founder member was Sammy Duddy, who achieved fame as the transvestite 'Samantha' on the entertainment circuit and used his female persona to evade the attentions of patrols and Nationalists. The UDA basic principle was that if the Provisionals ended their campaign, the UDA would do the same. But if Westminster withdrew, the UDA would use its majority democratically or fight, as 'the IRA in reverse', to stay within the United Kingdom governed by a devolved Stormont. Its military wing, the Ulster Freedom Fighters (UFF), emerged in 1972 as loosely organized firebrands prepared to take the law into their own hands. It is thought to have shot Sean McConville, aged 17 years, on 14 April in the first of many random and retaliatory sectarian killings. After being forced out of the UDA because of his militancy, John McKeague formed the Red Hand Commandos in the Shankill, which integrated into the UVF but retained its independence. The Loyalist Association of Workers, set up in 1971, illicitly manufactured several hundred simple firearms in the predominantly Loyalist Harland & Wolff shipyards in East Belfast.

When the Protestants protested that the No Go areas were not part of the United Kingdom, they placed Stormont on notice to do something about them. Stormont was unable to meet the conditions of the Downing Street Declaration and still refused to transfer power to Westminster until, on 30 March, Prime Minister Heath announced that, under the Northern Ireland (Temporary Provisions) Act, the Province would be governed by Direct Rule from London. William Whitelaw arrived as the first Secretary of State for Northern Ireland. On 6 April, Lord Scarman issued his report of the causes of the 1969 violence and concluded that the RUC had misjudged the situation on several occasions. Appreciating that Direct Rule was a sensitive issue, Army commanders adopted a low key approach. Nevertheless, internal insecurity deepened on 14 April when the Provisionals exploded twenty-three bombs throughout Northern Ireland, escalated their insurgency by attacking Army patrols and had their first major engagement with Loyalists in the Oldpark district of Belfast a month later. On the same day, Colonel Gaddafi announced that he had supplied arms to the 'revolutionaries' in Ireland. The number of weapons captured in searches was steady at seventy-eight, seventy-four and ten in the same months. The 1 RRW casualty list included six killed in a month. The kidnapping and murder by the Officials on 21 May of Ranger William Best, when he left his parent's home to use a public telephone while he was on leave in Londonderry from the 1st Royal Irish Rangers in West Germany led to outrage so widespread that they declared a ceasefire nine days later and won the release of almost all their prisoners. While the intimidation by the IRA of the UDR and RUC is well documented, far less acknowledged is the bullying of soldiers and families of Irishmen and women serving in the British Army. At least, seven Regulars were murdered while on leave in Northern Ireland, a statistic that does not figure on the official Roll of Honour. Private Thomas McCann, of the Royal Army Ordnance Corps (RAOC) was abducted by the Officials while he was visiting his mother in the south and executed on 14 February 1972.

When on 13 June, the Provisionals invited Whitelaw to meet them in Free Derry, he warned that he intended to re-establish a lasting legitimate presence throughout Ulster until a political solution was achieved. Nevertheless in spite of the gun battles, secret talks between MI6 and the Provisionals on 20 June led to a ceasefire being agreed for the 26th to allow negotiations to take place. As midnight approached on the 26th, about 150 men from 23rd Engineer Regiment, which was on an infantry roulement tour, and several others units were crammed into the Short Strand Bus Depot when, at 11.57 p.m., a gunman shot Sergeant Malcolm Banks, a 16 Squadron Troop Sergeant. He had just returned from ensuring that all patrols were off the streets with several men from other units. The soldiers were furious at this lack of goodwill, however RSM Mick Turner ordered that they remove their flak jackets and helmets, as a sign of good faith, and confined them to the depot before returning to HMS *Maidstone* next morning. Banks, who left a wife and two children, had seen service in Kenya, when the King's African Rifles mutinied, and in Aden and had been leading a project to create a playground for handicapped children. He was one of two soldiers killed on 26 June.

Included in the Provisional delegation that went to London on 7 July was Gerry Adams, who was released from internment after being arrested in March, and Martin McGuiness. Born in Derry, McGuiness began work as a butcher's assistant. Following the emergence of the civil rights movement, he became involved in Republicanism and was second-in-command of the Londonderry Provisionals by 1972. When the delegation refused to consider a settlement that did not include the Army retreating to its barracks and the release of Republican prisoners, Whitelaw again warned them that 'liberated areas' in any part of the UK defaulted from the normal standards of law and order and government and then signalled that the No Go areas would be challenged. He refused to release Adams from internment but did give interned prisoners, sentenced to more than nine months imprisonment and claiming political status, to be Special Category. This permitted them to wear their own clothes, exempted them from work and segregated them into sectarian compounds where the internees regarded themselves as prisoners of war and organized themselves along lines reminiscent of Second World War prison camp films with command structure and escape committees. Granting the internees this status gave the paramilitaries credibility and would prove a running sore for years to come.

Chapter 5

Defeat of IRA Insurgency
1972 to 1973

When the talks stalled on 9 July over the housing of Catholics in the Lenadoon in the Suffolk area of West Belfast, the 2nd (Ballymurphy) Battalion was quick to return to hostilities by opening fire from prepared positions on 20th Medium Regiment and 40 Commando preventing homeless Catholics occupying houses in Horn Drive. The forlorn hope of the first glimmer of a negotiated settlement had disappeared with too many hidden agendas, particularly by Seamus Twomey, of the Belfast Brigade, who was spoiling for a fight on the grounds of 'one big push to finish once and for all'. With Westminster insisting that the rule of law must be applied throughout Northern Ireland and the influence of the hardliners must be neutralized, by mid-July, the Army was finalizing plans to dismantle the No Go areas in Operation Motorman.

Military intelligence is the conversion, storage and timely dissemination of analysed information to commanders and is the currency for firepower – knowledge adds strength to the arm. With RUC intelligence proving unreliable, the Intelligence Corps reorganized its Northern Ireland structure into four strands of operational and strategic intelligence, protective security, intelligence liaison and covert operations. In a strategy masterminded by HQ Northern Ireland, in between the gun battles, patrols had been carrying out a discreet census by collecting information on virtually every household, business and community activity listing political leanings, habits and interests meticulously written or typed onto index cards and cross-referenced to other reports, photographs and newspaper articles assembled into an intelligence 'doomsday book' database and analysed by Battalion and Brigade intelligence sections and at

HQ Northern Ireland. Why was there an extra milk bottle on a doorstep? Someone 'on the run', perhaps? National, local and organization media outlets, such as the Republican *An Phoblacht*, were trawled for items of intelligence interest. Research Offices attached to the Brigades sowed the seeds of source and informant handling. Royal Engineers Military Surveyors from the HQ Northern Ireland Map Store combined the intelligence with photographs produced by the Joint Air Reconnaissance Information Cell (JARIC) at RAF Aldergrove to produce 'Tribal maps' showing demarcations – green for Catholic, orange for Protestants and white for mixed. At last, troops could see at a glance the sectarian structure of Northern Ireland.

On 14 July, three British soldiers were killed, as were two IRA. Four days later, Kingsman James Jones, aged 18 years and of 1 King's, was shot outside the Vere Foster School, New Barnsley Estate, West Belfast, as was Kingsman Brian Thomas, aged 20, six days later in the same place. Fifty-seven soldiers had been killed since 1 January. The Provisional Belfast Brigade retaliated to the breakdown of the talks with an attack on Belfast on Friday 21 July. Described on the Channel 4 programme *Car Bomb* by a former bomber as a 'spectacular' ordered by Provisional leaders, over a ninety minute period, a mix of twenty-two car and package bombs wreaked havoc across Belfast killing nine people and injuring seventy-seven women and girls and fifty-three men and boys. Although warnings were received every few minutes, the Provisionals badly underestimated the ability of the Security Forces to deal with so many bombs in a small area over a short period. Outside the Ulster Bank Limestone Branch in North Belfast, a Catholic woman lost both legs and a VW estate car bomb exploding outside the Ulsterbus depot in Oxford Street killed Sergeant Philip Price from the Welsh Guards and Driver Stephen Cooper, as they were clearing the area, and four Protestant employees. A car bomb outside shops on Cavehill Road killed the teenage son of a Protestant vicar and two Catholic women, one of whom, Mrs Margaret O'Hare, was the mother of seven children. Her 11-year-old daughter was badly injured. At Nutts Corner west of Belfast, a driver of a bus full of children avoided the majority of a landmine blast intended for a British Army vehicle. The Provisionals were roundly condemned for the murderous mayhem of Bloody Friday.

The Belfast Telegraph:

> This city has not experienced such a day of death and destruction since the German blitz of 1941. With the callous lack of remorse now so typical of the Provos they audaciously accepted responsibility for what was an operation clearly requiring considerable planning and manpower.

The Irish Times:

> Throughout the 32 counties Irish men and women should ponder how a virulent Nazi-style disregard for life can lodge in the hearts of our fellow countrymen; all the more virulent in that once again the innocent have been the main sufferers. Hitler in his Berlin bunker decided that the German people were no longer worthy of him and deserved not to survive. Yesterday's dead and injured are testimony to something similarly rotten in our philosophy of life.

It took Gerry Adams thirty years to apologize for the outrage, and to claim that there had been no intention to cause civilian casualties is unbelievable. If correct, Bloody Friday was an extremely badly planned operation. Ed Moloney suggests that Adams then took command of the Belfast Brigade from Seamus Twoomey and appointed Ivor Bell as his adjutant.

The failure of the talks and Bloody Friday led to the Army realizing that the pendulum had swung in their favour for the first time since mid-1970 and HQ Northern Ireland planned Operation Motorman to flood the No Go areas with a strong military presence and challenge Republican and Loyalist paramilitaries to fight or flee. It was not intended to be punitive, more the restoration of democracy against revolutionary insurgency. Public announcements giving the areas the opportunity to dismantle the barriers were generally ignored and the gun battles continued. On 26 July, 1 LI, on their third tour, took over from 1 RRW in the Ardoyne and was equipped with Saracens, as opposed to the Humber Pigs they had in 1971. Two days later, a platoon based in Flax Street Mill was deploying in response to a warning of a bomb at the shop at 100, Alliance Avenue when it came under fire. 10 Platoon was giving covering fire with a GPMG and, as his men doubled past him to prevent the gunmen using Berwick Road and Etna Drive to escape, the Platoon Commander noted their anxiety. A section came under automatic fire from another position and as the rounds ricocheted off his Saracen, in the confines of the narrow street, he found it impossible to tell the difference between echoes and the crack – thump of bullets overhead and then, suddenly, the firing ceased, as though by agreement.

In preparation for Operation Motorman, Great Britain was permitted by NATO to release troops from West Germany. HQ 5 Infantry Brigade, which was commanded by Brigadier Richard Trant, and seven battalions arrived from BAOR and UK in Operation Glasscutter, the 12,000 troops involved bringing the total in theatre to 21,290 – roughly 40 per cent of the Army – the largest deployment of the Armed Forces since Suez in 1956. Some arrived on board the assault ship HMS *Intrepid* deployed from a major refit at Portsmouth. The deployment was as follows:

39 Infantry Brigade
Resident
Holywood
1 PWO on its second tour. Arrived May 1972.

Roulement
City Centre
1 Welsh Guards on its second roulement since June 1972.
Suffolk
2 RRF on roulement since July. Lost Major Snow killed in the New Lodge in December 1971.
Beechmount
3 R Anglian on roulement tour since April.
Springfield Road
1 King's on roulement since April. Second tour since September 1969. Three soldiers killed in action in May and two in July.
New Lodge
40 Commando since June. Lost Marine Allen killed in July.
East Belfast
Life Guards. Roulement tour since 24 July.
Musgrave Park
19 Field Regiment RA.

Emergency
Ardoyne
1 LI arrived on 26 July. Third tour.
1 Para arrived in July. Third tour since October 1969. Had left as

66

Holywood Resident Battalion in June.

Springfield Road

2 Para arrived on 29 July. Lost a para killed in Anderstown in July 1971.

Ligoneil

42 Commando arrived on 28 July.

8 Infantry Brigade
Londonderry

Roulement

20 Medium Regiment. First roulement tour.

Creggan

1 Royal Scots. On fourth roulement tour since March 1970. Arrived in June 1972

Bogside

2 Queen's. Emergency tour. Third tour since March 1969.

Ballykelly

33 Independent Field Squadron. Resident Squadron.

Emergency Tours

1 Coldstream Guards. Arrived on 27 July having completed third roulement tour in February since December 1969

2 Scots Guards. Arrived on 28 July on second roulement tour since 1970.

3 RRF. Having departed in May after its first roulement tour, returned in July.

2 LI. Having departed in February 1972 after its third roulement tour, returned in June.

26 Armoured Engineer Squadron. Arrived on 30 July from West Germany.

15 Squadron RCT arrived from Osnabruck to join 1 Squadron providing drivers for the 110 Saracens.

Ballykelly

7 Field Squadron. Arrived July.

39 Field Squadron. Arrived March.

Antrim

59 Independent Commando Squadron RE. Arrived 24 July.

3 Infantry Brigade
Ballykinler

1 King's Own Borderers. Lost Colour Sergeant William Boardley

shot in Strabane in May 1975.

Roulement
Bessbrook
1 Argyll and Sutherland Highlanders
Long Kesh
4 Light Regiment RA
8 Field Squadron RE
Castledillon
32 Field Squadron RE
Emergency Tour
Dungannon
1 Queen's Own Highlanders arrived on second tour on 28 July.
Armagh
1 Gordon Highlanders arrived on 28 July on second tour since November 1971. Had lost three killed in a booby-trapped house in Lurgan in June 1972.

The assault ship HMS *Fearless* was off Cape Wrath with elements of 3 Commando Brigade and 846 Naval Air Squadron preparing for a naval gunfire support exercise when she was instructed to sail at best speed to Rhu on the shores of Gare Loch and lift 2 Scots Guards to Belfast, which she did on 28 July. She then returned to Rhu where a troop of four 26 Armoured Engineer Squadron Armoured Vehicles RE (AVRE) and a couple of Ferrets under the command of Captain Steve Taylor were embarked. The AVREs had been transported from Hohne garrison in north-west Germany and then ferried on the Army Landing Ship Tank HMAV *Audemer* to Marchwood Military Port near Southampton. They had then been driven by a tank transporter unit to the RCT slipway at Rhu and were embarked on HMS *Fearless*. In order to deflect the accusation that the Army used tanks to quell civil disturbance, as the Soviets had done in Czechoslovakia in 1968, the word 'Royal Engineer' was painted in white on their bazooka plates. Two naval recce teams from the ship flew by civilian aircraft to Northern Ireland with orders to find a suitable beach near Londonderry. Meanwhile, HMS *Fearless,* which was loitering off the east coast of Islay in order to avoid inquisitive questions about the AVREs, was joined by the minesweeper HMS *Gavington* to finalize landing the AVREs. Although not strictly an opposed landing, snipers could be disruptive. By 30 July, the recce team had selected a beach near the Army base at Fort George on the west bank of the River Foyle about two miles north of the Foyle Bridge. After dark,

Royal Engineers arrived and over the next five hours in pitch darkness laid three layers of Class 30 trackway on top of each other from the waterline across the beach and up a steep bank and pegged it to firm ground. As midnight approached, Captain Taylor and his HQ and the Beachmaster Party were flown ashore and the four landing craft skippered by four Royal Marine colour sergeants carrying the AVREs slipped out of the dock of HMS *Fearless*. HMS *Gavington* lurked at the mouth of the river to suppress gunfire. In poor visibility and rain, the coxswains kept to the deep water channel a few hundred yards from the Irish border and then, shortly before midnight, the Beachmaster switched on two dim, beach lights indicating the landing gate. Immediately after the ramp of the first landing craft crunched onto the trackway and a Ferret plunged ashore, the first AVRE trundled across the beach and up the steep bank without damaging the trackway. Twenty-six minutes later, the Troop was formed up waiting for H-Hour. By 3 a.m., the beach was clear.

Operation Motorman commenced at 4 a.m. on 31 July. The troops encountered little resistance because the IRA had no answer to the power of the Army and the nucleus of hardliners had gone 'on the run' to the sanctuary of Ireland. Military restraint ensured that civilian casualties were avoided. By 11 a.m., Royal Engineers' bull-dozers had destroyed No Go Area barriers in East Belfast, the markets and city centre. Residents in some Catholic estates offered to scrub slogans from walls. In Londonderry, the AVREs supported 3 RRF and 1 Royal Scots, choking the Creggan and Bogside by trampling over barricades and obstacles. Two gunmen were killed. When a Blues and Royals Ferret Scout Car commanded by Corporal of Horse Chris Hughes in the Enclave area was damaged by a mine and came under small arms fire, the driver immediately dropped the side hatch with the intention of hitching a tow rope to a Saladin Armoured Car, until he was reminded by Hughes to wear his helmet. In another incident, the exhaust manifold of a Saladin exploded and when spilt petrol from the fuel tank at the rear caught fire, the commander and gunner abandoned the burning Saladin, but its 76mm gun was in low elevation over the front hatch and the driver was unable to open it and escape. The commander returned to the armoured car and told the driver that he was going back into the turret to elevate the gun. If he failed, then he would shoot the driver so that he would not suffer. Reportedly, the driver was 'non-phased' about this suggestion but mentioned that it was getting a little warm.

Fortunately, the commander elevated the gun. Elsewhere, Nationalist and Loyalist strongholds in Armagh, Coalisland, Lurgan and Newry were entered. Royal Engineer search teams, targeting properties from the meticulous intelligence collected before the operation, recovered thirty-two weapons, including a Thompson and several M1 Carbines, over 1,000 rounds of ammunition, 450lb of explosive and twenty-seven prepared devices. Thirty people were arrested, of whom twenty were charged. The day was marred when three bombs planted by the Provisionals exploded without warning in the tiny border village of Claudy, killing six people and mortally wounding three. By 3 p.m., the AVREs had been recovered from the Fort George beach and the tired sappers were welcomed on board HMS *Fearless* with a cake. The ship then sailed for Plymouth, safe in the knowledge that the Royal Navy had played a key role in the success of Operation Motorman.

Army commanders had expected the Provisionals to resist but they had not and they had seized the initiative. The former No Go Areas were still dangerous places and would remain so until the end of Operation Banner.

On 8 August, a 1 LI platoon was moving across waste ground between Etna Drive and Jamaica Street in the Ardoyne. On the parallel axis in Berwick Road was the Platoon Sergeant leading a section. When several shots were heard, the Platoon Commander had trouble locating the gunman in the narrow, echoing streets. When his sergeant reported that he had a casualty and had located the gunman, as he led his men across the Berwick Road junction to outflank the gunman, the Platoon Commander saw a private lying in a front garden, his combat trousers dark red with blood and surrounded by a small crowd, some with blankets and bandages. One woman was punched by a man when she spat at the soldier while another pointed to a wall over which the 'bastard escaped'. The arrival of a Catholic priest horrified the soldier and then, when Knights of Malta paramedics turned up in an ambulance, the sergeant let them treat the wounded man. The Platoon Commander had no intention of allowing the vehicle of an organization known to evacuate IRA casualties take one of his soldiers. Eventually, a military ambulance appeared, having got lost.

On 29 August, the Platoon provided the inner cordon for an arrest operation to pick up Martin Meehan, the 3rd Battalion commander thought to be at 19, Jamaica Street. A tough docker, Meehan had the reputation of being the most aggressive of the hardliners and usually

70

resisted arrest. His father had been imprisoned for IRA activities in the 1940s and his grandfather was killed at the Somme. During the 1969 riots, he was one of the few IRA who did not run away and had been captured by 1st Green Howards in January 1972 and was detained after being implicated in the deaths of five members of the Battalion killed in the Ardoyne in 1971. In December, he and another hardliner Tony Doherty had escaped from Crumlin Road Prison by crouching knee deep in an exercise yard drain before scaling the wall with a sheet and reaching Dundalk. A month later, he was one of seven Provisionals acquitted of possession of weapons by an Irish Court after a four-hour border battle with the Royal Scots Dragoon Guards during which he claimed to have 'pasted them. You could have heard them squealing for miles'. In fact, the only casualty was a prize winning pig. Meehan then returned to Northern Ireland. Dropped from Saracens, as the Platoon took cover in doorways along Jamaica Street, surprised long-haired IRA lookouts fled and women screamed. When the Platoon Sergeant saw Meehan scurrying into No. 32, the soldiers detailed to make the arrest ran to the house under fire, barged through the door and unceremoniously dumped the belligerent Meehan into a Saracen. The LI covered the withdrawal from Jamaica Street and, in spite of retaliating with baton rounds, several soldiers needed stitches after being injured under a hail of paving slabs, stones, and bottles. The Platoon Commander fired two shots at a gunman seen near the junction of Herbert and Butler Streets. Meehan spent the next twenty-two years mostly behind bars on various charges, including the first person to be charged with membership of the Provisionals. He was the last internee to be released and later delved into politics until he died in 2007. The Platoon later protected a Royal Engineer bulldozer clearing a barricade at the top of Etna Drive and retaliated against a coordinated and relentless volley of bottles, bricks, stones, ironmongery and steel pipes masquerading as javelins, with baton rounds until a bullet smacked against a wall about two feet from a private's head. The Platoon Commander noted that whenever gunmen opened fire, while 'eight terrified men on the edge of life and death in a desperate firefight' were in one street, in the next street mothers with toddlers in pushchairs were oblivious to the shooting. He was once followed by two women deciding on the size of his coffin.

On 30 September, the Battalion lost Private Thomas Rudman shot while on patrol in the Ardoyne. A year earlier on 15 September 1971, his elder brother, Private John Rudman serving with 2 LI, was killed during an ambush while travelling to Coalisland. Both came from West Hartlepool and are thought to be the only brothers killed in Northern Ireland.

On 11 October, the Platoon had just finished restoring order at 100, Alliance Avenue after a bomb had wrecked the shop, when the crowds suddenly dispersed and the soldiers were ambushed by automatic fire from several positions. Covered by the .30 inch Brownings on their two Saracens, as the men ran for cover, a private tripped into a barbed wire entanglement. An Army sniper who climbed onto the roof of Young's burnt out garage was spotted by gunmen but still coolly returned fire. Believing that the Provisional position was at the south end of the waste ground and, with covering fire from 1 Section, the Ring OPs and the 3 Section Saracen, the Platoon Commander led his Assault Group of two Saracens through Etna Drive, their Brownings chattering noisily. Turning onto the waste ground, as the Saracens lurched over two cars blocking Stratford Gardens, he learnt over the radio that the gunmen had bugged out. The Assault Group then came under fire from the east end of Stratford Gardens, bullets pinging off his Saracen. With speed essential, 1 Section tried to outflank the gunmen by driving down Etna Drive, Berwick Road, and Stratford Gardens. Although the soldiers claimed several hits, no blood trails were found. When the Platoon occupied the three Ring OPs during the night of 18/19 October and came under single shot and automatic fire from several firing points, the bullets peppering the observation slits of the northern and centre OPs, the soldiers tempted the gunmen with a uniformed tailor's dummy. A private fired four shots at a gunman in the ruins of the shop and watched as he buckled backwards. During a lull, a woman washed blood from the street with a mop and bucket, a sure sign of a confirmed hit.

On 3 November, while the Platoon was searching the waste ground for weapons, two soldiers ran from a path to Etna Drive shouting 'Take cover!' And then one fell wounded in the leg by a nail bomb exploding in front of them. The Platoon Commander instinctively kicked the door into the backyard of the nearest house and, running through it onto Etna Drive, he saw a gang of children in the middle of the street, none of them aged more than 10 years, swinging paint tins packed with nails.

And then in October 1972 the first time that the public, and indeed most of the Armed Forces, were aware that the Army was engaged in intelligence operations, the story of the Four Square Laundry broke. Instigated by Brigadier Frank Kitson, 39 Brigade began joint RUC/Army plain clothes surveillance patrols in April 1971, mostly in Belfast. After the intelligence debacle surrounding Internment, the Brigade formed the Military Reconnaissance Force (MRF) from mostly soldiers with Irish backgrounds. With a remit to operate in the shadows of conventional activities from Palace Barracks, the MRF used 'pseudo gang' counterinsurgency techniques that had been used in Kenya and Cyprus. One method involved driving around Nationalist estates with turned informants known as 'Freds' identifying active IRA. Although the system was always at risk of compromise and mischief by the Freds when they left the compound, valuable intelligence was gained. Another activity was to destabilize paramilitary activities; for instance on 12 May, the MRF opened fire on Catholic ex-Servicemen's League VCP in Anderstown with a Thompson. In a controversial incident on the day of the IRA truce, a captain and a sergeant were arrested by a RUC patrol shortly after they had shot at a group of men in Glen Road, one of whom was named as having been involved in the murder of the three Royal Highland Fusiliers in March 1971. Smelling a scoop, editors targeted the MRF, in particular a year later when Sergeant Clive Williams was found not guilty of the attempted murder of three gunmen who, he claimed, had opened fire on his car.

The IRA also regarded intelligence as a key issue and Volunteers released after arrest were usually debriefed. When the D Company, 2nd (Ballymurphy) Battalion in the Lower Falls learnt that Seamus Wright was apparently spending time in England, he admitted under interrogation that he had actually been in Palace Barracks and iden-tified another D Company Volunteer, Kevin McKee, as an informer. The Belfast Brigade mounted a counterintelligence operation and learnt that several married quarters in Palace Barracks were occupied by a shadowy military organization. Reports then surfaced from Twinbrook that a personable brother and sister employed by the Four Square Laundry had been doing brisk business from a Bedford van for several days but no-one knew where the clothes were laundered. It seems likely that when a Fred saw the van in Palace Barracks, by the end of September, the Belfast Brigade had become deeply suspicious that offices at 15 College Square East and above the Gemini Health Club massage parlour at 397, Antrim Road, being used by a man and two women, were linked with the Four Square Laundry. During the morning of 2 October, the Brigade launched a coordinated attack; 2nd Battalion gunmen ambushed the

Bedford, killing the 'brother', Sapper Ted Stuart, an Irishman from Co. Tyrone. His 'sister', Lance Corporal Sarah Warke, WRAC attached to the Royal Military Police, managed to radio their controller in the College Square office, an Intelligence Corps corporal, who evacuated it with weapons, equipment and documents shortly before it was attacked by 3rd Battalion gunmen. The Gemini Health Club was also attacked soon after it had been evacuated.

The Four Square Laundry was part of the intelligence census, and cover for collection of laundry, which was then forensically examined for evidence of explosive or ammunition handling. The roof of the Bedford was fitted with a compartment as a mobile OP. A technical surveillance operation targeting clients using the Gemini Health Club had identified three IRA involved in the murder of the three Royal Highland Fusiliers; one would die in a gun battle with the Army in June 1973. Wright and McKee were executed by the IRA – their value of no further use. In claiming that the ambushes were as devastating a blow against military intelligence as the attack on the Cairo Gang in 1920, the Belfast Brigade leadership gave themselves too much credit. The willingness of the Army to employ covert operations caused suspicions throughout the Belfast IRA that lasted for years, particularly in the elitist 2nd Battalion. Provisional propagandists cried foul and encouraged sympathetic political and social organizations to believe that covert military operations would lead to sectarian hostility. Insisting the revolutionary drive would prevail, they continued to persuade Catholics to believe that they were at war and only the Provisionals were capable of defending them.

In spite of the setback, the MRF had proven the value of covert intelligence operations and, when Kitson heard that HQ Intelligence and Security Group (Germany) had formed a surveillance detachment, he asked if it could be transferred to Ulster. Nicknamed 'The Det' and commanded by Captain Stewart Small, 8 Detachment was formed by the Intelligence Corps to monitor the Soviet Military Mission (SOXMIS) shadowing NATO activities in the British zone and also supported Intelligence Corps counterintelligence sections in West Germany. Several WRAC were attached to the surveillance teams. But surveillance of the unarmed but expert Soviet intelligence officers in West Germany was markedly different from Northern Ireland and, when asked, Small believed his men needed at least three months' retraining. It would also mean that SOXMIS would not be shadowed. Another factor was that the Intelligence Corps did not have sufficient men to raise a quick reaction force to rescue surveillance detachments in trouble.

The SAS was the only Army unit not involved in Ulster and although it was involved in Dhofar, it had the capability to provide a quick reaction force but not expertise to provide surveillance although this was not the opinion of SAS Sergeant Major Connors. Accompanied by a major he had visited 8 Detachment and concluded was 'it was less professional than they could have been'. He seems to have ignored the role the Detachment and the vast experience the Intelligence Corps had assembled worldwide through Field Security and its successors since 1940. Interestingly, Connors also concluded the intelligence 'doomsday book' to be 'staggeringly inefficient' and a 'colossal waste of time'. That good intelligence had defeated Provisional insurgency seems to have escaped him. Nevertheless, the SAS took full control of surveillance, except training which fell to Captain Small running a two week course on the SAS selection course initially at Lydd and then as at the SAS training camp at Pontrilas. The final surveillance exercise took place in Bristol and those who had the aptitude were assembled in the Special Reconnaissance Unit (SRU) under direct command of HQ Northern Ireland. Its remit was to conduct surveillance as a preliminary to arrest by uniformed Security Forces and to protect people and property under threat. Its detachments were organized into several units with cover titles, such as 4 Field Survey Troop RE in Castledillon and the Northern Ireland Training and Advisory Team (NI). Crucial to surveillance throughout Operation Banner was informant handling.

The Protestants had watched the internal security situation without serious response until October when the Ballymacarret UDA in East Belfast rioted to remind Westminster that Loyalist views should not be disregarded. Unfortunately their timing was poor and two 1 RGJ companies and the dismounted Life Guards quelled the disturbances. 1 Para dealt with more unrest on the Shankill Road.

The last major event of 1972 took place on 26 November when a bomb exploded in the Film Centre Cinema in Dublin. An investigation, suggesting that Republican extremists were responsible, led to the Offences Against the State legislation being enacted in Ireland. Four days later, two car bombs exploded in the centre of the city, killing two bus conductors and injuring 127. Again Republicans were blamed.

The inability of the Army to interrogate for military information, as opposed to evidence presented in court, forced a rethink. When the Northern Ireland (Emergency Provisions) Act 1973 was enacted, giving soldiers the right to arrest and hold suspects for a maximum of four hours from the time of arrest until release or be handed to a RMP Arrest Team, the strategy that emerged was screening. Instructions for making an arrest were contained on the Blue Card – 'Instructions by the Director of Operations for making Arrests in Northern Ireland (Army Code No 70772)' – in which soldiers making the arrest must say 'As a member of Her Majesty's Forces, I arrest you'. Where appropriate, the soldier making the arrest left a white card (Army Code No. 70773) giving guidance to relatives that to obtain details of the arrested person, enquiries should be made with the local RUC station. Nobody below the age of 10 could be arrested. Suspects were taken to a Screening Centre to be searched and property formally logged before a period of questioning by screeners. With intelligence embedded into their tasks, patrols knew the quicker that arrested persons were taken to the centres, the longer the interviews and therefore improved opportunities for gathering information. Suspects lifted in rural areas had the advantage of the clock. Everything was meticulously logged in the knowledge that lawyers circled looking for opportunities for compensation. As the years rolled by, some suspects were lifted so many times that they became resistant. Others betrayed their IRA membership by employing resistance to interrogation techniques and were quickly handed over to the RUC. One Screening instructor, visiting Northern Ireland to audit methods, became slightly exasperated by the silence of one well known suspect that he suggested they exchange places. After a short period of silence and role reversal, the suspect asked a question, which then led to fruitful discussion. Informers and informants were also lifted to be debriefed and tasked in the safety of Security Forces bases.

By 1972, Prime Minister Heath, fearing that the judicial system in Northern Ireland was close to collapse because of intimidation, non-appearances in court and partisan juries, appointed a senior judge, Lord Diplock, to investigate. The next year, Diplock Courts were introduced in which judges sitting alone dealt with 'scheduled offences' including terrorism. It was another example of the adaptation of counterinsurgency principles employed since 1945 to Northern Ireland. In the 1970s, the Courts dealt with about 300 cases a year decreasing to sixty in 2007 but at the cost of several judges and magistrates murdered. By 1976, clever prosecutions were seeing an increasing number of convictions. In 1988, the Criminal Evidence (Northern Ireland) Order instructed that refusal to answer and the right of silence could be held against terrorist suspects.

Chapter 6

The Thin Red Line: The Border

There is no doubt that the average Irishman was collectively bemused by the depths to which his beautiful country had dropped, particularly as international investment and tourism had virtually disappeared. The border had been a source of political, strategic and tactical indecision since 1922 and it was not until the mid-1970s that Dublin could be persuaded to increase its security. About half the military and RUC casualties lost during Operation Banner occurred along the border.

Extensive local knowledge and intelligence was lost when the B-Specials were disbanded and into the vacuum stepped the IRA, no longer facing a formidable opponent. Quickly developing support and intelligence networks from sympathetic communities along the border, they took measures to ensure that cached weapons, ammunition and equipment from previous campaigns, perhaps stored in watertight milk churns buried in the banks of roads or tracks, were readily available. When Rory O'Brady said after the Border Campaign that IRA weapons had been 'dumped', he really meant hidden for future use.

The border meanders for 301 miles from Lough Foyle south to the western slopes of the Sperrin Mountains in Co. Londonderry to Strabane and then wanders across high ground toward Lower Lough Erne in Fermanagh. Turning south-east on high moorland north of Co. Leitrim, it skirts Upper Lough Erne, heads north to the border town of Aughnacloy and then edges south-east past Monaghan through lush farmland bordered by hedges, south to Slieve Gullion and then strikes east to the beautiful Mourne Mountains and Carlingford Lough which stretches ten miles south to the Irish Sea. At its widest, the inlet is about three miles with the border following the deepwater channel. Because of the historical threat from the IRA, numerous RUC stations and HM Customs and Excise posts dotted in border towns and villages covered, as best as they could, the 285 approved crossings and innumerable tracks and paths, streams and watercourses. Smuggling was widespread and exploited in the 1980s to take advantage of tax and currency differences between the UK and Ireland until European integration began to bite.

Strabane is separated from Lifford by a bridge and Belleek in Fermanagh is partly in Co. Donegal. South of Newry is Dundalk which has a long history of resistance to the English. Warrenpoint is separated from Omeath by about 150 yards of Carlingford Lough. The discontinuance of the ferry between the two towns meant a thirteen mile drive. Railways that once spread throughout the country were reduced when the border divided Ireland to the line between Dublin and Belfast. It inevitably became the focus of bombs and hoaxes designed to disrupt passenger travel and economic trading, and tie up the Security Forces.

When in October 1971, 3 Infantry Brigade was formed to take responsibility from Carlingford Lough to Co. Fermanagh with 8 Infantry Brigade taking over north to Lough Foyle, it faced a formidable task of patrolling 269 miles and covering 242 crossing points. The insurgents frequently initiated gun battles with patrols in the knowledge that south of the border they were relatively safe, even from the Gardai and the Irish Army, because Dublin could not risk the destabilization of an IRA uprising.

On 10 August 1972 when a VCP south of Crossmaglen manned by a 1st Argyll and Sutherland Highlanders platoon came under fire from two positions, a section forced the gunmen to retire to a derelict house close to the border. A Sioux helicopter then guided the second Argyll section to the scene until it came under fire and returned to Crossmaglen to refuel. When it returned, both sections had reached the house just as all but three of the gunmen were crossing the border in a small car. They then chased the three down a track until they crossed the border.

Early Army helicopter operations centred on regimental flights, for instance the Siouxs of the 17/21st Lancers Air Flight, which arrived in May 1970 as the Omagh Resident Battalion, and the 16/5th Lancer Flight which took over in March 1971. The increasing need for helicopters saw 8 Flight, Army Air Corps (AAC) of four Scouts and two Sioux forming at Ballykelly with a role to patrol the border, insert and extract patrols and provide a 'taxi service'. A Beaver, and then a Britten-Norman Islander, Flight provided air photographic

80

recce. The light helicopters were supported by Wessex medium helicopters from 72 Squadron RAF deploying a flight from RAF Odiham in 1969. Capable of carrying sixteen fully-equipped soldiers and able to deliver underslung loads, they were ideal for internal security operations. 845 and 846 Naval Air Squadrons of the Fleet Air Arm also provided medium helicopter support. RAF Aldergrove, located eighteen miles north-west of Belfast, shared the runway at Belfast Airport. The principal air station throughout Operation Banner, it had opened in 1918 but did not become operational until 1925. It was an important Coastal Command base hunting U-Boats in the Battle of the Atlantic during the Second World War. In the 1950s, Aldergrove was designated for V-Bomber dispersals until 1962 when No. 23 Maintenance Unit arrived to support RAF F-4 Phantoms

In early combined operations, when the light helicopter pilot saw something suspicious, he summoned the Wessex-borne quick reaction force. During searches of derelict buildings in rural areas, a Sioux identified the first target, loitered until a Wessex had dropped half of the search team and then flew to the next building and again covered the Wessex dropping the remainder of the search team before it collected the first half-section and then kept leapfrogging until the operation was complete. 'Eagle Patrols' of four lightly-armed soldiers in a Scout and then Gazelles and Lynxes swooped on roads to set up snap and planned VCPs and carry out searches. In 1979, 655 Squadron arrived from 1st (British) Corps in West Germany with nine Scouts and six Gazelles to form the nucleus of the resident 5 Regiment AAC at Ballykelly. It was reinforced by roulement squadrons from the three regiments attached to the three Armoured Divisions in West Germany. In 1981, 72 Squadron finally moved to Northern Ireland and was equipped with Pumas in 1991 until it was disbanded at Easter 2002. In March 1986, 665 Squadron was resurrected with Lynx and Gazelle helicopters until 1991 when it became a Gazelle only Squadron with twenty-one helicopters. 5 Regiment reorganized in October 1993 with 665 Squadron arriving with Lynxes. In early May 1992, 230 Squadron, which was reformed at Aldergrove after being disbanded in Germany, rotated its eighteen Pumas HC.1s with No 33 Squadron to flatten the flight hours of the fleet. 7 Squadron began helicopter operations in 1982 with Chinooks HC 1s until it converted to HC-2s in 1993.

Terrorism in the late 1970s led to the greater use of helicopters to move troops, equipment and supplies. Accidents were few but did happen. In October 1992, a RAF Puma and Army Gazelle collided, killing three RAF personnel. When, in March 2002, a RAF Puma experienced catastrophic engine failure and crashed onto Slieve Gullion near Jonesborough, injuring five soldiers and two civilians, the South Armagh Farmers' and Residents Committee, in their campaign for a complete cessation of helicopter operations, demanded that the flights should be grounded and claimed that since their representatives had not been permitted near the crash site, there must be a cover-up. Probably the most well known incident occurred on 2 June 1994 when HC 2 Chinook ZD 576 crashed into the Mull of Kintyre killing the four aircrew and twenty-five intelligence officers en route from RAF Aldergove to a conference in Inverness. The incident remains controversial.

Aircraft are always at risk from machine-gun fire and surface-to-air missiles. The Provisionals feared helicopters and are thought to have purchased Soviet SA-7 Grail surface-to-air missiles from Libya and also flirted with firing arrays of rockets into flight paths. There is a possibility that a missile was fired at a Wessex near Kinawley in July 1991. On 17 February 1978, machine-gun fire brought down a Gazelle at Bessbrook killing Lieutenant Colonel Ian Corden-Lloyd OBE MC, the 2 RJG Commanding Officer, during the follow up to a contact report and, in February 1990, an Army Lynx was shot down near Clogher. Corden-Lloyd had been accused of allowing his troops to stub cigarettes on suspects during Operation Demetrius. IRA propaganda suggested in 1973 that he had been involved in an incident involving a prisoner in Borneo. Three years later, when two 566 Squadron Lynxes came under fire from two Soviet 12.7mm heavy anti-aircraft machine guns mounted on lorries covering a flight path in South Armagh, both sides flirted with each other until the helicopters forced the lorries over the border where they were found by the Gardai. The IRA is thought to have used a helicopter at least once. On 20 January 1974, Eddie Gallagher, the maverick Provisional commander, and his girlfriend, the former English debutane Rose Dugdale, hijacked a helicopter in Co. Donegal and loaded it with two milk churn IEDs. The story goes that when the helicopter approached its target, RUC Strabane, there was pande-monium in the back because Gallagher had lit the fuses but was then unable to open the doors. When they did, the churns fell harmlessly in the river.

Faced with the dilemma of defending the border against the insur-gency, the Army first deployed strings of ZB 298 ground surveillance radars patrolled by the Royal Armoured Corps regiment based at Omagh. A patrolled fence, as that dividing East and West Germany, was rejected because it required a border force of perhaps 16,000 men. A minefield was impractical. During the early 1970s, Royal Engineers cratered several approved and unapproved border crossing points and latticed them with spikes, however, this proved unpopular because many locals had legitimate reasons to cross – farmers, business interests and families. Indeed within hours, most of the obstacles were dismantled. In November 1972, in Operation Ashburton, Royal Engineers blew deeper craters but these were soon filled in with hijacked cars and covered with rubble and earth. An attempt to use concrete anti-tank 'dragons' teeth' failed when they were blown up. In November 1973, in a major operation, Royal Engineers and battalion assault pioneers protected by the UDR and the Irish Army, deployed on both sides of the border, cratered and blocked unapproved roads and motorized tracks with large Braithwaite tanks filled with concrete, and demolished several bridges. In 1974, a BBC crew filming Royal Engineers cratering a track protected by Irish infantry were relieved of their film. When bad weather dogged operations near Castlederg and lorries were bogged down on tracks, Wessex helicopters lifted the blocks into place. They were covered by the 1 RTR Air Flight Sioux watching for IRA reactions and 651 Squadron Scouts flying Eagle patrols. Several authorized crossing-points were protected by Permanent Vehicle Check Points (PVCP), for instance, the Hump covering the bridge at Strabane. Initially, the soldiers manning the PVCPs were covered by GPMGs in sandbagged bunkers until they were converted into concrete pillboxes, equipped with automatic barriers controlled by intercom systems. Some were equipped with .50-inch M2 Brownings resurrected during the Falklands Campaign and French Close Light Assault Weapons. Despite these measures, the border was simply too long and difficult to defend. Nevertheless, 3 Infantry Brigade gradually developed an intelligence picture of the parts of the border critical to the Provisionals and ambushed tracks and paths, thereby forcing the insurgents to risk transporting people, arms, explosives and equipment using approved crossings.

One important development was closer liaison with the Irish Army, which had first deployed along the border in 1969 following suggestions that it should protect the Nationalist community. After 1972, the 2 (Eastern) and 4 (Western) Brigades were tasked to prevent the Provisionals crossing the border and, in 1975, conducted about 800 patrols, 5,500 VCPs and sixty-four searches but for a limited yield of three RPGs and twenty-four rifles. The Army also escorted cash-in-transit consignments to prevent thefts by paramilitaries obtaining funds. One soldier was killed in December 1983 when the Army and the Gardai released the supermarket executive Don Tidey, held hostage at Ballinamore in Co. Leitrim. Tidey had been seized in a wave of kidnappings masterminded by Kevin Mallon, the charismatic leader of the IRA East Tyrone Brigade, Border War veteran and member of the Provisional Army Council. British information on the Irish Army was limited and 3 and 8 Brigade Intelligence Sections set about gathering information by encouraging meetings with Irish patrols. When, in 1975, a 4 Cavalry Squadron sergeant reported having his photograph taken on a border bridge by a British patrol, actually from 124 Intelligence Section, 3 Brigade, this resulted in a minor diplomatic rumble when a complaint, made to the British Embassy in Dublin, was forwarded to the Foreign and Commonwealth Office and then the Ministry of Defence and finally HQ Ireland from HQ 3 Infantry Brigade explaining that it was an innocent meeting between allies.

When it became evident that weapons were being smuggled into Northern Ireland in 1972, the Royal Navy began Operation Interknit by stationing two Fleet Tenders in Carlingford Lough acting as a 'mother' ship for Dell Quay Dories coxswained by Royal Marines. Royal Marines also patrolled the River Foyle and Lough Foyle to deter gun running from Ireland. The Army and the Royal Marines provided boarding parties and shore patrol. Vessels on Lough Neagh were checked by UDR maritime patrols. Royal Marines from the Special Boat Squadron sometimes served with the Commandos and were attached to the SAS on covert operations.

When Operation Wolverine was launched in mid-1975 to investigate activity between Co. Tyrone and Belfast, duck hunters literally fell over the SBS Klepper canoes tucked into the reeds of the southern foreshore. In the offshore Operation Grenada, Ton-class coastal minesweepers initially operating from HMS *Maidstone* patrolled the Northern Ireland three mile territorial limit and conducted 'hot pursuits' of suspect vessels. Submarines collected coastal intelligence while the Irish Naval Service covered the southern coasts.

By the 1980s, maritime operations had increased and the Northern Ireland Squadron was formed with three Bird-class patrol boats for offshore operations and the two Loyal-class tenders, HMS *Alert* and HMS *Vigilant*, patrolling Carlingford Lough. Lough Foyle was similarly patrolled. In 1993, the Squadron patrolled from Faslane Naval Base with three River-class Fleet minesweepers, including HMS *Blackwater* and HMS *Spey*. HMS *Arun* and HMS *Itchen* replaced the Ton-class minesweepers and were, in turn, replaced in 1998 by Hunt-class Mine Counter Measures vessels, including HMS *Brecon*, HMS *Cottesmore* and HMS *Dulverton*, until naval operations ceased on 19 July 2005. The only naval casualty was Lieutenant A.R. Shields when a bomb planted by the Provisionals on 22 August 1988 exploded underneath his car at traffic lights as he was driving from the Royal Naval Recruiting Office in Belfast.

The East Tyrone IRA Brigade was a formidable organization that had a long history of border operations. It was deeply loyal to Kevin Mallon. The Brigade pursued its revolutionary zeal by attempting to 'liberate' parts of Fermanagh and Tyrone with ambushes, sniping and short occupations of border villages. On 30 August 1973, during coordinated attacks against several border villages, eight Provisionals placed an IED in a garage in Pettigoe and then lined several people against a wall and asked their names and religions. When Private Mervyn Johnston, a part-time 6 UDR, gave his name and a gunman put a pistol to his head, Johnston knocked it aside and, under wild fire from the gunman who had managed to wound Thomas Johnstone, aged 13 years, ran to his house where he collected his Sterling and engaged the insurgents as they withdrew across the border pursued by police and Army patrols. A few minutes after the IED exploded, a 1 RTR patrol arrived and was followed by Staff Sergeant Ron Beckett, an ATO from Omagh. Deciding to defuse a device placed in the Post Office only twenty-five yards from the border, when his controlled explosion failed and he went back into the building, Becket was killed as the device exploded. He left two small daughters.

Belcoo was also a typical border village that saw several incidents. Two cars containing 6 UDR soldiers were leaving the RUC station early on 15 May 1976 when they were ambushed from waste ground. Follow up patrols found Armalite and Garand cartridge cases and then a patrol with a tracker dog picked up the spoors of the insurgents and followed them to a disused railway bridge across a border stream 600 yards from Belcoo. Meanwhile, three RUC were killed and a fourth was blinded by a 10lbs HME bomb buried in an earth bank while they were searching a wall near the Provisional firing point. It took most of the day to clear the area. At the beginning of June, Condor Troop, 59 Independent Commando

Squadron collapsed the fifty year old bridge into the stream with 450lbs of plastic explosive.

Full and part-time members of the RUC and UDR living in rural areas, particularly those living near the border, were at continual risk from the Provisionals taking every opportunity to undermine their commitment, morale and determination. Between September 1971 and April 1988, 4 UDR, which was based in Fermanagh, lost twenty killed. 6 UDR based in Co. Tyrone had thirty killed, between August 1971 and June 1988, including the first UDR soldier and first Greenfinch to be killed. In the region covered by 8 UDR, the Battalion lost thirty-one between December 1972 and March 1989, only one being killed in action. Several bodies of UDR and RUC seized by the Provisionals were dumped on the border after brutal interrogation and often booby-trapped. It required many hours of waiting and checking for ambushes before they were recovered. This inhumanity was rarely, if ever publicly challenged. In March 1972, four gunmen intercepted Private Johnny Fletcher of 4 UDR on his way to work as a farmer near Garrison, took him home where they searched his house and then forced him into a car, telling his wife that he would not be harmed. Fletcher was later found brutally murdered near Killyclogher. An even more callous event occurred on 21 September 1972 when a car arrived at the home of 4 UDR Private Thomas Bullock, aged 53, near Derrylin and his wife, Emily, opened the door. She was gunned down. A gunman then entered the house and murdered Bullock. In a coordinated attack, a second car arrived at the home of Private Darling, however he was at work and although the gunmen ransacked the house, they did not find his Sterling, hidden by his wife under their bed with their children.

The 200 square miles of South Armagh bordered by Forkhill, Crossmaglen, Jonesborough and Newry was a battlefield in the conventional sense. The joint Army/RUC bases at RUC Crossmaglen, Forkhill and Newtownhamilton commanded from the roulement battalion at Bessbrook Mill were a red rag to the South Armagh Brigade, who regarded the area as 'liberated', as did many of those who lived in the area, in particular in Forkhill and Crossmaglen, or XMG as the latter village was known to the troops. Running through Crossmaglen was Concession Road from Dundalk to Monaghan. At first, conditions inside the bases were basic with usually 200 soldiers living in accommodation about the size of the average house in tiers of three bunks crammed into each room. Cooking was difficult and there were just three showers. When the first battalions deployed to patrol the area, 3 Queen's as the resident battalion in Ballykinler from May 1970 to February 1971, 3 Para from January to June 1971 and 1 KOSB for three months from March 1971, it was soon clear that the area would be hotly contested by the South Armagh Brigade setting out to dominate the 'bandit country'. The phrase 'bandit country' was coined by Secretary of State for Northern Ireland Merlyn Rees after the Drummuckavall ambush on 22 November 1974 when a 3 RRF section, establishing an OP, was attacked in the late afternoon and three Fusiliers were killed. Although seriously injured, the lance corporal in command wisely refused an IRA offer to surrender. Rees's comment damaged Security Forces credibility because it implied that the Army and RUC had lost control of the area and helped convince the Provisionals that liberating the area was worthwhile.

Throughout Operation Banner, the Provisionals able to rely on efficient local intelligence networks and consequently patrols, were at continual risk from ambushes, sniping, mines and bombs. Artillery was the only major all arms military resource not used. Sometimes troops blocked a village with VCPs and supported the RUC checking driving licences, vehicle tax and insurance to emphasize that they had greater control over local daily activities than the Provisionals. The first Security Force fatalities were two RUC officers killed by a car bomb at Crossmaglen on 11 August 1970 and then on 27 November, two HM Customs officials accompanying an Army patrol investigating a bomb attack on a post near Newry were shot dead. In 1973, a Saladin Armoured Car used its .30-inch Browning to shoot up a wanted car, until it resembled a sieve, near Forkhill as it sped south across the border after an incident and then its crew watched amazed as four men sprinted from the wreck. Friendly fire incidents were relatively rare in Northern Ireland but they did happen.

During the chill of the New Year Night 1980, Lieutenant Simon Bates, of 2 Para, was commanding an ambush at Tullydonnell, near Forkhill. A cardinal principle of ambush orders is never to leave the position. However for some reason, Bates and his radio operator, Private Gerald Hardy, left the ambush and were killed by their colleagues while returning to their positions.

When 1 Grenadier Guards took over from 42 Commando in November 1978, Battalion HQ and Queen's Company moved into Bessbrook Mill, No. 3 Company went to Forkhill, No. 4 Company at Newtownhamilton and, patrolling from Newry, was a 2 LI company from the Resident Battalion at Ballykinler. Adopted by No. 2 Company in Crossmaglen was a part Corgi, part Jack Russell stray dog called Rats, who accompanied patrols in which he challenged bigger dogs harrying soldiers and was shot, injured by a fire-bomb, stabbed in the stomach and lost two attacks on cars. He loved helicopter flights. When Rats achieved celebrity status and became an IRA target, he was retired in 1980.

In line with the policy of Criminalization and Ulsterization that evolved in 1976, a joint military/RUC Operations Room established at Bessbrook Mill enhanced cross-border coordination. As was traditional, the Provisionals usually bid farewell to, and welcomed, units with a demonstration. On 20 November, a joint Royal Marines and Grenadiers patrol from Crossmaglen was caught by a 50lbs gas cylinder RCIED hidden in a crevice between a derelict house and pig sty, fatally wounding Marine Gary Wheldon and wounding two Grenadiers.

After the Warrenpoint ambush in 1979, restrictions on military vehicle movement meant that the bases were reliant on helicopter support and, in 1980, Bessbrook was reputed to be the busiest airport in Europe with a constant flow of light and medium helicopters bringing about nine underslung loads each day, as well as deploying patrols and scouting for terrorist activity. When over four years from 1978, Crossmaglen in Operation Entity/Magistrate, and Forkhill in Operation Consult, were refurbished by 33 Field Squadron and several Royal Engineer roulement squadrons, about every two months, convoys of Army lorries driven by 26 Squadron RCT drivers ferried about 3,000 tons of bulk material, pre-cast concrete, steelwork and tippers plant from Castledillon to storage points in the overcrowded bases. The convoys required meticulous brigade-level planning with usually two battalions providing the advance, flank and rear guards along the main supply route, which had been cleared by RE Search Teams. Men and light equipment were flown in by helicopter.

In late November, after nine IRA had hijacked a goods train and jammed it underneath a bridge, in one of the coldest winters for several years, Queen's Company cordoned the area for five days until two 150lbs milk churn IEDs were defused and the train declared safe. Several days later, on 3 December, a Scout, providing cover for the insertion of a No. 2 Company patrol, disappeared in heavy rain and high wind. When a search party found oil slicks and debris at Lough Ross, the bodies of Captain Alan Stirling and Corporal Roger

Adcock, both Army Air Corps, were extracted from the wreckage by Royal Navy and Royal Engineer divers.

During the mid-morning on 21 December, with everyone hoping for the near traditional Christmas truce by the Provisionals, a No. 2 Company 'brick' was approaching Crossmaglen Square along the Newry Road when its commander, a sergeant, became suspicious of a lorry parked opposite the Catholic Church. Ordering his men into cover, as he approached it to check it, several gunmen in the back opened fire with three Armalites and an AK-47, mortally wounding three Guardsmen. Disregarding his safety, the sergeant returned fire, picked up the rifle of one of the wounded, emptied its magazine, and then using up the patrol LMG dropped by Guardsman Duggan fired at the lorry as it disappeared. For this act of gallantry, the sergeant was awarded the Military Medal.

When a patrol was caught in a car RCIED blast in Castleblaney Street, Crossmaglen, a soldier, his uniform ablaze, ran across the street into a house where he soaked himself in a bath, nevertheless he suffered 33 per cent burns. About half an hour later, a No. 2 Company patrol was scrambled to the area by helicopter when the Gardai reported that they were under fire after intercepting a suspicious car close to the border but found no one. The Gardai later recovered an Armalite, bomb-making and other equipment from the car, indicating the occupants were probably involved in the incident.

The No. 2 Company Commander was in a Gazelle with another Grenadier on 22 February 1979 when two cars were noted close to the border. The pilot landed the two Grenadiers to investigate and was flying top cover when he saw a van and about twenty armed men in a field gathered around a mortar on a lorry. Collecting the two Grenadiers, he landed them in a field from where they opened fire on the lorry but were unable to prevent it crossing the border. Two days later, it was found east of Crossmaglen. Shortly before another RCT convoy arrived at Crossmaglen, the terrorists blew up two pylons carrying the electricity grid from Northern Ireland to Ireland and placed a device on another pylon. On the 25th, a No. 3 Company patrol was attacked near Jonesborough but avoided being ambushed by eight gunmen in the village. At the beginning of March, as the Grenadier Guards was handing over to 3 Queen's, the Provisionals escalated their operations by hijacking several cars during the afternoon. During the early evening, a Scout making a low pass over two suspect vehicles near Glasdrummen came under heavy automatic fire from a hijacked lorry and the pilot and a 3

Queen's officer and Grenadier major were wounded. On 7 May, the Grenadier Guards battle group handed over to the 3 Queen's having lost three Guardsmen and a Royal Marine killed in action and two killed in the helicopter crash. Six men had been wounded in its tour.

By the early 1980s, defending the border with a string of tactically deployed and mutually supporting watchtowers in much the same way as the East German Border Force covered the Demilitarized Zone between West and East Germany, had become politically acceptable. In another major Royal Engineers and RCT operation, several watchtowers were erected along the border and in other parts of Ulster, including urban areas, and fitted with hi-tech imagery surveillance, high resolution cameras and binoculars and CCTV. In South Armagh, the watchtowers were prefixed with the letter R for 'Romeo', for instance, Romeo 21 at Jonesborough covered the Pass to the North. Low lying towers were prefixed with G for 'Golf'. The watchtowers were located in bases with staked and coiled barbed wire entanglements and protected by machine-gun bunkers and Claymore mines. The venerable ZB 298 radar was replaced by MSTAR. The troops, offices and stores were accommodated in steel containers that offered protection from mortar fire. The improved surveillance equipment allowed patrol activity to be coordinated and maximized observation into the previously dead ground of valleys and behind wooded areas to such an extent that the defence of the border was significantly enhanced. One drawback emerged when observers sometimes concentrated on covering the progress of patrols as opposed to watching their flanks. Boredom was also an issue. Suspect farms and premises were watched and information gathered on people and personal characteristics, something that does not emerge with still images. When the South Armagh IRA Brigade and also smugglers found that their activities were hampered by the towers, Sinn Fein and local councillors suggested that radiation from the antennae was causing illness among the local population and animals, a charge rejected as unlikely.

Chapter 7

The Armed Forces in the mid-1970s

By 1972, vaguely bemused soldiers, sailors and airmen and their families observed politicians struggling to find the distant dream of a solution to an ancient problem. Army commanders had recognized that Operation Banner was not a colonial campaign in some far off land and had successfully adopted military principles to counter IRA revolutionary and insurgency ideals. With Belfast a sixty minute flight from Heathrow, it was going to be a long haul from the expectations of a short stay when they had arrived in 1969. Although a shooting war was underway, changes in society, the promotion of civil rights and the increasing unwillingness of politicians to reject minority opinion had emasculated the natural power of the Armed Forces; for instance inability to interrogate captured insurgents had affected intelligence processes.

Until 1969, the Armed Forces had lost one man killed in action every year since 1945 except 1968, the year that the Soviet Union crushed the Pink Revolution in Czechoslovakia and possibly the closest that Europe came to war. The British Army of the Rhine was on standby for several months with a maximum of 17 per cent of unit strength permitted to be absent on leave and courses. More casualties had been taken in Northern Ireland than in any campaign except Korea because politics prevented patrols from using support weapons, such as mortars and grenades, to winkle gunmen from houses or suppress ambushes in rural areas. The troops had shown remarkable restraint and high discipline and recognized that over-shoots could cause civilian casualties, quite apart from international complaints. The Provisionals had no such restrictions. In spite of the best efforts of the IRA, partisan editors and subversives, such as the Troops Out Movement, discipline held and drugs were not an issue. Although few politicians regard Northern Ireland to be a war, few of those who served between 1969 to 2007 and their families would agree. Behind the blue and green ribbon of 1962 General Service Medal and its single 'Northern Ireland' bar were usually several tours. This is now recognized by an Accumulated Service Medal recognizing 1,000 days in Ulster.

In between tours, veterans would fight in the 1982 Falklands War, the 1990 Gulf War, in former Yugoslavia, Sierra Leone, Iraq and Afghanistan in between supporting the civil community driving Green Goddesses in firemen's strikes and removing rubbish and a host of other activities, including maintaining the UK contribution to NATO force levels. Even with the four, then three, Royal Marines Commandos and RAF Regiment squadrons, the infantry was at full stretch from the first day to the last and was reinforced by armoured, artillery, engineer, signals and transport units converted to infantry. Since Operation Banner was not a war, the Territorial Army could not be mobilized to fill gaps, although it also suffered soldiers murdered, as did the Army Cadet Force.

HQ Northern Ireland at Thiepval Barracks in Lisburn set out the basic military strategies to:

Deter and prevent the movement of illegal arms, ammunition and explosives.

Seize Republican and Loyalists active in insurgency and terrorism.

Maintain public confidence in the Armed Forces with its presence and patrols, in other words, hearts and minds.

In overall command was the General Officer Commanding (GOC), a lieutenant general, who reported to the Chief of the General Staff at the Ministry of Defence as Director of Operations, and not the Secretary of State for Northern Ireland, as some politicians assumed. During internment, successive secretaries released internees at the same time as the Army was re-arresting them. The Director of Operations, as had been common in the colonial campaigns, meant that contentious issues between the organizations that made up the Security Forces, for instance, standardizing police and military boundaries, could be resolved relatively quickly. Police boundaries were usually historical and based on the law enforcement while military boundaries were based on tactical needs. When military boundaries eventually matched police boundaries, improvements in information exchange were marked. Using practices from previous campaigns, descending levels of military committees established in 1969 prevailed until 2007. At the top was the Security Policy Committee chaired by the GOC down to the Security Coordinating Committee at CLF level and then district at battalion and Sub-District Action Committees at company levels. All were joint to promote coordination between the law enforcement of the RUC, politics through the Northern Ireland Office, local authorities and the Army. The CLF had operational control of the three brigades but not of air and naval operations, which were represented by the senior Royal Navy and RAF commanders.

After Operation Motorman until the late 1980s, the brigade commanders rarely directed the activities of their units and consequently regimental, company and platoon commanders wielded significant operational independence. At the height of Operation Banner in 1972, the troop levels were about 21,800 men. This had dropped to 10,000 by 1990. Resident battalions were based in barracks with most of the expected operational, recreational and welfare facilities for the soldier and his family, although internal security limited some activities. Companies usually rotated with one guarding the base; another the Brigade reserve; and another on leave and training. A significant number of combat and logistic support personnel also served two year tours. Roulement tours (translated from the French as 'rotation') were largely but not entirely confined to Belfast, Londonderry and South Armagh, with the troops usually based in requisitioned buildings, such as the Short Strand bus depot where, in 1971, some Grenadier Guards slept in buses. Basic facilities were just about adequate. Emergency short tours were usually as reinforcements or for a particular operation. Boards adorned with regimental colours and badges with dates of occupation screwed to walls of bases are as much a part of Northern Ireland's history as the impressive murals found in Nationalist estates. Some bigger bases had a canteen run by men from an enclave of several small villages in Pakistan providing a near twenty-four hour shop that included providing hamburgers and hot coffee to early morning patrols. Two Pakistanis were murdered, one manning a fish and chip van in Londonderry in 1973 and Mohammed Adbul Khalid shot seventeen times by gunmen in Crossmaglen in 1974. As an example of deployments, 2 Queen's was as follows:

March 1969 to August 1970	39 Infantry Brigade	Resident Battalion – Holywood Barracks
August to September 1971	39 Infantry Brigade	Roulement – East Belfast
29 July to November 1972	8 Infantry Brigade	Roulement –Londonderry
November 1973 to March 1974	8 Infantry Brigade	Roulement –Londonderry
7 to 14 January 1976	3 Infantry Brigade	Spearhead Battalion Emergency Reinforcement – South Armagh
February to June 1977	39 Infantry Brigade	Roulement – Andersonstown
April to August 1980	3 Infantry Brigade	Roulement – Armagh
January to November 1984	8 Infantry Brigade	Roulement - Londonderry
April to September 1988	39 Infantry Brigade	Roulement – Belfast

Roy Millard, serving with 1 Glosters, first arrived in December 1971 in Albert Street Mill in the Lower Falls before finishing in April 1972 at Mulhouse, still in the Lower Falls. During the tour, the Battalion lost three men killed in action. In one of the last occasions before security restrictions prevented similar public parades, the Battalion marched through Bristol, Cheltenham, Tewkesbury and Cheltenham. Millard, aged 19 years, returned to Mulhouse in April 1973 as the youngest Section Commander for a tour that ended in August 1973. During this tour, two soldiers were killed by a booby trap in the Divis Flats. His final tour was for the third time to Mulhouse between July and November 1974. Millard would serve more tours but not with the Battalion.

For the Royal Marines officer Jeff Niblett, his first tour was with 45 Commando on a roulement tour between October 1971 and January 1972 in the Lower Falls. This was followed, eight months later, by a three week emergency tour immediately before Operation Motorman during which a Royal Marine was killed by friendly fire in the Turf Lodge. Following successful completion of helicopter flying training with the Army Air Corps, Niblett returned with 845

Naval Air Squadron, flying Wessex helicopters from RAF Aldergrove, between October and November 1977 and January to February 1978. He returned with 40 Commando at Ballykelly between March and July 1979.

Early training for roulement units deploying from West Germany, using their spacious pre-1939 German barracks, was haphazard and bore little relation to the narrow streets of Belfast. The Northern Ireland Training and Advisory Team UKLF (NITAT) was established on the beach ranges at Shorncliffe/Lydd in 1972 and extended to the Sennelager Training Area in West Germany and the Northern Ireland Reinforcement Training Team (NIRTT) at Ballykinler, each with 'Tin City' representing part of an estate to exercise patrolling, riot control, searching and ambushes. Units deploying from the United Kingdom to rural areas often spent a week at Thetford Training Area in Norfolk. By the mid-1970s, attendance at NIRTT was mandatory with those on trickle postings expected to undertake 'special to arm' training. In the early 1990s, the Operational Training Advisory Group took over the training. Since Operation Banner was fought largely at section and platoon level, it was less easy to prepare company and battalion commanders in the management of their areas of operational responsibility. Initially battalion-level commanders had considerable independence to dominate their areas. How they did it depended on the characteristics of their commands. The Parachute Regiment robustness was equally matched by the relative tranquillity of the county infantry.

Patrols varied from foot to APCs, Land Rovers, Assault Boats, Rigid Raiders and helicopters. By 1973, the standard eight-man infantry section, commanded by a corporal, had been broken down into four-man 'bricks' patrolling as a square to ease command and control in urban areas. Patrols were critical in collecting intelligence, dominating areas of responsibilities with searches, convincing insurgents that they risked capture if they engaged in terrorism and intercepting wanted people and smuggled equipment at quick, temporary and permanent VCPs. Probably the most common radio message was 'Papa Check, Over' indicating that a patrol wanted a Personality Check (P Check). Did the name match the address? Was the person wanted? In Northern Ireland driving licences doubled as identification documents. If there was one check that usually caused problems, it was the P Check in a pub full of Irishmen. Patrols had photos of the top ten suspects and sometimes of aggressive dogs. The montages were known as 'bingo cards' with photos crossed off when a person was removed from circulation. Restraint was expected, in the face of obscenities from swearing women banging dustbin lids, and firm under attacks by dogs. Inevitably, there was some heavy handedness from tired and frustrated soldiers, however the degree of self-discipline over a sustained period is a credit to the Armed Forces.

In November 1972, the rules of engagement were listed in the Instructions by the Director of Operations for Opening Fire in Northern Ireland (Army Code No. 70771) which was issued to all soldiers. Known as the Yellow Card, it also came in as a buff coloured document. Basic rules were:

Use no more minimum force than necessary.

Try to handle the situation other than by opening fire.

Only aimed shots.

Do not fire more rounds than absolutely necessary.

Where possible, a shouted warning such as 'Stop or I fire' should be given. This could be ignored if a person was running away after killing or injuring someone.

The Yellow Card did not give soldiers carte blanche to ignore Common Law, however some found themselves in situations in which it was impractical to give warnings before opening fire and consequently it became the subject of considerable controversy. Apart from military disciplinary action, several soldiers faced murder charges in Diplock Courts, the first being a soldier who shot a Catholic during an altercation in Strabane in the middle of the Ulster Workers Council strike. Between 1985 and 1989, eight British soldiers were convicted of offences, compared with six RUC officers and twenty-nine UDR.

Private Ian Thain of 1 LI was convicted after shooting Thomas Reilly, a road manager to the female pop group Bananarama, during a serious disturbance in West Belfast on 9 August 1983. Aged just 18 years, he was sent to the Walton Jail Young Offenders Wing until released in February 1987. Bananarama wrote a song titled *Rough Justice* commemorating Reilly and highlighting that Thain had served a short jail sentence, his time off for good behaviour and youth seemingly ignored. Thain left the Army in 1990, the year that another soldier found himself in trouble in a more celebrated case that tested the Yellow Card rigorously for the first time.

On 30 September 1990 Private Lee Clegg was part of a sixteen-man patrol from A Company, 3 Para, manning a VCP in the staunchly Nationalist Upper Glen Road, Belfast when a Vauxhall Astra stopped short of the checkpoint and then accelerated towards two paras as they approached it. For years, vehicles attempting to breach a VCP were regarded as suspicious and, although the driver was warned to stop, he ignored the instruction and the patrol opened fire bringing it to a halt and killing the driver, Martin Peake, and fatally wounding Karen Reilly in the back. Her father, Volunteer James McGrillen, had been shot dead in a stolen car by soldiers in 1976. In an unwise attempt to justify their act, the patrol claimed that the car had injured one of them but this later proved to be untrue. Nevertheless the Director of Public Prosecutions took no action. At the time, the intrepid BBC journalist John Ware was investigating the deaths of civilians he believed to have been shot by the Army and saw, in a 3 Para Junior Ranks Mess, a cardboard cut-out of an Astra with nineteen holes and a large red splodge in the driver's position. Underneath, parodying the contemporary Smith and Jones comedy advertisement sketch for Fiat cars of 'Made by hand. Built by robots. Driven by Italians' was 'Vauxhall. Built by robots. Driven by joy riders. Stopped by A Company.' In the July 1991 *Panorama* documentary *Lethal Force*, Ware suggested the incident was proof of a Security Forces shoot-to-kill policy and, when members of the patrol were charged, although Clegg maintained that he had applied his safety catch as the car passed, he was singled out as the soldier who had fired the fatal shots. In June 1992, a Diplock Court sentenced him to life, to be served in an Ulster prison. The conviction was based on the forensic evidence indicating one of the four shots that he fired from his position in the centre of the VCP was 'unreasonable use', particularly as the Astra had left the VCP and was no longer a threat. There was dignified fury in the Army at the sentence and with the BBC, not for the first time in recent years, and the Parachute Regiment formed the Clegg Committee to campaign for his acquittal. In March 1994, the Court of Appeal concluded that the Yellow Card had no legal force justifying a soldier opening fire where a person has been injured and dismissed Clegg's appeal. That Clegg had no idea of the injuries in the car until after the incident seems to have escaped the Court. In dismissing his second appeal in January 1995, the House of Lords concluded that there was little in English law concerning the rights and duties of a member of the Armed Forces acting in aid of the civil community and therefore the law should be applied to a civilian, even though that member may be required to risk his life, if ordered by his superior.

Meanwhile another incident had taken place. At about 10.15 a.m. on 4 September 1992, a 1 Scots Guards patrol in the New Lodge Road stopped Peter McBride, a father of two young daughters and known to the Battalion. The enclave was tense after Guardsman Damian Shackleton had been shot dead while on mobile patrol the previous day. While a P Check was radioed to Company HQ and McBride was being searched because he was suspected of carrying a coffee pot grenade, he suddenly ran off and was chased up Glenrosa Street by three soldiers shouting 'Stop or we'll open up' into Upper Meadow Street where Guardsmen Mark Wright, and Jim Fisher, a Gulf War veteran, shot him at a range of about seventy yards. McBride staggered into his sister's house and died soon afterwards. Under pressure of another perceived whitewash and with journalists already claiming the two soldiers had murdered McBride, next day Wright and Fisher were charged with murder by the RUC. At Belfast Crown Court, Fisher's claim that he opened fire because he believed that McBride was leading the patrol into an ambush was rejected. Wright said he believed McBride had opened fire on them. In February 1995, both soldiers were sentenced to life imprisonment and their appeals dismissed on the grounds that McBride was unarmed, amid more controversy, this time from former members of the Guards insisting that soldiers were being convicted for doing their duty.

Meanwhile, Private Clegg won his appeal to the Northern Ireland Appeal Court in November 1997 on the grounds that forensic evidence of the bullet found in Miss Reilly suggested that it had entered the side of the car. His conviction for 'attempting to wound' Martin Peake was upheld. In January 2000, ten years after the incident, during which Clegg had spent three years and nine months in jail, Mr Justice Kerr, at the Northern Ireland Court of Appeal overturned the lesser conviction, but accused Clegg of telling a pack of lies in suggesting that the car had hit one of his colleagues in the first place. Had the investigatory skills of the BBC correspondent been more comprehensive and focused on the weaknesses of the Yellow Card, then an innocent soldier would not have been disgraced. In 2007, Sergeant Clegg went to Afghanistan with his Battalion.

Strange as it may seem to Fleet Street editors, when the Armed Forces move into new combat zones about which little is known, it takes time to work out tactics to match operational requirements. By 1970, disruptive camouflaged uniforms had replaced green combat kit, which soldiers patrolling the grey streets of towns found bizarre. The 7.62mm FN Self Loading Rifle (SLR) with its long barrel designed to pick off Soviet soldiers at long range was not replaced until the 1980s by the short barrel 5.56mm SA-80. Lightweight patrol boots and gloves padded to protect knuckles appeared. The wearing of civilian clothes by soldiers in combat and service support roles was common. Most were armed with a 9mm Browning. Some in intelligence roles were equipped with Walther PPKs. Corporal Paul Harman, of the Intelligence Corps, was alone in a car on the Monagh Road in the Turf Lodge on 14 December 1976 when he was attacked by two men at traffic lights. Attempting to drive through the ambush, he was shot dead by a third gunman armed with a telescopic rifle and his body was dragged out of the car. With the Army trained in mechanized warfare and physical fitness unsuited to fighting in built up areas, the introduction of the Battle Fitness Test of running a mile and a half in a squad and then as individuals within a time limit according to age, and Physical Fitness Assessments of repetitive exercises, improved conditioning and marksmanship. By 1973, more uniformed servicewomen were being seen on the streets, mainly Royal Military Police and UDR 'Greenfinches' as searchers. In the hope they would not be targeted by gunmen, they wore skirts and were unarmed. While the policy was understandable, it meant, theoretically, that servicewomen working with other Corps, such as the Intelligence Corps, could not ride 'shotgun'. A wide range of civilian cars, vans and lorries were purchased anonymously by Ministry of Defence suppliers from mainland second hand car sales and shipped to Northern Ireland where a complex system developed by the RAOC ensured that they did not remain in too long. The Royal Electrical and Mechanical Engineers (REME) had a range of civilian recovery vehicles.

In 1969, since most of the Army's armoured fighting vehicles were tracked and would have chewed up streets, two types of wheeled APCs were hauled out of retirement. The six wheel 10-ton Alvis FV 603 Saracen, introduced into service in 1952, could carry ten troops and the commander and driver. They had proven their robustness in Aden where at least one had three wheels blown off and yet it motored out of trouble. Most were eventually fitted with anti-grenade and anti-RPG mesh screens. Its sister, the Saladin Armoured Car equipped with a 76mm gun, patrolled the border in the early years and escorted convoys. The four wheel GKN Sankey FV 1611 Armoured Humber One Ton could carry ten troops and underwent several modifications. Its two front hatches, overlooking a long snout, led to it being nicknamed the Pig. It was also quite difficult to drive. In Operation Bracelet, it was strengthened with Macrolon armour against 7.62mm bullets. When hinged wire mesh was hung at the back to protect dismounted troops in riots, it was nicknamed the Flying Pig and the Kremlin Pig when mesh cages were added to protect it from RPGs. Pigs supporting 321 EOD filled with foam to suppress an IED were known as Foam Pigs.

At first, units trained their own APC drivers. By March 1972, the growing unrest and the intensity of ground operations led to the RCT taking over the driving of the 490 APCs then in Ulster with 3 Tank Transporter Squadron being sent from West Germany to take over APC driving. The APC Regiment was then formed and moved into a camp requistioned from Shorts Brothers that had been used by the Ministry of Supply Communications Office (MOSCO) during the Second World War and became known as Moscow Camp. With the APCs deployed in over seventy loactions throughout Northern Ireland, a large REME APC Workshop achieved spectacular success by keeping 70 per cent of the venerable fleet available to meet operational requirements. Several unit and RCT drivers were accused of deliberately running down pedestrians during civil disturbances, usually by people who had never been in a closed down APC in which the driver peers through apertures measuring about 14 inches by 8 inches.

The RCT also played an important role in the provision of general transport, which had been initially organized by 26 (General Transport (GT)) Squadron. It was then reinforced at the roulement 65, 14 (Air Despatch) and 18 (Amphibious) Squadrons. Eventually 18 Squadron joined 26 Squadron to form 26/18 (GT) Squadron providing support from Lisburn and Londonderry. The roulement GT squadron was based at Antrim and Moscow Camp. A specialist Troop supported 33 Independent Engineer Squadron at Antrim and its detachments at Castledillon and Ballykelly with dumper trucks and vehicles used in construction.

In 1974, 6 Artillery Support Squadron, which supported the Royal Artillery in West Germany by ferrying ammunition, supported twelve units in Belfast, including 321 EOD. In its second tour, the Squadron supported fourteen units with one Troop attached to 8 Infantry Brigade and two with 3 Infantry Brigade with detachments at Bessbrook, Crossmaglen, Lisnaskea and Squadron HQ at Ballykinler. The distance driven amassed to over 37,000 miles. During its third tour in 1976, again with the two Brigades, the drivers clocked up 500,000 accident free miles and organized two convoys, one carrying equipment needed by 9 Independant Parachute Squadron RE in South Armagh. By 1979, pressures on the RCT led to a roulement troop reinforced 26/18 Squadron until during the year the roulement HQ 4 Armoured Divisional Regiment arrived to command transport operations.

Another vital role of the RCT was to move units by air and sea. From January 1969 to March 1971, Movement Staff from the three Services organized twenty-six major, twenty-three minor and thirty other unit moves which grew to 100 major, seventy-two and twenty-four other units totalling 100,000 troops between April 1971 and March 1972. In the following year the 'Movers' transferred 162,000 men, not far short of the total Army strength, including about 2,400 men going on rest and recuperation leave monthly and the TA and cadet forces deploying to their annual training camps . As Operation Banner wore on, greater use was made of civil air and shipping, for instance in 1979, 41,000 men flew by air while 49,797 were moved by civil airlines, 26,017 were lifted by ferries and 18,199 sailed in Landing Ship Logistics; 13,220 vehicles, 600 tons and 8,084 containers were moved in the same period. Some deliveries were made over the beach at Ballykinler.

Land Rovers, which the Army had been using since the Korean War, came in several variants. The airportable Half Ton Lightweight, that could be quickly stripped of excess weight, was replaced with long wheelbase vehicles fitted with armoured Vehicle Protection Kits. Skirts fitted to hulls prevented explosive devices being rolled under the vehicle and grills over windows minimized missile injuries. Displayed on the cargo compartment side was an invitation for people to telephone the Confidential Line with information. The Composite Armoured Patrol Vehicles emerged a cheap, convenient and speedy alternative to Saracens and Pigs during the 1980s and were known as 'Snatch' Rovers. Specifically designed to parol the border, the Shorland Armoured Patrol Car mounted a 7.62mm GPMG or LMG turret. On the disbandment of the B-Specials, most were handed to the UDR. It was replaced by the Shorland Hotspur (or Simba) Armoured Car, most of the 750 in service being built in Wales. The need for increased defences against explosives dropped from above, saw the introduction of the Tangi Land Rover on the

Defender 110 Chassis, which was capable of carrying seven officers, including driver and commander. Other vehicles included a forklift fitted with a wire screen known as the 'Paddy Pusher' and Salamander and Neptune water cannons. The Royal Engineers Scooby-Do armoured A-5000 Wheeled Tractor with its bucket was useful for clearing streets of rubble and burnt out vehicles. In Belfast, an armoured van distributed fish and chips to troops.

One problem faced by those on long tours was entertainment. Although the tendency was to focus on Protestant venues, Irish and Nationalist pubs were noted for their Guinness, rebel songs and hospitality. However most were out of bounds because of several incidents, notably the murder of three 1 Royal Highland Fusiliers on 10 March 1971. Fusiliers John McCraig, aged 17½ years, his brother, Joseph, aged 18 years, and Dougald McCaughey were executed in the Belfast suburb of Ligoneil after being lured from a pub on the promise of meeting some girls. The Army then ruled that only soldiers aged over 18 years could serve in Northern Ireland. The brutality of the murders shocked many into attending wreath laying ceremonies, however it was not the only time that soldiers were lured. Two years later, of four sergeants based in Thiepval Barracks, Lisburn, invited to an Antrim Road flat by a woman on the promise of a party, three were executed at the flat. The fourth escaped. A mother implicated in the incident fled to Ireland and was arrested. However proceedings were not taken because the murders were regarded as political. In the same year, four sergeants attached to the Army Air Corps attending a dance at the Knock Na Moe Castle Hotel in Omagh were killed when their booby-trapped car exploded. A fifth died three weeks later from his wounds.

Intelligence is a critical asset that requires coordination. Although the Armed Forces had developed several types of intelligence operations since 1945, Northern Ireland was different because internal wrangling developed almost from the start. When the Army arrived, it had very little intelligence on the IRA and was reliant initially on RUC information, which soon proved unreliable. The disarming of the police in 1970 damaged relationships to the extent that Special Branch frequently discreetly tested how the information they supplied was being used and sometimes led to information being withheld on a need to know basis. Some Army officers suspected that it was an attempt by the RUC to dissuade the Army from muscling in on its turf.

Overseeing national security and intelligence is MI5. As the Security Service, it manages the protection of the nation against espionage, subversion and, during the transition to war, sabotage from hostile intelligence services. Its forays before into domestic radicalism and terrorism were largely confined to a few home grown organizations, such as the Angry Brigade. Scotland Yard monitored the IRA, indeed during the late nineteenth century, it had formed the Special Irish Branch, which spawned into Special Branch. When radical Irish subversion in the form of the Marxist Provisionals surfaced in 1970 and MI5 failed to respond, in 1971 Prime Minister Heath instructed MI6 to lead in Northern Ireland. MI6, the Secret Intelligence Service, had vast international experience in counterintelligence and was familiar with the Armed Forces. A major strategy was to open negotiations with opponents. When its senior officers justifiably expressed concern at interfering in the preserve of MI5, Heath rejected their argument.

By the spring, MI6 was in Northern Ireland developing covert intelligence and developing contacts with the IRA. One officer based in Dublin, Michael Oatley, persuaded Brendan Duddy, the Londonderry businessman, to open up channels of communication with Provisional leadership, in spite of his earlier refusal to another MI6 officer seeking contacts after Bloody Sunday. The interface was Martin McGuiness. By 1972, MI6 assessed that Unionism was a hindrance and that while the IRA leadership might believe it was capable of guerrilla warfare, in comparison with some organizations that Great Britain had confronted since 1945, they were second-rate. By 1973, MI5 was leading intelligence operations in Northern Ireland. Its strategy was that the IRA must first be defeated before negotiation. MI6 reverted to undermining the IRA by provoking Dublin into taking action against them and formed a loose association with the Littlejohn brothers to act as agent provocateurs by raiding banks in Ireland and ensuring that when bombs rocked Dublin and Monaghan on 1 December 1972, the IRA was blamed on the grounds that Loyalists lacked the capability to mount such a sophisticated operation. These operations were closed down by the Gardai shortly before Christmas.

The lead intelligence and security agency for the three services is the Intelligence Corps. Established in 1940, it had gained experience fighting terrorists in the Malayan Emergency, Nationalists in Cyprus and insurgents in Borneo and was familiar with MI6, but not MI5.

12 Intelligence and Security Company supported HQ Northern Ireland and the Brigades with Intelligence Sections to collate, analyse and disseminate information and intelligence on two-year tours. Most gained detailed specialist knowledge about the paramilitaries.

In many respects, the Brigade intelligence sections laid the foundations for intelligence operations. A corporal joined a 1 Hampshire patrol and found himself commanding a Pig carrying out several snap VCPs and checking several 'tea stops'. A sergeant assessing the quality of the naval intelligence spent several days on the minesweeper HMS *Lewiston* and boarded vessels ranging in size from yachts to merchant ships. Brigadier Wallis-King, who commanded 3 Infantry Brigade from 1972 to 1974, frequently took a member of his 124 Intelligence Section on visits to units. One corporal clocked up about eighty hours helicopter flying during a year. An NCO regularly watched rugby matches with the brother of a UDA leader while another travelled alone through hardline Nationalist areas to visit a high level Loyalist political source. A sergeant spent a profitable twelve hour conversation with a Loyalist leader after arranging for his car to be intercepted and thoroughly searched by a REME workshop. 120 Security Section carried out security surveys of military installations, investigated subversion and vetted locally employed civilians. Since Intelligence Corps NCOs sometimes accompanied infantry patrols to familiarize themselves with localities and meet informants, they had to be competent infantrymen. Battalion Intelligence Sections usually consisted of an officer and eight soldiers trained at the School of Service Intelligence at Templer Barracks, Ashford, Kent, then the home of the Intelligence Corps, and later at Chicksands. Their critical intelligence came from patrol and observation posts (OP).

Despite some limitations, military intelligence adapted to the strategic philosophy that emerged in the mid 1970s of Find, Fix, Strike and Exploit, a doctrine that paralleled the conventional encounter with the enemy, carrying out a recce, attacking and then exploiting by rolling over him ready for the next task. While the Find was relatively easy, evidence and forensics proving terrorist and paramilitary involvement did not always exist and since intelligence does not stand up in court, it was easy for defence lawyers to blow holes in prosecutions. Almost since its formation, the Intelligence Corps had exploited willing informants and developing the unwilling into sharing information. By 1974, the number of uncoordinated Military Intelligence Source Reports (MISR) of source and informer information held in the Brigades research offices led HQ Northern Ireland to form the Force Sources Cell (FSC). Source handling was dangerous because it was face to face with opponents who could never be trusted, but without this recce, the strategy was weakened. By 1980, the FSC had been renamed the Force Research Unit (FRU). A selection course at the Special Military Intelligence Unit at Ashford and Chicksands tested their Human Intelligence skills. One involved extracting information in a pub without recording it in order to test retention and the ability to remain sufficiently sober to report the findings accurately.

In order to support the RUC and unit intelligence sections and improve the quality of intelligence and information without the bias often previously shown, the SMIU re-established the system of intelligence liaison officers and NCOs that had been so successfully developed in Borneo. Military Intelligence Officers (MIOs) from any Arm liaised with RUC Divisional commanders. Captain Fred Holroyd, who enlisted into the Royal Artillery in 1961 and was commissioned into the RCT, arrived as the RUC J Division MIO in the 3 Infantry Brigade area of operations. In his patch was the Mid-Ulster UVF with its headquarters at Portadown, which had strong links with Belfast and was quite prepared to take on the IRA. Rapidly achieving a reputation for commitment, he regularly helped the Brigade intelligence collators draft the weekly Intelligence Summary. Attached to Special Branches were Field Intelligence Non-Commissioned Officers (FINCO), who were only Intelligence Corps. Intelligence Corps Continuity NCOs (CONCO) and all Arms Liaison Intelligence NCOs (LINCO) provided the intelligence link between roulement units and with the prisons.

In relation to the Fix, this required surveillance to determine the routines, aspirations and associations of targets in such a manner that they had no idea they were on target lists. Offensive in nature, the surveillance sisters included recce patrols and OPs, air photo recce, intercept and electronic warfare intelligence and covert intelligence. Several permanent OPs had deterrent value, the position on top of the Divis Flats at the bottom of the Falls Road being one of the first. The heavily-defended Borucki Sangar in the centre of Crossmaglen was named after Private James Borucki, aged 19 years who was killed on 8 August 1976 by a 5lbs RCIED left on a bicycle. Deployed from information received or speculative to gain new information, a typical battalion OP was usually a short operation of about four men occupying such places as the upper floors of derelict houses, schools during holidays and woods and ditches in rural areas. Usual insertion and extraction was between 2 a.m. and 4 a.m. and usually camouflaged a patrol dropping and collecting the OP. During his tenure as CLF from 1977 to 1979 as intelligence became a major function, Major General Richard Trant developed the concept of converting battalion Recce Platoons into specialist Close Observation Platoons (COP) within battalion tactical areas of responsibility, thereby freeing up more men for patrolling. Training included recognition training to enable observers to identify makes of vehicles from their hub caps. When, several days before Queen Elizabeth II visited Northern Ireland in August 1977, a 1 RGJ COP in the Ardoyne reported suspicious activity in Cranbrook Gardens, a Battalion Search Team, hustled by hostile crowds, found detonators, incendiary devices, bomb making equipment and an illegal radio underneath a cot. Further searches led to an Armalite, a M1 Carbine, a Winchester Repeater, a Bren gun barrel and ammunition concealed underneath floorboards of a house in Highbury Gardens.

In 1975, the SAS was not particularly secretive, indeed its tough selection process featured in *Soldier* magazine, complete with photographs. D Squadron had been exercising in Co. Antrim in uniform in the spring of 1969 when it was instructed to search for Loyalist weapons after the UVF had sabotaged the water key points. One patrol boarded an Argentine freighter seeking 1,500 'pistolas', and found not pistols but a cargo of sides of beef. When the Regiment disappeared into the deserts of Dhofar in Operation Storm to support the Sultan of Oman tackling communist insurgency on his borders with Yemen, small detachments remained in Northern Ireland in the guise of other units, for instance 4 Field Survey Troop at Castledillon where there was also a sizeable Royal Engineers presence. When two members of B Squadron were convicted of a bank robbery in 1974, it endangered a statement made by Secretary of State for Northern Ireland, Roy Mason, in the House of Commons on 9 April that, 'No SAS unit has been or is stationed in Northern Ireland'.

As information technology (IT) appeared, HQ Northern Ireland, through 233 Signal Squadron, embraced the new systems. Integrating with the Northern Ireland Vehicle Licensing Office, Victor Troop managed Operation Vengeful that enabled patrols to confirm driver identities against registered owners and tracked known and unknown suspects using three processors known as 'Faith', 'Hope' and 'Charity'. The Troop was amalgamated with

Whiskey Troop in September 1987 to form India Troop, as opposed to the preferred name of VW (Beatle) Troop, and used two processors nicknamed 'Ignorance' and 'Bliss'. By the mid-1990s, in the belief that Operation Banner would continue for some years, 233 Squadron integrated Human, Electronic and Signals Intelligence into a single system. Even with several hundred terminals guarded by firewalls, the average response times for a single enquiry from a patrol was about ten seconds. In 1997, overt automatic vehicle recognition systems were introduced in Northern Ireland.

Chapter 8

Phase Four: Holding The Line
1973 to 1975

The first day of January 1973 saw a marked political change as the United Kingdom and the Republic of Ireland both joined the European Economic Community and were now duty bound to find a solution to the troubles in Northern Ireland. Internment and Operation Motorman, which had continued until 1 December, had proved a considerable strategic success in undermining Provisional insurgency to the extent that it was unable to mount a credible response to the smashing of the No Go areas. The leadership was emasculated and in disarray. The Belfast Brigade had been badly mauled and was reeling under sustained intelligence gathering attacks and 531 paramilitaries had been charged with various offences. The Armed Forces had adapted and, acting decisively and efficiently, had regained the initiative and, in spite of two years of intimidation, political dithering and journalistic and judicial meddling, were proving to be the best counterinsurgency force in the world. Many had experienced the 'Crack, thump!' as bullets, breaking the sound barrier, whistled overhead. The 1,756 shootings in 1971 had risen to 10,564 in 1972, most of them gun battles with Provisionals defending the No Go areas. 'Contact! Wait, Out' was a very frequent radio message. But the cost was high. One hundred and three Regulars had been killed in 1972 with sixty killed in the first seven months, the highest number of military fatalities in one year throughout Operation Banner. The RUC lost seventeen officers. Ninety-five gunmen and three Loyalist terrorists were killed. Of the 307 civilians killed and 3,553 bombs since 1969, 223 were fatalities in 1972, most killed in one of the 1,853 bombings. Of the 2,319 weapons seized since 1969, 1,264 were captured in 1972. About twenty-eight tons of explosive had been found.

On 18 January, an alert sentry shot a robber and wounded another during a Provisional raid on the bank at the Royal Victoria Hospital. It was not the only attack on a hospital. Two days later a car, hijacked in Belfast, exploded in Dublin killing a man and injuring seventeen. It was blamed on Loyalists, as were the deaths of two men found murdered in Bannfoot, Co. Donegal. During the weekend of 3/4 February, in the New Lodge, a 1 KOSB patrol armed with rifles fitted with the new Sight Unit Infantry Trilux night sight, shot six gunmen in a gun battle, the Provisionals claimed that they had been murdered, a claim that was refuted by the Army who said that the patrol had fired at identifiable targets. When two Loyalists were interned on 5 February under the Detention of Terrorists Order, the umbrella United Loyalist Council organized a general strike two days later to 're-establish some kind of Protestant or Loyalist control over the affairs in the Province, especially over security policy'. In Belfast, intimidation prevented people from going to work. Several RUC stations were attacked and two armed Loyalists were shot by the Army. On the 15th, Albert Browne of the UDA was sentenced to death for murdering a RUC officer on 15 October 1972; the sentence was later commuted to life.

The Provisionals launched a counterattack in the summer but quickly came under the cosh when a 39 Infantry Brigade intelligence-led operation that began on 26 June led to the arrest of fifty members of the Belfast Brigade. On 18 July, acting on information received, 1 Glosters swooped on a house in the Falls Road and captured several senior Belfast Brigade officers. Also arrested was Gerry Adams. A few hours later the entire 3rd Battalion command structure was captured in a raid in Ardoyne.

Another operation on 2 August saw twenty-eight more Provisionals arrested and more disaster followed in South Armagh when Michael McVerry, who commanded the Crossmaglen Provisionals, was shot dead by police officers during a raid on RUC Keady in November. In total, 621 IRA were arrested between June and August, of whom 373 were charged with offences and sixty-one were interned.

The destruction of the Provisional leadership meant that when 3 RGJ took over the hardline Ballymurphy sector for a four-month tour on 27 July, the period was quiet with four shootings against eight in 1973 and fifty-seven in 1972 and just two casualties.

On 13 August, a 'brick' stopped a suspect van in Beechmount Avenue and before agreeing to give it a bump start, the corporal asked to check the van. When the driver opened the back doors and the corporal saw 700lbs of HME, the driver admitted to being the Belfast Brigade Explosives Officer. Two days later acting on intelligence, another brick found 650lbs of explosive in Healey's Funeral parlour. On 31 August, a two-man OP in the attic of a building in Ballymurphy reported that they had seen Jim Bryson, a senior commander of the 2nd Battalion, and four men in a Hillman Hunter set up an ambush. Bryson, something of a cult hero, was reckless and particularly ruthless and, according to Moloney, had worked with Adams to convert the battalion into an elite unit during faction fighting with the Officials. As the corporal in charge was moving a tile to get a better view, he dislodged one which crashed to the ground. After an exchange of fire, the Hillman returned a few minutes later, possibly because they had no idea where the OP was. The corporal fired at the car several times and watched it crash into the garden of 99, Ballymurphy Road and then both soldiers left the OP to engage three gunmen in the car until S Company arrived and found that Bryson was mortally wounded and Paddy Mulvenna, brother-in-law to Adams, dead. A week before the battalion returned to Shoeburyness on 1 November, acting on confidential telephoned information, a patrol stopped a Hughes Bakery van on the Springfield Road and found three mortars and twenty-eight bombs, three weapons and a large quantity of detonators and ammunition for bomb-making. A Royal Engineer Search Team found more explosive and detonators in a cache. Earlier in its tour, the battalion had found twenty-one weapons including a .303-inch sniper rifle and a RPG-7, 2,600 rounds of ammunition and a considerable quantity of HME. By the time it left, 3 RGJ had destroyed the Ballymurphy Battalion.

On 24 February 1974, Support Company, 1 Welsh Guards, searched a house in Andersonstown after reports that several Provisional commanders were to meet there. The swoop proved fruitless, however as the company commander and Battalion Intelligence sergeant were leaving, they noticed the back door of an adjacent house was open and the curtains had been opened. When they had arrived, they had been closed. Although the house was known to be fiercely Nationalist, patrols had reported the occupants to have become particularly amenable during the previous days. The two Welsh Guards searched the house and upstairs found a young man claiming to be a plasterer estimating the cost of some work. However, the soldiers were suspicious and handed him to the RUC where it turned out that he was Ivor Bell, close ally to Adams and the fifth Provisional Belfast Brigade commander to be captured since 1972. Brendan Hughes took over command but was captured a few weeks later in a house in Myrtlefield Park in the Malone suburb being used as the Provisional operational HQ. In spite of the attrition, the Provisionals seemed slow to acknowledge the extent to which the Army had penetrated their operational security and that it would blight their activities for years to come. Some regard the handling of informants as unethical and ruthless, nevertheless it is a fact that coordinated, meticulous intelligence was exposing the vulnerability of the Republican groups to exploitation. Motives varied. Some were disappointed by the sectarian and faction fighting, others wanted to save their skins in the belief that the Army would destroy the IRA and others accepted gratuities and benefits. Some informed because they disliked someone. When several senior Provisionals, locked up in Long Kesh, investigated the destruction of the Belfast Brigade, they concluded that Eamon Molloy, the Brigade Quartermaster, was responsible. Critically, his account that he had 'escaped' from the RUC Headquarters at Castlereagh was believed by Brian Keenan, an influential member of the Belfast Brigade staff and close ally of Gerry Adams, who would lead the bombing campaign in England. Two years later Molloy was executed.

The removal of so many Provisionals sometimes led to young people becoming actively involved. The murder of Constable McClinton in March 1974 by a boy, aged 14 years, led to scathing criticism of the IRA by Roman Catholic priests. In October, two boys, aged 12 years, who fired a sub-machine gun at a 2 Scots Guards patrol in Springfield Road, were unable to control their aim. Two days after a 1 Queen's Own Highlanders company sergeant major had been wounded near the Divis Flats, a patrol stopped a girl aged 16 years and found in her possession the M1 carbine that had been used. In 1973, over 130 juveniles were arrested for terrorist-type offences.

The Northern Ireland Office made some political progress and during the Border Poll referendum in March 1973, which was boycotted by Nationalists, of the 57 per cent who voted, 98 per cent favoured the Union. On Polling Day, Loyalist paramilitaries 'overpowered' a UDR section protecting an East Belfast polling station and 'stole their rifles'. After three bomb and gun attacks on Catholic public houses in Belfast on 31 May killed two and injured about twenty people, it emerged that the Sterling sub-machine gun used in the attack on Muldoon's had been stolen from 10 UDR on 23 October 1972. A power-sharing Executive to govern Northern Ireland, agreed on 21 November, was rejected by Loyalists and when, on 9 December, London hosted the Sunningdale Agreement to discuss power sharing, patrolling soldiers were astonished to learn it was the first occasion since 1925 that London, Dublin and Stormont had discussed Northern Ireland. With the negotiations focused on the 'Irish Dimension', of Dublin contributing to the governing of Northern Ireland, it was a red rag to the Loyalists and flexing their majority muscle, in January 1974 they formed the Ulster Army Council (UAC) to resist the proposals. In a bitter General Election summoned by Prime Minister Heath, the winning of eleven of the twelve seats by the Unionists effectively undermined the Agreement. Nationally, Labour won and Prime Minister Harold Wilson appointed Merlyn Rees as Secretary of State for Northern Ireland on 5 March. We now know from recently released documents that Wilson examined the possibility of severing the constitutional links between Westminster and Stormont, and also that Northern Ireland join the Commonwealth. A week later, Taoiseach Liam Cosgrave admitted the majority must decide the future of Northern Ireland.

In early April, Rees proposed to de-proscribe the UVF and Sinn Fein and phase out Internment. He then met with the Ulster Workers' Council (UWC), an emerging political group calling for elections to the Northern Ireland Assembly and threatening civil disruption unless the Executive was dissolved. At the beginning of May, the UDA declared its opposition to the Sunningdale Agreement and a fortnight later, after the Assembly rejected the Council of Ireland, the UWC announced to a surprised British Government that a general strike would start the following day. Although the momentum was slow, the strike was sufficiently effective that when, on 19 May, HQ Northern Ireland warned it could not protect fuel supplies and also maintain internal security, Rees announced a State of Emergency.

As with Operation Motorman, 29 Movement Regiment at South Cerney and just twenty-four RAF and one RCT Movers at Aldergrove swung into action by controlling the delivery of an additional 3,200 troops in 125 flights. The RAOC played a crucial role in organizing their accommodation. 1 LI arrived almost direct from training in Florida and a hastily assembled 500-strong Royal Navy/Army unit, tasked to maintain essential public services, brought troop levels to 16,500. HQ 3 Armoured Division Transport Regiment arrived direct from exercising in England to manage fuel distribution and the RAOC sent the strengthened 180 Petroleum Bulk Operating Platoon from 10 Ordnance Battalion. The RFA *Sir Lancelot* was unloaded three times at the military jetty at Kinnegar Ordnance Depot. By 1974, the muddy lanes and leaky huts of the Depot had disappeared in favour of modern sheds lined with neat racks, tarmac roads and a decent perimeter fence. The Supply Depot at Lisburn and Vehicle Depot at Long Kesh had both moved to Holywood. The Command Ammunition Depot was still at Ballykinler. To reduce the shortfall in drivers, servicemen serving in Northern Ireland with HGV licences were attached to 26 (General Transport) Squadron and among the vehicles issued to 60 Squadron RCT from England were fifteen Second World War fuel tankers, which later provided valuable service as storage units. The Army distributed 120,000 tons of fuel from three oil depots to twenty-one petrol stations abandoned by their managers. Mediation by Trades Union Council, British politicians and General Idi Amin of Uganda, attempting to enhance his status with a conference, were unproductive. After Merlyn Rees had refused to meet the UWC and Brian Faulkner then resigned as Chief Executive on 28 May, the Sunningdale Agreement was dead. During the strike, Wilson, who was under pressure from Army commanders dubious about fighting the IRA and Loyalists on two fronts, was so angered by the Loyalists that he accused them of 'sponging' from the United Kingdom and investigated the possibility of Northern Ireland being arbitrarily given Dominion status. The implications of the scheme could have been serious – civil war in the north and the 12,000-strong Irish Army unable to prevent the IRA stepping into the political vacuum as Dublin wobbled, resulting in a Marxist state across the Irish Sea at London's back door. Fortunately, Wilson backed off, however his unwillingness to challenge Loyalist muscle displayed during the UWC strike arguably led to thirty years of conflict until the power sharing that they had opposed led to peace.

Throughout the strike, bombings, sectarian murders and assassinations continued unabated. When 1st Royal Horse Artillery (RHA) arrived for its third roulement tour of four tours on 7 March, for the second time it was based at the Grand Central Hotel with responsibility for the security of Belfast City Centre. For most of the next six months, the Gunners dealt with bombs. Literally within hours, an explosion littered James Street South with glass and chunks of

1969. An early photograph of soldiers in Northern Ireland. Dressed in green combat with shirt and tie, the SLR has its bayonet fixed. (*Anon*)

1970. Belfast. A thin advance guard during a riot. Note the small size of the shields and the amount of stones and bricks surrounding the soldiers. (*Military Intelligence Museum*)

1971. Londonderry. While a water cannon soaks a crowd, soldiers equipped with shields pass through a gate in the fence to make arrests. (*Military Intelligence Museum*)

January 1972. Royal Engineers of 1 Troop, 8 Field Squadron demolish a border road near Drumcully, Co. Londonderry. (*Source Unknown*)

Bloody Sunday. C Coy, 2 Para crosses a barrier and advance along Chamberlain Road. Note the accompanying camera crews. (*Source unknown*)

20 March 1972. LCpl Wayne Evans of 1 Para cradles a woman who has just lost both her legs in the IRA car bomb in Donegal St, Belfast which killed six people and injured 100. Another para administers first aid. (*Military Intelligence Museum*)

1972. Lower Falls, Belfast. A soldier of D Company, 1 Gloucesters extinguishes a gas light in Plevna Street. (*Roy Millard*)

1972. A soldier with a baton gun slung across his back carries his SLR in the iconic position of the butt resting on his hip. His flak jacket is not in good condition.

1972. Londonderry. A rare image of an Army sniper. He is equipped with a 7.62mm L42 bolt action rifle fitted with a Sighting Telescope and a special sling that gives improved stability. His position is screened with a small piece of camouflage netting. (*Anon*)

Operation *Motorman*, Londonderry. The crew of the Blues and Royals Saladin Armoured Car that caught fire when its fuel tank exploded. (*Brigadier Andrew Parker-Bowles*)

Operation *Motorman*, Londonderry. A 26 Armoured Squadron AVRE smashes a barrier. The turret is reversed and the words 'Royal Engineers' are painted on the bazooka plates. Behind the AVRE is a Saracen. (*Source unknown*)

1972. Londonderry. A Humber APC 'Pig' driver usually based with 2 Squadron RCT in Nienburg, West Germany at the 'Saracen Factory', Lonemore Rd, Londonderry. (*Chris Cronk*)

1974. An Army Landing Ship Tank beached at Ballykinler Camp is unloaded by 26/18 Squadron RCT. (*Major Gerry Webb*)

HQ Northern Ireland, Thiepval Barracks, Lisburn. (*Military Intelligence Museum*)

1974. The 'Knicker Factory' at Lurgan with housed HQ 3 Infantry Brigade and several other units. The approach road has been dug up to restrict traffic and lined with concrete-filled anti-parking 40-gallon oil drums. (*Author's Collection*)

1974. The Long Kesh Mutiny. A Saracen smashes through a fence. The soldiers are unarmed, wearing respirators and carrying wooden coshes. (*Author's Collection*)

1974. Two 39 Brigade and HQ Squadron signallers on top of a building in Belfast. The rifle butt number '128' can match the soldier over the radio without giving his name in the event that he becomes a casualty. In September 1989, Staff Sergeant Froggett was killed while repairing a radio mast at RUC Coalisland. (*Royal Signals Museum*)

Royal Engineer Antrim Bridging Camp, 1974. 33 Field Squadron RE and 124 Intelligence Section train for waterborne operations on Lough Neagh. (*Author's Collection*)

RCT Corps Day 1975, Thiepval Barracks, Lisburn. Major Alan Tapp takes the salute of the march-past of 26/18 Squadron led by the Pipes and Drums of 152 Regiment RCT (V). (*Major Gerry Webb*)

South Armagh. An Army Air Corps Scout lands to collect a patrol assembled from HQ 3 Infantry Brigade. (*Author's Collection*)

July 1975. The naval boarding party on the coastal minesweeper HMS *Lewiston*. The helmets were often dispensed with as being cumbersome. (*Author's Collection*)

1976. RUC Kinawley after the East Tyrone Provisionals had left a bomb in a horse box against a wall. (*Tom Priestley*)

1977. Carlingford Lough. The converted motor fishing vessel HMS *Alert* with a Rigid Raider manned by 1st Raiding Squadron, Royal Marines and 40 Commando at the stern. An unseen helicopter delivers a netted underslung forward of the bridge. (*Chris Baxter*)

1977. A UDR patrol boards a 72 Squadron Wessex. The soldier at the rear carries a General Purpose Machine gun. (*Source unknown*)

17 March 1978. The capture of the severely wounded Francis Hughes by the SAS. His first comments were that the search dogs were no good. (*Source unknown*)

1979. Captain Robert Nairac GC who was murdered by the Provisionals. This photo was used in the search for him. (*Author's Collection*)

1980. Company Sergeant Major Downey of F Coy, 41 Commando, a Special Branch Officer and an ATO after an attempt to bomb a patrol. (*Brian Downey*)

1980, Londonderry. UDR 'Greenfinch' searchers and soldiers from 2 Royal Regiment of Fusiliers at a vehicle check-point. (*Source unknown*)

1980. A soldier from 1 Kings Own Borderers leads a patrol from RUC Newtownhamilton accompanied by the stray dog, *Drummer*. He has no flak jacket and his rifle is equipped with a sight. In the background is a Ferret Mark 2 fitted with a turret equipped with a .30-inch Browning machine gun. (*Source unknown*)

1987. Belfast. A soldier from 1 Queens Lancashire Regiment alongside a 'Flying Pig'. On his back is a Remote Control Device used to detect electronically-controlled bombs and a Federal Riot Gun. Note the RUC officer sitting on the wall. (*Sean Metcalfe*)

1991. A patrol from E (Home Service Force) Company, 2 Wessex (V) consisting men who had served in Aden, Borneo and Northern Ireland. Twice, this Company deployed in England on anti-terrorist operations. (*Author's Collection*)

1992. Lisburn. Brigadier Alan Ramsey, the last UDR CO, with his Chief of Staff, his 26 Squadron RCT driver and close protection escort from 177 (Support) Platoon RMP close protection team. (*Des Green*)

1993. North Belfast. A 9/12th Lancers patrol accompanied by a RUC officer. The searcher on the left was later shot in her face and upper body by a gunman equipped with an AK-47 semi-automatic rifle. (*Rob Millington*)

1993. Belfast. A view from an Army sangar viewing toward Crumlin Road Courthouse. (*Rob Millington*)

The Borucki Observation Post in Crossmaglen named after Pte James Borucki, 3 Para (killed 8 August 1976). Built by 33 Field Squadron RE between 1976 and 1983, the 200mm of reinforced concrete and 2.5 metre thick armour-plate walls were surrounded by weld mesh anti-rocket screens. (*Author's Collection*)

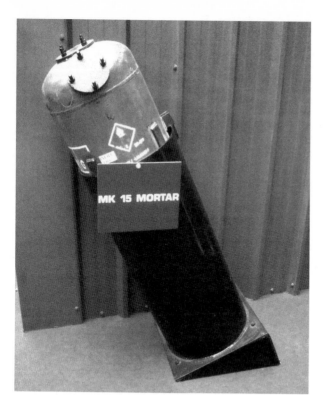

An IRA Mark 15 'Barrackbuster' mortar and its Kosangas domestic cylinder projectile. (*Author's Collection*)

2000. Watchtower G40A at Forkhill. Fitted with sophisticated cameras and surveillance equipment, it was one of a series that restricted IRA activity in South Armagh. (*Harry Long*)

building and then half an hour later, after a failed attempt to defuse it, a proxy car bomb exploded at the corner of the hotel causing extensive collateral damage to a distance of 300 metres. The Regiment's only fatality during the tour was Gunner David Farrington shot on 13 March by a gunman firing from the sanctuary of St Mary's Catholic Church. Two other Gunners were seriously injured in the same burst. The fourth soldier chased the gunman through the church but lost him. Three weeks later, the Provisionals again attacked the Grand Central with a 600lb bomb loaded on a furniture lorry that injured twenty-eight civilians and caused collateral damage up to 800 metres away. The most serious incident was the Chichester Street bomb in May in which a hijacked van, containing a 1,000lbs bomb and ten mortar bombs, was driven over a fuel storage tank underneath the forecourt of Charles Hurst's garage. Using a Foam Pig, it took the ATO over eleven hours to neutralize the device by hauling a large pile of sacks from the van. Had it exploded, it would have devastated the area. April was quieter except for E Battery in Ballymacarret, where violence and aggression was normal. On the 14th, a man was relieved of a Sten when he was seen to be walking peculiarly. Three weeks later, a man was arrested in a bar, however his appearance did not match the photograph of the name he gave and then an Intelligence Section screener noticed that the address he gave matched that of a senior terrorist questioned about three weeks earlier. It turned out the suspect was in disguise. By the time 1 RHA left Belfast on 4 July, it had made 399 arrests, which resulted in five terrorists being charged and had dealt with thirty-six bombs and 596 hoaxes, scares and false alarms. Four hundred and thirteen unoccupied houses had been searched. There had been forty-eight shootings at patrols, which had resulted in one gunner killed and two injured; a markedly different statistic from 1972 and 1973. Compared with previous tours, things were sufficiently quiet for the 1 RRW Band to entertain shoppers, an event that was greeted enthusiastically.

At about 4 p.m. on 27 October 1973, Sergeant Watts RAMC was inside RUC Crossmaglen when a bomb exploded in the street. Rushing outside, he was directed to a badly wounded and distressed private lying on the road experiencing difficulties in breathing. Fashioning an airways tube from a syringe casing, Watts performed an emergency tracheotomy with a scalpel, inserted the tube into the soldier's throat and for the next two hours used a small syringe to suck blood from his airways until a helicopter arrived to fly him and the casualty to Musgrave Park Hospital in Belfast. When surgeons operated on the soldier, they found twelve wounds, the most dangerous being a penetrating neck wound and a larynx full of blood. Unfortunately his vocal cords were damaged beyond repair but this did not stop him marrying a year later with Sergeant Watts as his best man.

Not included in the statistic of 6,116 Service personnel wounded are those injured in road traffic accidents, sports injuries and illness. Every soldier needs to be assured of efficient medical services beginning at the point of being wounded, to surgery, through to the recovery process and beyond to rehabilitation. For the first time since 1945, the Royal Army Medical Corps (RAMC) did not have to contend with tropical diseases. Broadly, for every soldier killed in action, one was discharged from wounds received. Most wounds were from gunshot or blast and the worst injuries generally from IEDs and mines filled with nails and bolts adding to shrapnel provided by the casing. Since it was not unknown for military ambulances to be held up by hostile crowds, Saracens were converted into ambulances and fitted with blood transfusion and intravenous fluid equipment. Difficulties experienced evacuating casualties from rural areas, particularly along the border where roads and tracks were always in danger of being mined, ambushed or blocked, led to helicopters being used. Unlike the battlefield where the wounded pass through a military triage process that leads to the seriously wounded being treated in general hospitals, wounded and injured soldiers were initially taken direct to NHS hospitals in Northern Ireland. A Military Wing was then established at Musgrave Hospital in Belfast. Essentially a field hospital staffed by male and female medical staff from the three services, it had resuscitation and intensive care bays and a theatre run by a full surgical team tasked to stabilize the wounded, injured and ill before the more serious were flown to England in the care of RAF aero-medics and transferred to the Queen Elizabeth Military Hospitals at Woolwich, the Cambridge at Aldershot for the Army and the naval Haslar Hospital for the Royal Marines and then onto rehabilitation at RAF Chessington. When the Defence Medical Services were reorganized in the 1990s, wounded soldiers were treated in NHS hospitals alongside hospitalized civilians and removed from their optimum comfort zone of recovering with other military casualties. It was not a popular decision.

Between 1972 and 1974 at the height of the fighting, of 454 soldiers shot in a limb, only one died, and of the fifty-six shot in the abdomen, eight died. Although flak jackets prevented some serious wounds, of the ninety-one soldiers hit in the chest, forty-three died, most because of fatal damage to the heart. One problem of clinical searches of penetrating wounds was evidence of the nylon content of the jacket. Sixty-five of 108 soldiers admitted with head wounds died. Until the mid-1980s, soldiers tended to wear berets until helmets became normal. Serious head wounds were usually first treated at the Royal Victoria Hospital where the theatre staff achieved international status as experts in treating terrorist casualties. Three soldiers admitted with limbs sliced by missiles that damaged femoral arteries survived with the help of multiple blood transfusions. Twenty soldiers suffered gunshot wounds to their spines and, of 281 that had multiple injuries from bombs and mines, 101 died. Those suffering psychiatric illnesses were usually evacuated to the military psychiatric hospital at Netley near Southampton. As always for some, post combat stress problems usually surfaced later in life.

In October, the second General Election of the year saw the return of the controversial Conservative politician Enoch Powell as the Unionist member for South Down. A month later, the Protestant Action Group (PAG), a cover name for the UVF, shot two Catholics at their workplace near Templepatrick, Co. Antrim and wounded Billy Hull, a former leader of the Loyalist Association of Workers (LAW), and Jim Anderson, a former UDA leader, during Loyalist squabbling. On the same day, the Ministry of Defence announced that the names of those killed in Northern Ireland would not be added to war memorials because the conflict was not classified as a war.

On 29 November, Home Secretary Roy Jenkins announced the Prevention of Terrorism Bill and gave the RUC powers to detain suspected terrorists for up to forty-eight hours in the first instance and for up to seven days on application to the Home Secretary. Originally a temporary measure, the Act was renewed annually until made permanent in 1988 by Prime Minister Thatcher. Three days later, when Dublin introduced legislation permitting prosecution for terrorist offences committed outside the jurisdiction of the Republic of Ireland, theoretically the IRA had nowhere to hide. On 10 December, in a Secret Intelligence Service operation engineered with the assistance of Brendan Duddy, several senior Provisionals secretly met eight Protestant clergymen from Northern Ireland acting as intermediaries at Smyth's Village Hotel in Feakle, Co. Clare to discuss proposals from the British Government. Although the meeting broke up when the Provisionals were tipped off that Irish Special Branch were on their way to arrest them, the clergymen presented Rees with the Provisional response on 20 December. This included the announcement of a ceasefire between midnight on 22 December and midnight on 2 January 1975. When Rees suggested on New Year's Eve that Westminster would respond positively if there was a 'genuine and sustained cessation of violence', for the first time since 1969 there was a feeling that a military withdrawal was a possibility. But exploratory talks between the government and the Provisionals collapsed on 17 January 1975 after Rees said that the government would not be swayed by the politics of bomb and bullet. The ceasefire ended, however, three weeks later; the weakened Provisional leadership, in spite of simmering opposition of rising stars, had no real alternative but to announce another ceasefire. The Army reduced its patrols and several Incident Centres were established to monitor military and paramilitary activity.

'On the run' in Ireland were significant numbers of IRA living in comparative safety. Also in Ireland were several training camps teaching recruits explosive handling, weapon training, tactics and an introduction into Marxism. John Francis Green, a prominent figure of the 2nd (North Armagh) Battalion in Lurgan, had escaped from internment in Long Kesh three years earlier by exchanging clothes with his brother, who was a priest. On 10 January, a farmer returning home after milking the cows of a neighbour on the slopes of Mullyash Mountain in Co. Monaghan found his body on a track and ignited one of the most controversial episodes in the troubles. Benny Green, an aide of John Francis, was also found shot not far from Monaghan.

By 1975, the turf war between MI5, who favoured defeating the IRA, and the Secret Intelligence Services, who backed negotiation, was reaching a climax. There had already been casualties. An Intelligence Corps Warrant Officer had taken his life after seeing his network of informants in Belfast destroyed within days of handing over to civilian handlers. Throughout Great Britain's withdrawal from the colonies, the Secret Intelligence Service had employed a twin track of supporting individuals and groups supportive of democracy, including dissidents, and undermining opponents. In early 1975, Captain Holroyd, the 3 Infantry Brigade MIO, had recognized that the Secret Intelligence Service was seeking a political solution, however he believed that the military strategy favoured the

118

views promoted by Brigadier Kitson of combining the subversion of Republican activists and infiltration with a dirty tricks campaign. The phrase 'dirty tricks' is frequently used to describe unconventional and irregular warfare, even though history gives countless honourable examples, notably the Second World War Special Operations Executive. Holroyd began to suspect collusion between military intelligence and Loyalists, particularly on 17 May, the third day of the UWC Strike, when Dublin was rocked for the second time by three bombs exploding almost simultaneously in the evening rush hour, killing twenty-six people, followed by an explosion in Monaghan ninety minutes later that killed seven people and injured twenty-eight. The operation was too sophisticated for Loyalists, particularly when Sammy Smyth, UDA and UWC Strike Committee press officer, commented 'I am very happy about the bombings in Dublin. There is a war with the Free State and now we are laughing at them.'

In July 1993, the Yorkshire Television documentary *The Hidden Hand – The Forgotten Massacre* accused the Security Forces of helping the UVF to deliver the bombs. A week later, the UVF reiterated it was responsible. In spite of his suspicions, Holroyd continued to act diligently until, he alleges, in early 1975 he was shown a photograph by Lieutenant Nairac purporting to be that of the body of John Francis Green.

One of the most controversial personalities in Operation Banner, Robert Nairac was born in 1948 in Mauritius, the younger of a brother and two sisters born to a father who was an eye surgeon. After attending the Roman Catholic public school Ampleforth, Nairac read medieval and military history at Oxford University, played for the 2nd XV and revived the boxing club. In one match, he boxed Martin Meehan. Commissioned into the Grenadier Guards, he was a postgraduate at Dublin University before joining his battalion. Described as having a strong belief in Catholicism, Nairac's first tour in Northern Ireland was with the 2nd Battalion in Shankill and the Ardoyne from July to October 1973 where he became involved in community activity, in particular at an Ardoyne sports club. The battalion captured fifty-eight weapons, 9,000 rounds of ammunition and 693lbs of explosive and saw 104 men interned at no loss. At the end of the tour, Nairac stayed on as liaison officer to 1 Argyll and Sutherland Highlanders. When his Battalion was posted to Hong Kong, a former Guards officer who had joined the SAS invited Nairac to be a liaison officer between 4 Field Survey Troop RE in Castledillon and HQ 3 Infantry Brigade.

In his conversation with Holroyd, Nairac described how he and two SAS had crossed the border, waited in the lane until the farmer left the house and then broke in and shot Green. Several weeks before the killing, a small unit of British soldiers had been politely escorted north across border by the Gardai after raiding the farmhouse of an Irish citizen and a British Army helicopter circling the farmhouse drew little response from Dublin. With his knowledge of the Mid-Ulster UVF, Holroyd was convinced that once the government sanctioned collusion with Loyalists, the support of the majority of the community would be at risk and the struggle in Northern Ireland lost. But his views landed him in trouble and one dull morning in the spring, 124 Intelligence Section at Lurgan was told that he would be leaving his post as his loyalties lay elsewhere. Holroyd left Northern Ireland under acrimonious circumstances and resigned his commission. Largely isolated, he has spent years defending his reputation by attempting to undermine claims that the SAS was not in Northern Ireland. After serving with the Rhodesian Army, he returned to England where he elicited support from the anti-Establishment on a high after the shoot-to-kill revelations in the early 1980s and contributed to Justice Barron's 2003 investigation in Dublin into alleged collusion between the British Security Forces and Loyalist groups.

In the spring, simmering sectarian tension in mid-Ulster exploded into violence in an area roughly encompassing East Tyrone and Co. Armagh. Plotting the incidents on maps, HQ 3 Brigade nicknamed the area the Murder Triangle and concluded from the patterns of incidents and movement of weapons that the violence was a fierce turf war by about thirty terrorists from the South Armagh Provisionals and Mid-Ulster UVF. The Provisional claim that a hardline splinter group opposing the ceasefire was responsible was rejected as nonsense. It was nothing more than extreme sectarian violence in which the casualties were the innocent. May saw five bombings, a Catholic stabbed ten times and three shootings. June began badly with the murders near Killen of three Protestants returning from a dog show. A train was robbed. The two shootings and seven bombings in July ended with an atrocity that shook Ulster, even today.

In the 1970s Irish bands were at the height of their popularity and regularly performed in the north, usually from Thursdays to

Sundays. The dancehalls in which the bands performed were vibrant, especially in the border counties. To a certain extent, the bands helped the Catholics retain their cultural heritage, although Protestants and, indeed, soldiers found the bands entertaining, if they half-heartedly accused them of playing nothing but infectious rebel songs, such as *Behind the Wire*. During the evening of 31 July, the Miami Showband had performed to a small, mixed audience at the Castle Ballroom in Banbridge and by 2.30 a.m. had packed their equipment into a van driven by their road manager, Brian Maguire. In the second van driven by Brian McCoy, who was the lead singer and Ireland's latest heart-throb, were Francis O'Toole, Anthony Geraghty, Stephen Travers and Des McAlea. The drummer Ray Millar drove to Antrim to see his parents. On the road to Newry, Maguire, a few minutes ahead of McCoy, ignored a blue Triumph 2000 that pulled out from a lay-by and indicated that he stop by flashing its lights. McCoy, however, obeyed the directions of the Triumph driver and stopped at a UDR VCP in a lay-by. The band was unconcerned as soldiers checked the van until one of them, later identified as Private James McDowell, became impatient with his colleagues' relaxed attitude and ordered the band to line up along a hedge. A soldier, apparently with an English accent, then instructed the soldiers to take the personal details of the band. When Travers then saw two soldiers searching the back of the van, fearing they might damage his guitar, he broke from the line-up to help them and was being pushed back into line when the van exploded, hurling McAlea over a hedge. As he picked himself up and ran across dark fields, the soldiers opened fire, killing O'Toole, Geraghty and McCoy. Travers pretended to be dead and later recalled someone saying, 'Come on, those bastards are dead. I got them with dum-dums.' When a Security Forces patrol arrived at the scene, they found body parts strewn over 100 yards from the wrecked van and recovered two guns, three magazines and UDR berets. When the forensics on the weapons linking several to sectarian killings in the Murder Triangle was shared with the Gardai, their investigators concluded that a Spanish Star pistol found at the scene was linked to four murders south of the border between 1973 and 1976, including John Francis Green. The funeral cortege of two dead soldiers, both serving with 11 UDR, passed provocatively through the Catholic Garvaghy estate in Portadown on their way to paramilitary funerals at Drumcree Church, complete with a volley. Three members of the battalion were later sentenced to life for their part in the attack and released under the 1998 Good Friday Agreement. The soldier with the distinctive English accent cast suspicion that a Regular was involved.

August was also a bad month in the Murder Triangle with an attack on an elderly people's outing minibus at Gilford and four attacks on UDR soldiers in three days in South Armagh. In September, shootings included the Provisional attack on Tullyvallen Orange Hall resulting in five killed and seven injured and eleven injured in the second bombing of McGurk's Bar in Belfast. Faction fighting led to further casualties. Public loss of confidence led to 1 LI, the Spearhead Battalion, being flown to South Armagh for a month to reinforce 3 RRF, which had relieved 1 Green Howards at Bessbrook Mill, in August. The LI were in turn relieved by 42 Commando. Violence in Belfast and the UVF rampant resulted in twelve people killed on 2 October and five on 19 December, three in Silverbridge and two in Dundalk. A political solution now seemed a distant dream. Nevertheless, Internment ended on 5 December and with it went the ability to remove individuals from circulation that intelligence strongly suspected to be involved in paramilitary activity. It would now need to be proven in court.

Some returned to paramilitary activity. Since 9 August 1971, 1,874 Catholics and 107 Protestants had been interned and while it remains fashionable to criticize the strategy, to the soldiers patrolling the streets and lanes expecting to be ambushed, the combination of improved intelligence, good luck and the removal of hardline IRA, in particular, had been welcome. Clearly missed in the drive for civil and human rights was that the Provisional IRA was a military force in name, composition and culture. Military casualties had dropped from fifty-eight in 1973 to twenty-eight in 1974. Gun battles and shootings had dropped from 5,018 to 3,206 in the same period. Internment worked. The 145 civilian casualties in 1974 rose to 196 in 1975, most concentrated in the Murder Triangle.

Chapter 9

The Beginning of the Long War

Meanwhile, a deep rift had developed in the Provisional Belfast Brigade IRA over the depreciation of military capability during the ceasefire between the Old Guard led by such veterans as Rory O'Brady and New Guard dissidents, mostly from the Belfast Brigade, led by Gerry Adams languishing in Compound (Convicted) 11 in Long Kesh. Adams had been transferred from Compound (Internees) 6 after attempting to escape. The South Armagh and East Tyrone Brigades had generally not abided by the ceasefire and were still militarily sharp. By the end of 1975, Brian Keenan, fresh from a year in prison in Ireland, after being convicted as a member of the IRA, had rejoined the Provisional Army Council as Quartermaster General and Director of Mainland Operations. His political philosophy veered toward left-wing groups in Central and South America. Frustrated by events in the Murder Triangle and the murders of the three Reavey brothers in Glenane and the three O'Dowds at Ballydugan, near Gilford, the previous day, he convinced Seamus Twomey, who was Chief of Staff, that retaliation was essential. On 5 January 1976 this resulted in the slaughter of twelve Protestant textile workers at a Provisional roadblock near Kingsmill.

Two days later, Prime Minister Wilson unexpectedly announced that the SAS would deploy to South Armagh for 'patrolling and surveillance' tasks. The announcement came as something of a surprise to SAS commanders because the Regiment was still engaged in a counter-revolutionary war in Dhofar, albeit near the end, and a squadron was winter warfare training in Norway. Nevertheless the eleven soldiers available, which included several recovering from wounds received in Dhofar, were formed into Ulster Troop. The Ministry of Defence was equally destabilized by the announcement, particularly as the Regiment had little experience in Ulster and that some SAS officers believed that the counter-insurgency experience gained in the deserts of Dhofar, where the rule of law was generally summary, could be transferred to the narrow streets and fields of Northern Ireland, where the rule of law prevailed. HQ Northern Ireland and the RUC were distinctly uncomfortable with the idea of the Regiment being let loose in an internal security environment and thus when SAS senior officers arrived, they were slightly taken aback not to be invited into the Intelligence corridor.

Meanwhile, Secretary of State Rees had finished working on his paper entitled *The Way Ahead*, in which he envisaged a strategy of 'Criminalization, Ulsterization, and Normalization'. In a concept not markedly different from British strategies employed in its post-1945 campaigns, the idea was to transfer responsibility for internal security back to local government and its armed forces, as quickly as possible and that the Army would gradually disengage, as much as possible, because British soldiers being killed was politically less acceptable than the deaths of local security forces. In March, Rees took the first step in the criminalization process by announcing that the special category status for those convicted of terrorist offences would end and from henceforth anyone convicted of political violence would be treated as criminals and accommodated in the eight new H Blocks being built at HMP Maze at Long Kesh. Some prisoners lost their special category status literally within several hours; for instance Brendan Hughes for attacking prison officers. The Republican leadership did not like the loss of the status and, in September 1976, Kieran Nugent was the first terrorist to be sent as a criminal to the H Blocks for refusing to wear prison uniform; he used a blanket. So began a long confrontation with Westminster that ended in bitter tragedy. After Rees had announced in the House of Commons on the 25th that Ulsterization would lead the security policy and, importantly, that the RUC would re-assume police primacy, HQ Northern Ireland changed its military strategy to:

Gain detailed knowledge of specific areas by dominating with a military presence.

Protect the RUC carrying out their normal activities. The policy remained to arrest suspects and transfer to the RUC.

React to incidents.

Carry out specialist operations – search, air and naval support, bomb disposal and logistics surrounding the refurbishments of bases.

Undertake static operations – guarding key points and manning Permanent VCPs.

Direct covert operations – source handling, surveillance and direct action.

With the RUC taking the lead, the failure to appoint a Director of Operations to oversee Security Forces' operations meant that contentious issues took ages to resolve and led to some intelligence agencies competing. RUC intransigence, and unwillingness by military commanders to adjust, also led to disagreements and distrust. Political interests often affected military decision-making because of an increasing lack of understanding of the purpose of the military, particularly after 1997. On 1 January, the Army deployment was:

39 Infantry Brigade

Resident
Holywood Barracks
1 King's Own Scottish Borderers on its fifth tour since May 1970. Three killed in action and one non-battle fatality.

Roulement
Ballymurphy, Springfield, Whiterock
1 Coldstream Guards. Fourth tour since December 1970. Seven killed in action, one in 1972, three in 1973 and two in 1974.
Falls Road, Divis and Sandy Row
1 Argylls and Sutherland Highlanders. Fourth tour since July 1972. Seven fatalities of five killed in action, one killed by a train and one by friendly fire, all in 1972.
Anderstown, Suffolk and Twinbrook
3 Queen's on its fourth tour since April 1970.
Ardoyne and New Lodge
47 Light Regiment RA as infantry. Second tour since July 1973.
Belfast City Centre and Markets
17/21 Lancers as infantry on its second tour since May 1970, the first as the Omagh Resident Regiment. Three men killed in booby trap bomb in Crossmaglen in May 1973.

125

East Belfast

3 RHA on its sixth tour since September. Disbanded on completion of the deployment.

8 Infantry Brigade

Resident
Londonderry

1 King's. Third tour since September 1969. Seven killed in action, all in 1972.

1 Worcestershire and Sherwood Foresters. Second tour since March 1972.

Roulement
Londonderry

3 LI. On its fifth tour since August 1969. Three killed in action and one battle fatality.

42 Heavy Regiment RA. On its sixth tour as infantry since April 1970.

Ballykelly

37 Field Squadron RE. On its second tour since November 1973.

3 Infantry Brigade

Resident
Ballykinler

1 Queen's Lancashire Regiment. Fourth tour since May 1970. Six deaths, including one of natural causes.

Omagh

15/19 Hussars. Second tour since August 1971, the previous being at HMP Long Kesh.

Roulement
Bessbrook

1 Royal Scots on its fifth tour since March 1970.

Armagh and Aughnacloy

13/18 Hussars. On its second tour since September January 1972.

Armagh

Queen's Dragoon Guards as infantry. On its second tour since February 1972.

Long Kesh Guard Force

39 Medium Regiment RA. Second tour since October 1973.

Castledillon
8 Field Squadron RE. Sixth tour since January 1970.

Emergency
South Armagh
2 Queen's. Fifth tour since March 1969.
1 Duke of Wellington's on its fourth tour since June 1971. Five killed in action.

After the departure of HMS *Maidstone*, Moscow Camp had been expanded to include the Senior Naval Officer, Northern Ireland and transit accommodation to include the hundreds of serving and former soldiers giving evidence in the courts. Most were transported in APCs. The average APC deployment saw about twenty Saracens and 100 Pigs of the City Squadron attached to 39 Brigade and about sixty Saracens attached to the County Squadron based at Long Kesh.

Part of Ulsterization was an increase in establishments of the RUC and RUC Reserve and an extension of RUC operations to include 'mobile support units' for special operations. To their great credit, the relentless murder of police officers on duty, at home and at their places of work did not dissuade recruitment. In support was the Royal Military Police (RMP), 1 Regiment RMP had been formed in Thiepval Barracks in November 1971 and by June 1973 numbered about 700 all ranks, which included 181 Provost Company WRAC, formed in 1972, to assist the searching of women and children. Replacing their familiar stiff red-topped caps with distinctive red berets, the RMP had powers as constables under the 1954 Interpretation Act and regularly joined RUC foot and mobile patrols. Their expertise in criminal investigation meant they were a valuable resource collecting forensic evidence after bomb incidents and terrorist shootings. The RMP also investigated every instance of opening fire. In June 1973, 2 Regiment RMP was formed in Londonderry from 1 Regiment until reductions in troop levels in 1978 resulted in its disbandment. In March 1985, 1 Regiment was disbanded with 175, 176 and 181 Provost Companies split between 39 and 8 Infantry Brigades. The RMP also provided close protection for the GOC and CLF.

In spite of limited subversion by Loyalist paramilitaries and the murder of soldiers, the combination of UDR soldiers attending courses at the Schools of Infantry, Intelligence and Military Engineering, its links with infantry regiments providing a steady flow of key personnel and its experiences since 1970, led to the UDR emerging as a valued force. Fifty-six soldiers had been killed since April 1970. As part of the Way Ahead, UDR took primary tactical military responsibility for the quieter parts of Northern Ireland and formed full-time operational platoons in each company to support part-timers. Recruiting resulted in 300 extra soldiers although the persistent shortfall of full-time officers meant that some full-time SNCOs acted as Operations Officers at UDR bases. The decrease in violence by 1984 resulted in two amalgamations of the 1st/9th (Co. Antrim) and 7th/10th (City of Belfast) Battalions.

When Ulster Troop arrived in South Armagh to support 1 Royal Scots at Bessbrook with instructions to apply pressure on the Provisionals by striking at selected targets, it took over the offices of the disbanded 4 Field Survey Troop at Castledillon but first there was retraining and familiarization before being committed to operations. One RCT corporal trained the SAS in the seamless delivery and exchange of OPs without stopping, by fitting a civilian van with sliding doors and a red light – 'Prepare to exit' – and a green light – 'Go!' Much to their discomfort, the SAS were expected to abide by the Yellow Card rules of engagement and it would take time for the Regiment to acknowledge that they were unlikely to defeat the IRA without some help from the existing command, control and intelligence infrastructure. After returning to his battalion in 1976, Captain Nairac was again invited to liaise with the RUC and Special Branch on behalf of the SAS, however he began to infringe their guidelines by taking on tasks outside his role and visiting pubs in South Armagh. By March, the Strike element of Find, Fix, Strike and Exploit was ready.

On 12 March, a 1 Royal Scots patrol, reporting that they had arrested a drunken man staggering around a field near Entubber, was not quite correct. During the night, in its first operation, a SAS patrol seized Sean McKenna, a prominent Newry Provisional, from a house 250 metres south of the border. Threatening to kill him if he resisted, his captors told him to jump over the Flurry stream – straight to a waiting Army patrol. McKenna was a member of a hardline Republican family and had been interned between 1971 and 1974. His father was one of the 'hooded men' picked up in Operation Demetrius. Sentenced to twenty-five years, he took part in the 1980 hunger strike. His capture was a clear message to those 'on the run' that they were no longer safe. However the SAS aura was dented on 8 May when two soldiers, one a Fijian, were arrested in a Triumph

Toledo by the Gardai about half a mile inside the Republic near Border Crossing Point Hotel One, south of Crossmaglen, claiming that they were testing the car. This naïve claim was not believed by the incredulous Gardai or indeed most of those serving or who had served in Northern Ireland. When six more SAS in two cars 'searching for their colleagues' were then arrested nearby, all eight were taken to Dublin much to the embarrassment of the British Government. After this incident the 'Instructions to Soldiers who May Accidentally Cross the Border into the Irish Republic' was issued in July. They were to:

Contact its headquarters by radio.

Ensure that the people with whom they were dealing are Irish Security Forces and say they have strayed in error. It was not unknown for uniformed Provisionals to mount military-style patrols and road blocks.

Give the Irish number, rank and name and unit telephone number and ask that the RUC be advised.

If the patrol is to be taken to a Gardai police station, then cooperate and ask to contact the British Embassy in Dublin. A telephone number was supplied.

Patrols were permitted to open fire either if they came under attack or there was no other alternative.

After a day in custody, the eight were charged with possession of firearms, bailed on £40,000 and returned to Northern Ireland where they took considerable teasing from the rest of the Army. In March 1977 in Dublin, each was fined £100 on the lesser charge of possession of unlicensed weapons.

Two months after Lance Corporal David Hinds, of 1 Royal Highland Fusiliers, was killed in an ambush near Crossmaglen on 2 January, a car suspected of being used in the attack crossed the border into Ireland. Two weeks after the capture of McKenna and soon after Operation Vengeful had reported that the car had returned north, a SAS patrol ambushed a column of armed men, during which Seamus Harvey, a well known member from Crossmaglen, was shot dead, probably by his colleagues. The rest of the column escaped. A fortnight after three 1 Royal Scots had been killed by a landmine on 15 April, the scrap dealer and IRA treasurer Staff Officer Peter Cleary was seized from his fiancée's house near Forkhill. However, after the patrol commander had shot him when he resisted as the helicopter landed to take him away, the Provisionals promised revenge. In June, the British Ambassador in Dublin, Christopher Ewart-Biggs, was assassinated. Provisional Quartermaster Patrick Duffy died in a hail of bullets as he checked an arms cache while his daughter and granddaughter were waiting in his car nearby.

With their operational security in tatters, Nationalist estates patrolled by the RUC and Army, Ireland no longer a sanctuary and improved detection seeing more convictions, the Provisionals had fewer safe havens and their survival was at risk. Most of their casualties had been sustained in gun battles with the Army and in the vicious sectarian war with Loyalists, although sixty-one bombers had scored 'own goals' by 1973. The silenced Officials had been replaced by other radical Republican groups, such as the Irish National Liberation Army (INLA), which preached armed removal of the British from Northern Ireland and the united Ireland withdrawing from Europe to practise Marxist-Leninist socialism, in much the same way as Pol Pot was doing in Cambodia. In Compound 11, with little to do but plot and scheme, Adams and several dissidents, including Brendan Hughes, Ivor Bell and Danny Morrison, drafted plans and tested opinions to reinvigorate their drive for a thirty-two-county Irish socialist republic governed by a revolutionary council. By mid-1976, draft proposals were circulating among the Provisional Army Council. The 1977 edition of the Green Book describes the strategy:

> Attrition against the British Army by causing as many deaths as possible and induce the British public to demand their withdrawal.

> A bombing campaign aimed at making the enemy's financial interests in Ireland unprofitable while at the same time curbing long term investment.

> To make Ulster ungovernable except by military rule.

> To sustain the war and gain support for its ends by national and international propaganda and publicity campaigns.

In many respects, the dissidents acknowledged that their campaign of insurgency had been defeated and the next evolution was terrorism. In converting, the Provisionals lost the protection available to resistance groups under the Protocols of the Fourth (Protection of Civilians) Geneva Convention that four principles must be followed. First, the Provisional IRA had a commander accountable for its activities. Secondly, the IRA had an identifiable insignia – a lily. Thirdly, arms were generally carried openly during engagements, although crowds were sometimes used as shields before and after opening fire. It was this belief that led to Bloody Sunday. Fourthly, paramilitaries must conduct operations in accordance with customs, traditions and laws of armed conflict that had evolved over the centuries.

Petty Officer Fred MacLaughlin, a 45 Commando medic, was severely wounded in the face while treating another medic, who had just been shot while treating a civilian. Their marked Saracen ambulance then came under fire.

The adage that one man's terrorist is another man's freedom fighter is insufficient. An international definition of terrorism had not been agreed by 1977 and where a nation had developed legislation, common themes in definitions were 'political', 'violence' and reflections of that nation's experiences. The Israeli definition was 'the deliberate and systematic murder, maiming and menacing of the innocent to inspire fear for political ends' while the British Prevention of Terrorism Act was typical – 'the use of violence for political ends ... the use of violence for the purpose of putting the public of any section in fear'. To the average citizen, terrorism is an act by those who fail to get their way by lawful means reverting to violence, no matter how long it takes – the Long War.

In 1976, the Revolutionary Council confirmed the establishment of Northern and Southern Commands to coordinate operations, share technology and resources and centralize training. The dominant Northern Command consisted of the six counties of Ulster and the three border counties but did not include the Belfast Brigade, which was still commanded by the popular Billy McKee. The decimated brigades and battalions were replaced by the communist model of small independent cells of four or five ideologically sound activists grouped into ASUs with commissions to carry out attacks supported by local companies who gathered intelligence, provided logistics, managed weapon caches, stole vehicles and raised funds through sales, donations, robbery and extortion. Communication was through a single point of contact, thereby reducing the operational insecurity impact if an ASU was compromised.

Although the Gardai found a draft of the proposals in December 1976 when Seamus Twomey was arrested in Dublin, after his release from Long Kesh in February 1977, Adams, now appointed Chief of Staff, set about reinvigorating the Provisional campaign. In November, the changes in styles of attacks to bombings indicated that the Provisionals had reorganized and were the beginning of The Long War. However, his tenure was cut short when he was swept up in arrests after the brutal bombing of the Le Mon Hotel in February 1978 when twelve people, seven of them women, attending the annual Irish Collie Club dinner-dance were burned to death when an incendiary bomb suspended in front of a window exploded. The casualty list was one more than killed on Bloody Sunday, about which the Republican movement stills crows. Public outrage added to a string of public relation disasters. Martin McGuiness took over as Chief of Staff and the replacement of McKee by Ivor Bell and the rejection of David O'Connell and Rory O'Brady on the Army Council cemented the takeover by the Compound 11 dissidents for Northern Command to dictate strategy. When Adams proposed permanent commanders replicating the Army Council at all levels, this led to suggestions that not only were they accessories to breaking the law, it also broke with the tradition of IRA leaders fighting alongside the Volunteers. It also illustrated his relative aloofness from the rank and file. Strategically, the command structure of the Provisionals had not changed markedly.

Appointed by the Executive to the IRA General Army Convention, the Provisional Army Council appointed a Chief of Staff to command General Headquarters. The female Cumann Na mBan, which was not represented on the Council until the 1990s, provided intelligence collectors, couriers, arms and explosives smugglers and temptresses encouraging soldiers into situations which resulted in the execution of several. The youth Fianna Na hEireann provided lookouts and instigators of riots.

The Director of Operations was responsible for planning. Recces had to avoid attracting the attention of Army patrols and OPs searching for suspicious activity. Routes to and from operational areas needed to be cleared, warnings of Security Forces activity arranged and covering forces briefed to divert or hinder patrols, particularly when weapons needed to be dismantled and cached quickly. Forensic evidence, such as clothes, needed to be removed

132

and credible cover stories developed. Rehearsals always risked operational security pressure because of the number of people involved.

The Quartermaster General organized the supply of arms, ammunition, explosives and war stores. Since caches ran the risk of discovery, relatively small stocks were held in Northern Ireland with permanent caches in the southern border counties under the control of Northern Command. Southern Command controlled the delivery of war stores from rear area dumps in Ireland where the chance of discovery was less likely and dispersal easier. Technical ground and airborne surveillance led to the concealment of caches in concrete bunkers inside farm buildings and under silage pits. Most bomb factories found by the Gardai were concentrated in the border counties and Dublin suburbs. Initially, the Officials controlled weapons stockpiled from previous campaigns, such as the .303 Lee Enfield and .30 M1 Garand rifles, Thompson sub-machine guns, Webley revolvers and a few Bren light machine guns. One intelligence report suggested that in 1970, the Provisionals had about thirty weapons and £100. Quartermasters General also developed their sources. In the US, the IRA veteran George Harrison used NORAID funds to buy over 2,500 weapons, including Colt Armalites, which became a Nationalist symbol, 9mm Browning pistols, M-60 general purpose machine guns and C4 plastic explosive, some smuggled to Southampton on board the *Queen Elizabeth II* and taken to Belfast. Libya was also a prime source. On 28 November 1972, the Provisionals fired a RPG-7 at RUC Belleek. The RPG-7 was a Soviet light anti-tank weapon derived from the shoulder-fired Second World War German *Panzerfaust*. It was not unknown for IRA rocketeers to forget that the RPG had a 25-metre back blast. When a 1 RTR Troop deployed to a RUC station came under RPG-7 and small arms fire from two positions two years later, Trooper Graham Wooley drove his Ferret Scout car and used its .30-inch Browning to suppress the insurgency position on the ridge 300 yards to the south-west that other defenders were having difficulty engaging. For this act of gallantry, Wooley was awarded the British Empire Medal.

While insurgents and terrorists regularly employ methods that are criminal and offend the rights of the individual, Security Forces are expected to keep with the governance of common law using minimum force and are held to be accountable. A major success of the Provisional Directors of Publicity, in particular Danny Morrison in the 1980s, was their ability to keep the Republican pot boiling.

This was achieved through Provisional Sinn Fein highlighting real and imagined 'unacceptable' Security Forces' behaviour by crying moral indignation and exploiting the European Court of Human Rights. This led to successive British governments meekly drawing standards expected of the Armed Forces well above the Common Law threshold. Morrison was helped by the inability of government information officers to mount an effective counter campaign. The Secret Intelligence Service's Information Research Department had played a vital role in undermining and discrediting the opposition of Great Britain from its colonies, however MI5 had very little experience in black propaganda to expose the fact, for instance, that Irish Republicans were responsible for about 70 per cent of the violence was hardly exploited and that its interrogation methods regularly used torture and brutality. Only one military prisoner survived – because he was in the Territorial Army. The Republican newspaper, *An Phoblacht*, was rarely challenged. Morrison remained largely unchallenged even when he suggested, at the 1982 Sinn Fein annual conference, that the Provisional political strategy was the 'ballot paper in this hand and an Armalite in the other'. Irish nationalism has a long association with Europe and the determination displayed by the Provisionals led to loose alliances with continental and international radicals and terrorists, including the Palestine Liberation Organization, the Sandinistas in Nicaragua and Basque separatists in Spain.

In 2001 three IRA, allegedly training guerrillas, were captured by the Columbian Army. In Ireland, sympathy for the IRA lapsed when several bombings and incidents were perceived to be atrocities. The BBC came in for considerable official and unofficial criticism. After several embarrassing moments during the early 1970s when soldiers were confronted by cameras and microphones in the middle of a gun battle, many soldiers attended short courses learning how to cope with the media.

Promoting the philosophy, politics, culture and history of the IRA was the responsibility of the Director of Political Education. The objectives for the 'liberation of Ireland from foreign occupiers' was set out in the Green Book, an instruction document distributed to Volunteers as a secret document not to be discussed with non-IRA. The first edition published before the 1956 Border War was influenced by the developments of insurgency and counterinsurgency by Lawrence of Arabia, Mao Tse Tung in his 1937 *On Guerrilla Warfare,* and the use of the Chindits by General William Slim in

Burma during the Second World War. Interestingly, the second edition in 1977 drew on Brigadier Kitson's 1971 *Low Intensity Operations: Subversion, Insurgency and Peacekeeping*. On leadership, there are interesting differences between the two editions. In the 1956 'Chapter Five – Organization and Arms', the reader is advised:

Leadership will not come so much by appointment as by the trust the guerrillas place in their commander. He must be worthy of that trust if he is to succeed. Instead of discipline of the regular army type there will be a more stern battle discipline: agreement on the job to be done, and the need to do it, and obedience to the guerrilla code, these take the place of the unthinking army type discipline. Breaches of the guerrilla code – desertion, betrayal, breach of confidence in any way – must be severely dealt with on the spot.

In 1977:

The Army as an organisation claims and expects your total allegiance without reservation. It enters into every aspect of your life. It invades the privacy of your home life, it fragments your family and friends, in other words claims your total allegiance. All potential volunteers must realise that the threat of capture and of long jail sentences are a very real danger and a shadow which hangs over every volunteer ... Another important aspect all potential volunteers should think about is their ability to obey orders from a superior officer. All volunteers must obey orders issued to them by a superior officer regardless of whether they like the particular officer or not.

The Director of Intelligence, as the name suggests, was responsible for the collection of information on the Security Forces and opposing factions.

The Director of Security protected the organization. This became increasingly difficult when it was infiltrated by Security Forces intelligence operations. The Internal Security Department investigated breaches of security, trained Volunteers in resistance to interrogation, into saying and signing nothing, and distributed punishments for collaboration. The fact that the Green Book devoted a considerable chunk to inquiries and courts martial reflects the success of penetration by the Security Forces. Although the rules of discipline advocated by Mao were regarded as 'idealistic', the Green Book rec-

135

ognized that the power of the media could undermine the reputation of the Provisionals.

The Director of Finance organized fund raising, including bank robberies and drug dealing. Sufficient funding allowed several smuggling projects in which ships were hired and airport staff bribed. In 1987, the trawler *Eksund* cost about £50,000. A hunting version of the Armalite cost £450.

The Director of Engineering managed research and development by exploiting the skills of sympathetic technicians and engineers. Projects ranged from designing bombs and booby traps using off-the-shelf electronic timers and initiation technology to develop anti-armour weapons, such as the 40mm anti-armour Improvised Projected Grenade and the Projected Recoilless Improvised Grenade (PRIG), and investigated anti-helicopter weapons. The Provisionals developed several mortars but since they lacked fire controllers, accuracy was often crude and overshoots causing collateral damage was not unknown. The mysterious 'Yankee Joe' Conlon, apparently a Vietnam veteran, was said to have been behind the early mortar developments in South Armagh. In the Mark 1, the bomb dropping onto a spike at the bottom of a copper tube was propelled by a .303-inch bullet. The danger of an explosion in the tube was solved by placing a metal plate over the mouth of the tube, which was then tugged with nylon fishing line from a safe distance allowing the bomb to drop down the tube. The Mark 6 with a range of 1,200 metres had a conventional appearance of a tube, tripod and base plate. The bomb was filled with Semtex. In one of several attacks on RUC Crossmaglen, on 23 October 1976, seven short, fat Mark 7 bombs fired from an array of ten gas cylinder tubes, fitted in a van, hit the target.

Nevertheless, the eighty attacks between 1973 and 1985 caused a few minor casualties although some damage was severe. This changed on 28 February 1985 when a bomb from an array of nine pre-loaded, electrically-fired Mark 10s hit the RUC Newry canteen and killed seven male and two female RUC officers. The mortar threat resulted in military and RUC bases being surrounded with large wire cages and walls strengthened to about seven feet thick. The Provisionals responded by developing the lorry-mounted Mark 13 short range spigot mortar that launched a 45-gallon oil drum containing 800lbs of explosive – not dissimilar to a depth charge.

In the early 1990s, the Provisionals combined the flexibility of the

Mark 10 and the power of the Mark 13 to develop the Mark 15 'Barrackbuster' of industrial gas tubes adapted to deliver a one metre long projectile containing 154lbs of explosive a distance of 150 metres. One concealed in a bale of hay in the bucket of a tractor parked outside RUC Crossmaglen hit a Lynx coming in to land.

The Director of Training had the difficult task of discreetly organizing military training in a climate of law and order. Most early training was done in the No Go areas, but when these were dismantled in July 1972, training was transferred to camps south of the border, some below ground in concrete bunkers complete with ranges. While weapon training and tactics were relatively easy to teach, the use of mortars, machine guns and surface-to-air missiles in an environment in which security was always in doubt required a high degree of skill.

Chapter 10

The English Department
1972 to 1984

While the IRA exploited media and civil liberty lobbies to criticize British military operations in Northern Ireland, it escalated its sphere of operations by attacking England, not the Celtic countries of Scotland and Wales, in a projected campaign that lasted until 2001.

The campaign opened on 22 February 1972 when a bomb in a Ford Cortina parked by the Officials outside the HQ 16 Parachute Brigade Officers Mess at Aldershot exploded at lunchtime without warning, very severely damaging the Mess and several buildings and killing an elderly gardener, five cleaning staff leaving the Mess and Captain Gerard Weston, a respected Roman Catholic chaplain, who had just parked behind the Cortina, and wounding nineteen. Most of the officers were at work. The next day, after the Officials admitted the attack to be revenge for Bloody Sunday and that it was the opening phase of a campaign to attack regiments that had served or were serving in Northern Ireland, the faction encountered criticism because casualties were civilians and a Catholic priest. Although the ease of the attack was a shock, barracks had been on high alert since the spring of 1970 and were able to control access at the Guardroom and regularly searched vehicles. Open camps with public access routes, such as Aldershot and Catterick, were far more difficult to protect. Nevertheless, a massive security review led to military establishments' perimeter fences being strengthened with barbed wire and patrolled by armed soldiers, supported by the latest security technology. Orders were issued that military personnel were not to wear uniform off base and thus the familiar sight of a uniformed serviceman hitchhiking disappeared in favour of civilian clothes and a beret carelessly left on a suitcase.

At a Provisional Army Council meeting in June, when Sean MacStiofain, who was born in London and had served in the RAF during the Second World War, proposed bombing England to 'take the heat off Belfast and Derry', there was disagreement because it was a step too far. However, when the ceasefire talks with William Whitelaw failed, he persuaded the Council that the English needed a 'short, sharp shock' to convince the public to press for a military withdrawal from Northern Ireland. The task was given to the 1st (Andersonstown and Falls Road) Battalion, who had assembled an intelligence cell not known to the Security Forces, with instructions that the bombing be confined to London. The cell included the sisters Dolores and Marion Price, both Cumann Na mBan who had met left wing urban guerrilla groups in Italy.

Selecting 8 March for the opening of the second campaign, Dolores planned that as the car bombs exploded, the group would be flying back to Dublin. On the 4th, after a final briefing from MacStiofan, five of the team boarded a ferry in two cars hijacked in Belfast and sailed to Liverpool. The second team in two stolen cars left two days later but briefly attracted the attention of a suspicious Customs and Excise officer because it had no tax disc. Four days later, two observant police officers, checking a suspicious Ford Corsair outside New Scotland Yard, saw a device and raised the alarm. 'Close England' was ordered but not before two bombs had exploded, killing one person and causing 180 casualties.

At Heathrow, Special Branch officers surveying passengers joining the Dublin flight noted that a man was nervous and arrested the entire bombing team except for one. Nevertheless, shortly before 2 p.m., the Provisional public relations machine, unaware of the arrests, claimed responsibility for the bombs and that the teams had returned to Dublin. On the defensive in Northern Ireland, the Provisionals continued with the strategy of attacking England, one unit targeting the Midlands and the North and another London, both returning to Dublin on the completion of operations.

The third campaign began on 29 August 1973 when a bomb exploded in Solihull and in Harrods, London. A nail bomb was thrown into Chelsea Barracks and then, on 23 September, the police bomb disposal officer Ronald Wilkinson was fatally wounded while defusing a bomb in Edgbaston. On 4 February 1974, shortly after midnight, a coach hired in Manchester to take British Army and RAF personnel and their families to Catterick Camp during a railway strike, was on the M62 between Chain Bar, near Bradford, and

Gildersome, near Leeds, when a 25lbs suitcase bomb deposited in a luggage locker reduced the bus to a 'tangle of twisted metal'. Corporal Clifford Haughton, of the 1 RRF, his wife Linda and two sons Lee, aged 5, and Robert, aged 2, were killed as were two Royal Artillery, three Royal Corps of Signals and two more Fusiliers. Over fifty passengers were injured, including a 6 year old boy badly burned. Linda's sister, Anne later commented that:

> We've come to terms with it, but we'll never ever forgive, and never ever forget. It will be with me to the day I die, that morning.

In the entrance hall of the westbound Hartshead Moor Motorway service area, which was used as a first aid station, is a memorial to those killed. Although the Provisionals were suspected, it has never accepted responsibility for the explosion. The reaction in Britain was fury, with calls for immediate action against the IRA. The *Guardian* described the incident as 'the worst IRA outrage on the British mainland' while the *Irish Sunday Business Post* described it as the 'worst' of the 'awful atrocities perpetrated by the IRA'. The investigation focused on Judith Ward, a former member of the WRAC, who had been a riding instructor in Dundalk before enlisting in 1971. Going absent without leave, she briefly returned to Dundalk and then surrendered to the Army in Aldershot several months later claiming that the IRA had attempted to recruit her. Discharged from the Army, she returned to Dundalk for a year, during which she was detained inside Thiepval Barracks, Lisburn and handed to the RUC. Ward moved to London in August 1973, where she worked as a chambermaid, and was briefly arrested after the Euston Station bombing. At the end of the year, she returned to her home town of Stockport and, in early 1974, was arrested while working for Chipperfield's Circus. Under significant pressure for a result, the police charged Ward after she claimed to have been involved in several bombings in Britain in 1973 and 1974, was married and had a baby fathered by an IRA member. Further evidence emerged when Dr Frank Skuse, a forensic scientist working for the North West Forensic Laboratories, exposed her to the Griess test, which indicated traces of nitroglycerine in her caravan, on her hands and in her handbag. These findings, combined with her confessions, led to Ward being sentenced to thirty years at Wakefield Crown Court in November for three bombing offences, even though she retracted the confessions and her testimony was rambling and incoherent. Ward was eventually released in 1992 when the Appeal Court voted that her conviction was 'a grave miscarriage of justice' and had been 'secured by ambush'. The true culprits have never been discovered.

In mid-1974, Brendan Dowd and Joseph O'Connell were selected to lead an ASU assembled in Ireland and sent to England with orders to avoid contact with the mainstream Irish community and carry out one attack a week. They established a base in Waldemar Avenue, Fulham and among their supplies was the odourless, easily moulded and powerful Czech explosive Semtex, purchased from the PLO and Libyans and smuggled through Amsterdam and Brussels. In October, Harry Duggan and Edward Butler arrived in Fulham. Cover stories were organized to explain their absence from Northern Ireland, Duggan's being that he was dead. Another ASU was activated in the Midlands.

The fourth bombing campaign of England began on 5 October with attacks on the Army when the two IRA and two trusted women left a 6lbs gelignite bomb in The Horse and Groom, Guildford, a pub frequented by soldiers. At 8.30 p.m., it exploded without warning, killing a plasterer, four off-duty Scots Guards and WRAC Privates Ann Hamilton and Caroline Slater, aged 19 and 18 respectively. A second device exploded in the town at 9 p.m. in The Seven Stars soon after the landlord had evacuated it. The Guildford bombings suggested that there was a group of dangerous Irish at large. A bomb killed one person and injured forty-one at the Tower of London and three staff were injured by a device at the Brooks Club, London, whose members include retired British military officers. Stricter anti-terrorism legislation gave the police power to detain suspects for up to seven days without charge and to extradite suspects to Northern Ireland to face trial in the Diplock Courts. Meanwhile, four of Prices' bombing team went on hunger strike demanding to be transferred to Northern Ireland, which inevitably led to establishment figures joining those voicing their support; not that the public were.

A month later, on 7 November, another military local, The King's Arms near Woolwich Arsenal, was the scene of carnage when a 6lbs gelignite bomb was thrown into the bar killing Gunner Richard Dunne of the Royal Artillery and Alan Horsley, a sales clerk. On 11 November, the ASU murdered the stockbroker Allan Quartermaine in Chelsea, seemingly in pursuit of the IRA Marxist political philosophy and campaign against capitalism.

On 21 November, the Midlands IRA team exploded two devices in the Mulberry Bush and in the Tavern in the Town in the centre of Birmingham, within two minutes of each other. Since the warnings were inaccurate, twenty-one people were killed and 182 injured. A third device outside a bank failed to detonate. It was the most serious act of terrorism so far. Meanwhile, five Irishmen had left Birmingham by train during the evening in order to attend the funeral of an IRA bomber in Belfast. He had scored 'an own goal' while planting a bomb in Coventry. At Heysham, they drew attention to themselves by failing to admit why they were travelling to Belfast and were being questioned by Special Branch when news arrived of the bombings. The five agreed to be taken to Morecambe Police Station for forensic tests and next morning were transferred to the custody of West Midlands Serious Crime Squad where they were later joined by a sixth man and charged with terrorism offences. When their trial began on 9 June 1975 in Lancaster, statements made by the men in November were deemed admissible, although evidence of their association with the IRA was largely circumstantial. Dr Skuse again concluded that from his findings with the Griess test, two of the men had handled explosives. In August, when the Birmingham Six were sentenced to life, they began a long and highly publicized appeal process, in particular concentrating on the claim that their confessions had been extracted under duress, that they had been assaulted by police and prison officers and the forensic evidence was flawed. The journalist Chris Mullins, later a Labour MP, campaigned on their behalf and even claimed to have met the actual bombers. Three years after their convictions were upheld in January 1988, their third appeal was successful on the basis that the evidence of Dr Skuse and the Griess Test was discredited. This case and other miscarriages led to the establishment of the Criminal Cases Review Commission in 1997. In spite of Mullins's claims, no one else has ever been prosecuted for the atrocity.

After the ASU had left three small bombs in letter boxes in Chelsea and deliberately targeted civilians, four days after the Birmingham bombs, IRA Chief of Staff David O'Connell warned them to desist from targeting civilians, but they ignored it and carried out a string of attacks deliberately setting out to cause civilian casualties and included lobbing a homemade grenade onto the balcony of the first floor flat of Edward Heath.

Ten days after the end of the Christmas ceasefire on 16 January 1975, the London ASU continued their campaign, including detonating seven bombs over a six hour period in London that injured twenty-six people. A teacher in Greenwich was mistaken for a brigadier and wounded. On 10 February, the Provisional Army Council called for a truce in Northern Ireland and England. On the same day, Liam Quinn, a middle class Mexican-Irish from San Francisco, a specialist in letter bombs with a romantic view of the IRA, joined the ASU. Brendan Dowd, the leader, returned to Dublin. When three detectives looking out for burglars in Fairholme Road on 26 February intercepted Quinn leaving a basement flat, he panicked and was pursued by the police officers. They were joined by the off-duty PC Stephen Tibble on his motorbike. When Tibble cornered the man in Baron's Court, Quinn shot him three times with a Colt revolver. Tibble, aged 22, who had been in the Metropolitan Police six months and was recently married, was posthumously awarded the Queen's Police Medal for Gallantry and a memorial was erected to him on Charleville Road. The search of the flat revealed the first IRA bomb factory to be found in London and forensic clues about the bombers. With the Anti-Terrorist Squad closing in, the ASU went underground in their flats at Crouch End and Milton. Quinn fled to Dublin where he was arrested after assaulting a Gardai. Although identified by one of the British police officers as the man he had intercepted in Fairholme Road, Dublin refused to extradite him. Quinn fled to San Francisco where he successfully fought extradition in US Courts sympathetic to the political nature of the Republican cause until, in 1988, he was flown to England and was jailed for life for the murder of Tibble. He was released under the Good Friday Agreement.

In June, Dowd returned to England to establish a cell in Manchester but was compromised by inexperienced supporters and was arrested. He was wearing the watch that he stole from PC Michael Lloyd in October 1974 when Lloyd disturbed him and O'Connell looking for a car to steal. When the Provisional Army Council abandoned their truce on 27 August, the London ASU left a device underneath a bench in The Caterham Arms in Caterham, Surrey, a pub frequented by the 1 Welsh Guards, that same night. The Battalion had returned from Northern Ireland on 8 March after their third tour since March 1971. No warning was given and one civilian lost a leg while a soldier lost both legs and an arm. Two days later, Captain Roger Goad, a police bomb disposal officer, was killed while defusing an IED device fitted with an anti-tamper device in the K Shoe Shop in Kensington and was posthumously awarded the George Cross. A week later, while his funeral was taking place, a bomb exploded in the London Hilton foyer, killing two and injuring sixty-three. The warning received by the *Daily Mail* was too late for a complete evacuation; indeed it was the last to be given by the group and marked a change in targets to those politically resented by the terrorists. Ten days later, among several letter bombs postmarked 'Dublin', one received by Lady Pamela Onslow in Notting Hill exploded. She was probably targeted because she had introduced Keith Littlejohn to MI6.

On 8 October, O'Connell was in the Green Park public toilets priming a device for use against the Ritz Hotel when a man in the next cubicle peered over to see what he was doing. O'Connell panicked and threw the device at a bus stop where it exploded, killing a man and injuring twenty. Four days later, a 27lbs gelignite bomb planted in Lockett's Restaurant, Marsham Street, Westminster, a popular haunt of Tory MPs, was defused with minutes to spare and gave the Bomb Squad important forensic evidence. On the 22nd, three men and a woman were sentenced to fifteen years for the Guildford bombings. On the same day, a bomb targeting Hugh Fraser MP was disturbed by the renowned cancer specialist Professor Gordon Hamilton-Fairley, as he was walking his dog, and he was killed in the explosion. The convictions for the Guildford bombings were overturned several years later when it was proved their confessions had been obtained under duress and evidence clearing them was not reported by the police. Although the Provisionals have admitted responsibility for the bombing, the killers have never been identified. An improvised grenade, thrown into Scott's Oyster Restaurant in Mayfair on 13 November, killed a customer and injured fifteen and was followed ten days later by Doherty and Duggan assassinating Ross McWhirter outside his home in Enfield in front of his wife. With his twin brother Norris, McWhirter was editor of the *Guinness Book of Records* and an active Conservative. On 4 November, he had advocated that Irish living in Britain register with the police and hand in signed photographs of themselves at hotels and hostels and when renting flats. He also offered a £50,000 reward for information leading to the conviction of the bombers. When it was suggested to McWhirter that he might be an IRA target, he replied, 'When you feel as strongly as I do about the need for the murderous and senseless bombings to cease, then that is not something you can worry about.' Duggan later said, 'The man thought he was living in Texas. He placed a bounty on our heads.'

By December, the London ASU had become over confident and, ignoring operational instructions to operate in pairs, the four set out to attack Scott's Restaurant because they were annoyed that the proprietor had the audacity to re-open his premises. During the evening of 6 December, the West End was being patrolled by over 400 police officers watching out for the terrorist activity. PC John Cook was near Scott's when he reported seeing a man lean out of a Cortina and fire at the restaurant with a M1 Carbine. Detective Inspector John Purnell and Sergeant Philip McVeigh, from the Special Patrol Group, then commandeered a taxi and pursued the car to Park Road in Marylebone where there was a short gun battle. As the police converged on the area, in a state of near panic, at about 9.45 p.m., the four IRA burst into Flat 22b, Balcombe Street and took its two residents, John and Sheila Matthews, hostage. Over the next six days in the glare of television cameras, they failed to negotiate with Detective Chief Superintendent Jim Nevill, then deputy head of the Bomb Squad, for £20,000 and a plane to fly them and their hostages to Dublin. The police, under pressure from MI5 and the Army to storm the flat, were determined to take the terrorists alive. Duggan and O'Connell were convinced the SAS would storm the flat and six days later, the four surrendered. After a lengthy investigation and thorough examination of their flats, they were sentenced to twelve life terms for seven murders, conspiracy to cause explosions and falsely imprisoning the Matthews. A photograph shows the gang were armed with a Sten gun, a M1 Carbine, a 9mm Browning and four .38-inch revolvers. During their trial, the four claimed responsibility for the Guildford and Woolwich bombings, however, in a decision that would result in an embarrassing miscarriage of justice, their claims were not investigated by the police. After serving twenty-three years in British jails, the four were transferred to Portlaoise Prison and, after being released as part of the Good Friday Agreement, were presented by Gerry Adams to a Sinn Fein meeting as 'our Nelson Mandelas'. The arrests effectively ended the fourth bombing of England.

The neutralization of the group was not a major setback for the Provisionals. By 1978, with Northern Command now in full control of operations, the English Department set about recruiting and training ASUs and smuggled explosive and weapons to caches, in particularly in the Midlands. Lock ups in London were too vulnerable in a country where the public and police were vigilant. The Internal Security Department vetted the ASUs for evidence of penetration. Several women were selected to provide communication with the ASUs. Among the recruits was Gerard Tuite and Patrick Magee, who was known to the Dutch police as suspect IRA. Patrick Magee was born in Ballymurphy in 1948 and had grown up in England. He had served time in Long Kesh and been involved in the M-60 incident in which the SAS Captain Westmacott had been killed.

The fifth campaign opened on 9 May 1981 when a bomb planted by a northern ASU was found in the Shetlands during the visit by the Queen to an oil refinery. In October, a blast at Chelsea Barracks killed two, including a bomb disposal officer, and injured thirty-nine and the following month, the house of Attorney-General Michael Havers was damaged by a bomb. At 10.35 a.m. on 20 July 1982, sixteen cavalrymen of the Mounted Squadron, The Blues and Royals providing, the Queen's Life Guard for the day, passed under the arched gate of Knightsbridge Barracks and walked along South Carriageway escorted by two police mounted officers front and back. The sun shone on the column as it headed towards Horse Guards to take over from The Life Guards. The Troop was commanded by Lieutenant Anthony Daly on his debut as Captain of the Guard after he had taken the place of a captain, who was taking part in a military showjumping competition. His mother was waiting at Whitehall to witness the ceremony. The Blues and Royals had lost seven men in Northern Ireland, including Sergeant Barry Cox, who was then attached to the Army Air Corps, at the Knock Na Moe Castle Hotel bombing. Two troops had just returned from the Falklands War. After about five minutes, as the column passed a file of parked cars opposite the Hyde Park Hotel, watching IRA detonated a remotely controlled 25lb gelignite bomb in a Morris Marina parked behind a camper-wagon that hurled 30lbs of 6-inch and 4-inch nails at the Troop. As the smoke cleared, an eyewitness described 'terrible silence' and watched as troopers led their surviving, shocked horses from the carnage on the road and were met by men running from the barracks. Lieutenant Colonel Andrew Parker-Bowles, the Commanding Officer, met the barely conscious Trooper Pedersen leading his horse Sefton, which had blood pouring from his jugular vein and nails lodged in his side. Corporal of Horse O'Flaherty, of The Life Guards, punched a shirt into the wound and the animal was led to a horse box, which took him to Knightsbridge where Veterinary-Major Carding was already working on the casualties. He gave Sefton a fifty-fifty chance of survival. A farrier

147

borrowed the pistol of the armed police officer posted outside the French Embassy and shot seven severely injured horses. Lieutenant Daly and Trooper Simon Tipper, both of whom had been married less than a month, and Trooper Jeffrey Young, who left two young children were killed and Squadron Quartermaster Corporal Roy Bright was very seriously wounded.

At about midday, thirty 1 RGJ bandsmen were assembled on the Regents Park bandstand playing excerpts from the musical *Oliver* to about 150 people relaxing in chairs and on the grass, some reading headlines expressing concern about the security situation, particularly as Michael Fagan had just managed to break into Buckingham Palace. The Battalion had returned from Bessbrook, having completed, on 27 July 1981, its seventh tour since 20 August 1969 in the Province, six of them in the hardest areas of Belfast. It had lost twelve soldiers, including four killed in a single incident at Camlough on 19 May 1981 when a Saracen ran over a mine. The same man who had organized the Warrenpoint bombing laid the mine. At 12.55 p.m., the centre of the bandstand erupted in a loud explosion, hurling the bandsmen, their instruments and chairs into the air, killing seven, including Bandmaster Graham Barker. One body was pinned to a fence thirty yards away. An hour later, a telex from the IRA arrived at several Northern Ireland newspapers claiming responsibility for the attacks and insisting that the Irish people had a sovereign and national right which no occupation force could put aside. It made no mention of the wishes of the Protestant majority.

A day later, in open defiance of the IRA, The Blues and Royals flying their tattered Squadron Standard, which had been carried by Squadron Quartermaster Corporal Bright, now lying horribly wounded in hospital, mounted The Queen's Guard. Bright died on 23 July. Within a week, nine of the RGJ Band were playing in public. Sefton became a symbolic celebrity of defiance, particularly as he had originated from Waterford in Ireland. Terence Cuneo painted him and he appeared on the BBC's *Blue Peter* and at fundraising events and during the finale of the 1982 Horse of the Year Show was led into the arena by Trooper Pedersen to a tremendous reception. In August 1986, Gilbert 'Danny' McNamee, an electronics engineer, was arrested in Crossmaglen accused of conspiracy to cause explosions on the strength that his fingerprints were found on electronic circuits in a cache linking him to the attack on the Queen's Life Guard. Claiming that he may well have handled them while working for a previous employer and denying that he was IRA, he was found guilty on all counts and sentenced to twenty-five years.

Harrods was attacked on 17 December resulting in six people, including three police officers, killed and ninety wounded. Although a warning had been received, the Chairman Alec Craddock decided not to evacuate the building and undoubtedly saved the lives of thousands of Christmas shoppers. On 12 October 1984, in an attempt to decimate the Cabinet, a sophisticated IED left by Magee in the Grand Hotel, Brighton six weeks before the Conservative Party annual conference, exploded with devastating effect and collapsed the centre of the building. Prime Minister Thatcher and her Cabinet survived, but five people were killed and several others were injured, including Margaret Tebbit, wife of Norman Tebbit, left permanently disabled. The Provisionals had previously planned to kill Thatcher at Blackpool in 1983. Far from intimidating her, the attack steeled her to defeat the Provisionals and the SAS were ordered to escalate their operations.

Chapter 11

Phase Five: Containment – Insurgency to Terrorism

Since terrorism was tackled by legislation and membership of the IRA was illegal in the UK and the Republic, from henceforth the Provisional IRA was a criminal organization.

In Northern Ireland, the Find, Fix and Strike strategy began to destabilize the Republican groups as, by 1978, the SAS was rotating its A, B, D and G Squadrons on six month tours. The SAS had full control of surveillance and the Special Reconnaissance Unit had been renamed 14 Intelligence Company. Their HQ was in Thiepval Barracks, Lisburn while East Det was at Palace Barracks, North Det at Ballykelly and West Det at St Angelo. J Troop supported South Det at Castledillon. The nomenclature was unhelpful to the Intelligence Corps because it had a total of twelve Security, Intelligence and Intelligence and Security companies throughout the world, including 12 Intelligence Company in Northern Ireland. Colonel Brian Parritt, the senior Intelligence officer in Northern Ireland, refused the new company to be entitled 13 Intelligence Company fin case it brought back luck. There was also some concern that the Corps would find itself in the limelight when it needed to be discreet. In the late 1970s, Ulster Squadron and 14 Intelligence Company were formed into Intelligence and Security Group (Northern Ireland). Once again the nomenclature was unhelpful to the Intelligence Corps, which had Intelligence and Security Groups in West Germany and the United Kingdom. The SAS rather compromised the cover by rejecting the suggestion from Lieutenant Colonel Small that he, as an Intelligence Corps lieutenant colonel with surveillance experience, should command the Group. The SAS developed a specific selection course to turn out surveillance operators. Strangely enough, about half of the non-commissioned ranks in the Intelligence Corps were known as Operators Intelligence and Security. The existence of 14 Intelligence Company was not well known until several books by former operators emerged, more than happy to broadcast their association with the SAS, leading to the usual media and political frenzy that it operated outside accepted conventions. In at least one Parliamentary debate, it was referred to as 14 Intelligence Regiment, which allowed ministers to deny its existence. A specialist flight of Gazelle helicopters with sophisticated surveillance devices, including cameras connected to the wire-guided missile sights, supported the Company.

On 18 April 1977, when three men in a car were directed to stop by a RUC patrol car near Moneymore, the driver lost control of a U-turn and the car careered into a ditch. As the men abandoned it and crossed a field, they opened fire killing two RUC officers and wounding a third and then opened fire on a second police car attempting to intercept them. Francis Hughes, from a well known hardline Republican family in Bellaghy, Co. Londonderry, and on the most wanted list, was identified as being involved. The other two, Ian Milne and Dominic McGlinchey, were arrested later in the year in Lurgan and Ireland respectively. In February 1978, a SAS ambush killed a terrorist accessing a weapons cache on a Co. Tyrone farm and then, on 20 June, a joint SAS/RUC patrol killed three bombers on their way to firebomb the Ballysillan Road Post Office depot in Belfast. Of two Protestants caught in the crossfire, one was killed. Three weeks later, the teenager John Boyle was searching for family headstones in the derelict cemetery in Dunloy Co. Antrim, near his father's farm, when he stumbled across a fertilizer sack containing uniforms and some weapons. Mr Boyle reported his son's find to the RUC who, in turn, reported it to the Army. When the SAS were tasked with establishing an OP in the cemetery, the police warned the Boyles not to return to it. During the night, two SAS moved into a barn overlooking two colleagues in a hide close to the cache. At about 10 a.m. next day, when the two in the hide saw a youth approach the cache and take an Armalite from the sack, they opened fire. It turned out to be John Boyle. In a controversial trial, although SAS claimed that John had pointed the rifle at them, the evidence suggested otherwise. The rifle was also not loaded. Although both soldiers were acquitted, the judge was highly critical of the operation and assessed their evidence as unreliable. On 12 December, Colin McNutt, of INLA, was shot in Londonderry allegedly by the SAS.

To a great extent, the Army operations had levelled into one of containment, nevertheless the Provisional change in strategy did not mean that they were less dangerous. In 1977, there were 1,803 shootings and 535 bombs. Fifteen soldiers were killed compared with fourteen in 1975, 1976 and 1978.

On 22 June, 45 Commando began their sixth tour in the Monagh district in Turf Lodge. Shortly after midday on 12 August, a shot fired at a mobile patrol cracked the Land Rover windscreen, wounded a lance corporal in the head, fortunately causing no lasting damage, and hit the windscreen of the following Land Rover. About eighty minutes later, during the follow up, after Marine Neil Bewley, aged 19 years, was shot while his troop was establishing a cordon and died in Musgrave Park Hospital, a 'hot pursuit' to the firing position recovered two Webley revolvers, ammunition and two radios. Shortly before 2 p.m., a homemade grenade thrown at a RMP patrol in Norglen Parade seriously wounded two lance corporals in the legs. At 3.15 p.m., a high velocity bullet punctured a window near some crouching Royal Marines and then, fifteen minutes later, a crowd tried to prevent a RMP team accessing the place from where the grenade had been thrown by placing a car across the road. At 3.45 p.m., another shot was fired at the cordon and, when military police were sent to collect a Webley 12-bore shotgun and imitation Thompson found in the follow up, the sergeant in command fired two shots with his Browning to disperse the mob stoning them. A sharpened stake had embedded in the Macrolon armour of their Land Rover. A few minutes after another shot was fired at the Royal Marines at about 5 p.m., two men were arrested at a VCP on suspicion of being the gunmen. Forty minutes later, six shots were fired at the cordon. 45 Commando had been under fire for over six hours, during which time two soldiers had been killed. A RCT Saracen driver was wounded. Sixty-two baton rounds had been fired at unruly mobs. One hundred and five houses had been searched, some sufficiently robustly to upset their occupants but balanced against this was the fact that somewhere in the Turf Lodge were gunmen determined to kill soldiers.

When, on 10 August, a patrol of Recce Platoon, 1 King's Own Border Regiment came under Armalite fire in Rosareen Avenue, Andersonstown, the two gunmen escaping in a Cortina almost collided with an Army Land Rover patrol. Soldiers fired four shots and then pursued the car into Finaghy Road where it ploughed into the Maguire family, killing three children walking with their mother,

Anne. The wounded passenger was captured and the driver was found to have been hit. The Provisionals were blamed, the deaths of the children condemned and several big rallies were organized by their aunt, Mairead Corrigan who, with Betty Williams and Ciaran McKeown, developed the Women's Peace Movement. It was then renamed the Peace Movement and became a focal point for Protestants and Catholics protesting at the violence, in spite of the Provisional media machine and intimidation attempting to undermine them. In October 1977, Corrigan and Williams were awarded the Nobel Peace Prize but within the year both had stood down as leaders of the organizations. Anne Maguire later took her own life.

In November, Brigadier James Glover, Director, Defence Intelligence Staff, analysed the intelligence aspects of Operation Banner in a document entitled 'Northern Ireland: Future Terrorist Trends'. He recognized that the Provisionals had dedication and an ability to escalate and de-escalate violence and that their political and social powerbase remained as a working class organization in the poorer areas of city enclaves – that is Catholic. Assessing that the composition of the emerging ASUs was not hooligans drawn from the unemployed and unemployable but consisted of experienced, well-trained extremists, many with ten years of operational experience, Glover suggested that if the word 'terrorist' was substituted by 'soldier', then his report on the Provisionals would equate to a positive analysis of an allied army. He predicted that while politicians dithered about 'overcoming terrorism', terrorism would continue as long as the Army remained in Northern Ireland and that for the next five years, there was no prospect of existing political changes removing the reason for the existence of the Provisionals. Although the report received some publicity in Irish Republican circles, it was largely ignored by British editors until it was leaked in a major breach of security a year later. When Major General Glover was promoted and appointed Commander, Land Forces, the Ministry of Defence signalled its support of his views. Those who were serving or had served in Northern Ireland also recognized that terrorism had to be contained until political success.

In March 1978, when intelligence was received that a farm west of Maghera was being used by INLA as a safe house, an SAS ambush was taken over by 3 Para, which was then deployed in the Monagh district of Belfast on their roulement fifth tour. Two paras in an OP in a lane covered two others in a hide near the house. During the night of the 16th, the paras in the hide heard movement in the field behind them and, believing that two uniformed figures seen in their night sights to be a UDR patrol, when Lance Corporal David Jones stood up to identify himself, he was cut down by a hail of fire and his colleague was seriously wounded. When patrols and dogs searched the area for another terrorist known to be armed, Francis Hughes, hiding in gorse and nursing a severe leg wound, was unearthed by SAS soldiers thirteen hours later. Sentenced to eighty-three years and commemorated in Boston, USA when a street near the British Consulate was named after him, he was the second to die in the 1981 Hunger Strike.

In the spring of 1979, Captain Nairac returned as the SAS liaison officer at Castledillon and again infringed SAS guidelines. However J Troop had become progressively full of men on their first tours who did not know Nairac or his methods and asked the question 'Who is this guy?' On 14 May, Nairac visited the infamous Three Steps pub in Drumintree and aroused suspicions by claiming to be an Official from the Ardoyne which, if correct, was rather unwise in a Provisional stronghold. He also asked a girl about the best way to cross the border without being detected and attracted attention by singing with the band. But the locals were suspicious and as he left at about 11.45 p.m., he was seized by seven men in the car park and hustled across the border to a field near Ravensdale where he was subjected to a typically brutal Provisional interrogation. In spite of making several attempts to escape, he was overpowered each time. One kidnapper posed as a priest to obtain information through a confession but all that Nairac said was 'Bless me Father, for I have sinned'. Liam Townson, a Provisional living in nearby Meigh, later confessed to executing Nairac and admitted to Gardai officers in November that, 'He never told us anything. He was a great soldier.' Within the year, two men were convicted of his murder, another for manslaughter, another for kidnapping and another for withholding information. On 13 February 1979, Nairac was posthumously awarded the George Cross for 'exceptional courage and acts of the greatest heroism in circumstances of extreme peril [and] showed devotion to duty and personal courage second to none'.

Controversy pursued Nairac even after death. One of several IRA victims whose graves remain undeclared, rumours suggested that his body was dismembered in a meat grinder and that it had been buried in a field and had been re-interred after being dug up by animals. Allegations persisted that he had links with the Mid-Ulster UVF and was the English speaker at the Miami Showband Murders. Ken Livingstone MP used his House of Commons maiden speech to suggest that Nairac had organized the Miami Murders. In 1993, the Yorkshire Television documentary *Hidden Hand*, investigating the Dublin and Monaghan bombings, used evidence from the RUC, the Gardai, the Army and Mid-Ulster paramilitaries to claim that Nairac had supplied the UVF with arms and ammunition and helped plan operations against Republican targets. In May 2000, allegations that he was alive and had fathered a child proved a hoax.

The fourth element of the Find, Fix and Strike was Exploitation. The Armed Forces knew from their experiences since 1945 that 'hearts and minds' operations were critical in keeping indigenous populations on side. But voices from aircraft circling villages reminding the people to remain loyal, leaflet drops, medics handing out aspirins and pulling teeth, and the distribution of footballs and pictures of the Queen, which was still happening in Belize, would have had few tangible results in Northern Ireland. In 1969, the Army had established several Boys' Clubs in Londonderry and soldiers had helped with Meals on Wheels and visited mental health wards. Soldiers of 1 Queen's had donated a day's pay to local charities and one soldier in full uniform had married a girl in Co. Donegal. In Christmas 1971, 1 Queen's Own Highlanders learnt that gas meters in the Ballymacarrett estate had not been emptied since June, because the collectors feared robbery, and had organized discreet military escorts so that the meters could be emptied and families assured of gas for the turkey. The 4/7th Dragoon Guards ran weekend mixed camps for Protestant and Catholic children from an area of East Belfast rife with intimidation. Virtually every unit tried to contribute to the local community by inviting local girls to discos inside bases, including some flown to Bessbrook by helicopter. All were vetted and proved a valuable intelligence resource.

Several weeks after Nairac had disappeared, locals in the Three Steps Inn were stunned into silence when the door opened and two uniformed SAS strode to the bar. When the sullen landlord refused to pull them pints and take their money, the pair helped themselves. After about thirty minutes and concern that they had not received a regular confirmatory signal from their two colleagues inside, the cover party of four charged through the door found their two colleagues propping up the bar. They had forgotten to send a signal that they were unharmed. Before leaving, the patrol helped themselves to a round and placed money on the bar to cover the drinks and the cost of the hinges. While the infantry at Bessbrook Mill could not send the same message, the presence of the SAS was a powerful psychological tool that sent a shudder through the Republican groups. Their anxiety was enhanced by images of black overalled soldiers abseiling down the walls of the Iranian Embassy in London. This secretive Regiment had become the most publicized unit in the Army. With their operational security leaking, the Provisionals knew they were up against a formidable opponent who practised direct, deadly action and their propagandists spent years attempting to undermine its operations.

Shortly before 11.30 a.m. on 27 August, a hot and sunny August Bank Holiday Monday in Great Britain, Lord Louis Mountbatten and a party of five left the turreted Victorian mansion of Classiebawn Castle overlooking the wild coast of Co. Sligo and drove to the tiny harbour of Mullaghmore with a Gardai escort. The party boarded a small green fishing launch, *Shadow V*, and Mountbatten, watched by holidaymakers, locals and two men in a yellow Cortina, steered it between two high Victorian moles and turned south. As the launch came alongside some lobster pots 200 yards offshore, the passenger in the car pressed the button of a transmitter and watched as the launch disintegrated into a hail of timbers, ropes, metal and cushions, in a cloud of smoke, as a 50lbs gelignite RCIED, secreted aboard the previous night, exploded killing Mountbatten and two boys, fatally wounding the 83 year old Dowager Lady Doreen Brabourne, and injuring the remaining two people to a greater or lesser degree. Within minutes, details were flashing around the world. Mountbatten's murder caused international outrage and his televised state funeral damaged IRA credibility. Two men were later sentenced to life for the assassination.

In Northern Ireland, 2 Para (Lieutenant Colonel Colin Morris) had begun its tour on 27 July, the eighth since February 1970, this time as the resident Battalion in Ballykinler. For a couple of days' familiarization in South Armagh, Morris was rotating his companies with 1 Queen's Own Highlanders which had begun a roulement tour on 5 July. A Company was replacing Support Company in Newry. The plan was for the exchange to be by lorry.

Several miles north of the picturesque port of Warrenpoint, below the Mourne Mountains, the River Newry funnels into a tidal stream about 200 yards wide known as Narrow Water. Across the dual carriageway from a small keep on the foreshore was the Gate Lodge at the head of a shallow drive that led to Narrow Water Castle. With woods spilling to the shore on the Irish side, the Army knew the stretch of road alongside Narrow Water to be vulnerable to an attack because ambushers had a clear view of the road and there was nothing to interfere with signals igniting RCIEDS. Convoy routes were therefore randomly selected at short notice but a major problem was that alternative routes connecting Newry and Ballykinler were limited.

At about 3.30 p.m., a Land Rover and two 4-Tonners carrying twenty-six men of A Company left Ballykinler. Several paras had recently completed recruit training. By about 4.30 p.m. the convoy had passed through Warrenpoint and was on the dual carriageway heading north towards Newry and approaching Narrow Water Castle. Across the lough, a South Armagh Brigade ambush in the woods was watching and, as the rear lorry passed a trailer loaded with hay about 100 yards south of the castle, they pressed a remote control device. The trailer erupted as 500lbs of explosive packed into milk churns hidden in the hay exploded, hurling the lorry onto its side, killing six soldiers and very severely injuring three; one would later die. The Land Rover crossed the central reservation and stopped facing north, its occupants running to the lorry to render assistance. The second lorry parked underneath a tree and while the paras sought cover, they believed that they came under fire from across the Irish side of Narrow Water and shot two men seen in the open. However, both were tourists. Michael Hudson, the son of a Queen's coachman, was killed and the other man was seriously wounded. Spotting movement behind a roadside wall, when a para shouted an order to come out with hands up, several shocked children picnicking with their mother appeared. Some witnesses claiming hearing the small arms fire while others alleged that it was exploding ammunition in the burning lorry.

1 Queen Own Highlanders was alerted to the ambush by a Royal Marines' patrol in Warrenpoint reporting an explosion. Major Barry Rogan, who commanded the 2 Para Support Company, assembled a medical team, signallers and drivers, and sent the Assault Engineer Platoon to the scene in two Land Rovers equipped with machine guns. Major Fursman also left Newry with two Land Rovers. As reinforcements arrived and road blocks were set up north and south of the burning lorry, the incident command post was established in the Gate Lodge. The Highlanders Quick Reaction Force in helicop-

ters arrived and covered a Gazelle landing a medical officer and two medics. At about 4.45 p.m., Lieutenant Colonel David Blair, the Queen's Own Highlanders' Commanding Officer and his radio operator, Lance Corporal Victor McLeod, landed from another Gazelle and joined Fursman at the Gate Lodge. The Royal Marines also arrived. At about 5 p.m., a 72 Squadron Wessex was loading several wounded when a 500lbs mine buried in the Lodge exploded, killing ten more paras, including Blair, Fursman and McLeod. Despite being showered with earth, granite and stone, the pilot coaxed the helicopter into the air and reached Bessbrook. Blair, standing on the seat of the explosion, took the full force, the only recognizable item recovered being an epaulette. From years of watching the Army, the South Armagh Provisionals had guessed that the Lodge would be used as the incident command post.

As reports of the ambush arrived at the 2 Para Operations Room at Ballykinler, there was disbelief because the route had been cleared by the Royal Marines several days earlier. As the extent of the casualties became known, a signaller collected rifle butt numbers from the Armoury so that they could be identified over the radio without naming names. Mrs Christine Fursman arrived ready to console the bereaved until a signaller informed the adjutant that her husband had been killed. As reports arrived at HQ 3 Infantry Brigade in Mahon Barracks, Portadown, Brigadier David Thorne flew to Bessbrook and sent Major Mike Jackson and his B Company to secure the scene. Jackson arrived about thirty minutes later and saw two large craters, scorch marks on the road and a horrifying scene of scattered body parts. Shocked by the carnage, his training instincts took over and he took command from Major Rogan, who had been wounded on the forehead by the mine. The final count of sixteen killed was the greatest loss the Parachute Regiment had suffered since Arnhem in 1944. Among them was Corporal Johnny Giles who had been in the Horse and Groom in Guildford when the IRA blew it up. The courage and bravery of wives and parents who lost their husbands and sons was epitomized when Mrs Fursman arrived at the scene escorted by Major Jackson. She was described by a para as, 'A brave lady in her time, like all of the wives of that period.'

Next day, the Provisionals admitted both attacks and the chant 'Thirteen gone but not forgotten; we got eighteen and Mountbatten' was celebrated in Nationalist circles, the thirteen referring to Bloody Sunday. In spite of reservations of how his Battalion might react,

Morris rejected any notion that 2 Para should be replaced. The ambush reinforced the use of helicopters to supply South Armagh bases, a tactic that led to the South Armagh Brigade claiming that they had denied the Army the use of roads in the region. It was nonsense. Soldiers had been driving around South Armagh for years, not always in uniform, and revelling in cocking a snoop at the IRA for having the arrogance to declare this part of Great Britain off limits.

Chapter 12

The Long Decade

The Way Ahead strategy was firmly entrenched and greater cohesion over the border had been developed with Dublin. Intelligence remained the leading operational weapon with technical surveillance running parallel to human intelligence. About one soldier in seven was involved in the intelligence process either as analysts or operators on the ground, or in support.

In 1979, Brian Keenan was arrested when he was noted associating with Martin McGuiness during Operation Hawk, a technical surveillance operation targeting senior Provisionals. Previously convicted in England after his fingerprint was found on parts of a device in the Crouch End flat, he was sentenced to eighteen years. By 1980, troop levels had been reduced to six resident and three Roulement Battalions. In June 1981, the deployment was:

39 Infantry Brigade

Resident
Holywood
3 RRF on its tenth tour since January 1972.
Aldergrove
1 Scots Guards on its sixth tour since August 1971, which included a week in August during the Royal Visit.

Roulement
Springfield Road, Belfast
1 Royal Welch Fusiliers on its eighth tour since 1972, all roulement. Had lost six killed, including two shot in 1972.

8 Infantry Brigade

Resident

Londonderry
2 Royal Anglians on its sixth tour since October 1970.

Ballykelly
1 Argyll and Sutherland Highlanders on its sixth tour since July 1972. Had lost nine killed, including one lost in the Guildford bombings.

3 Infantry Brigade

Resident

Ballykinler
1 Royal Scots on its seventh tour since March 1970. Had lost four killed in action and one died of a heart attack.

Omagh
Queen's Dragoon Guards on its third tour since April 1974, the previous two roulement tours being in the infantry role.

Roulement

Bessbrook Mill
1 RGJ on its eighth tour since 1972, all roulement, the last three in Bessbrook and the remainder in Belfast.

To meet the lower troop levels, 3 Infantry Brigade was disbanded in September 1981 and its area was taken over by 8 Infantry Brigade. The reduction was fortunate because, in 1982, the Falklands War broke out and two brigades were hurriedly assembled and sent south. Northern Ireland was a major contributor to the military overstretch in West Germany, Belize, Cyprus, Hong Kong and the United Nations.

The combination of the election of Mrs Margaret Thatcher's Conservative Party in May 1979, the murder of Mountbatten and the Warrenpoint ambush saw Lieutenant General Tim Creasey, the GOC, suggesting to Mrs Prime Thatcher when she visited after Warrenpoint that the time was not yet ready for police primacy. She disagreed, nevertheless the decade was one of continued British resilience and limited contact between Thatcher and the Republicans. The Provisionals were quick to test her resolve over the control of their colleagues in prison.

The Northern Ireland Prison Service, reinforced by military Guard Forces and Her Majesty's Prison Service staff from British prisons on two to three month tours, managed the prisons at considerable risk to their personal safety. The British volunteers at Long Kesh were usually flown from Aldergrove by helicopter and remained within the perimeter until flown out at the end of their tour. Since 1971, the Royal Armoured Corps had provided a regiment, the first being 15/19th Hussars from August to December 1971. Tasked to secure the prison perimeters by manning the 'goon' watchtowers, providing foot and mobile patrols, assisting the Governor by providing cordons during searches and collecting intelligence, tours could be tedious, interrupted by periods of activity. Twenty-seven prison officers were murdered by Republican and Loyalist terrorists. Officer Elizabeth Chambers, from HMP Armagh, was killed in October 1982 when her car collided with that of a UDR soldier who had been ambushed in an INLA attack.

By 1974, the prisons had become political hot potatoes, none more so than at Long Kesh where the internees and convicted prisoners were confined to Loyalist and Republican compounds each over-looked by 'goon' watchtowers and consisting of three huts, each accommodating forty men, an ablution hut and a canteen hut sur-rounded by barbed wire. Internees were allowed free association, extra visits, food parcels and could wear their own clothes. Loyalist compounds were noted for their barrack cleanliness and daily parades conducted with military discipline and wooden weapons. Republican compounds were less organized and often had their parades disrupted by Gaelic-speaking Loyalists shouting counter-manding orders. Shops dedicated to the 'prisoners of war' raised funds by selling handkerchiefs decorated with Loyalist or Nationalist logos, leather worked into belts and holsters and meticulous match-stick models of boats and houses. Claiming protection under the Geneva Conventions, the prisoners were visited by the International Committee of the Red Cross. Early morning raids by the Prison Service, Army intelligence and Royal Engineer search teams regularly found escape paraphernalia and, in Republican compounds, documents sent from Moscow relating to bomb making, political ideology and revolutionary warfare.

The Republicans made several spectacular escapes. On 17 November 1971, of the nine 'Crumlin Kangaroos' that scaled Crumlin Road Jail wall using rope ladders, seven reached the sanctuary of Dublin and a press conference. After several more incidents at Crumlin Road, including the discovery of three tunnels in C Wing and several weapons, in mid-January 1972, internees were transferred to HMS *Maidstone*, which was moored alongside a quay near Moscow Camp. When fifty detainees were transferred to the new camp at Magilligan and more were expected to leave, the 'Magnificent Seven' watched tide and currents and after smearing themselves in butter and black shoe polish, they cut through a porthole and clambering down a hawser then swam 400 yards across the icy Belfast Lough but came ashore fifty yards from the rendezvous with men from the Andersonstown IRA battalion. A member of the group who was a former bus driver hijacked a bus at Queen's Road, the escapees piled in and were pursued by a Royal Horse Artillery patrol to the Markets. A week later they also gave a press conference in Dublin. In April, the use of the ship as a prison camp was discontinued and it became spare accommodation for the Army. In mid-February, a breakout of 85 C Wing remand prisoners from Crumlin Road was foiled when soldiers arrived with orders to shoot.

Despite regular air photographic recces by Beaver and helicopter flights over Long Kesh, on 6 November 1973, thirty internees escaped through a tunnel from Compound 5 until Hugh Coney, from Dungannon, was shot by a sentry in a tower as he emerged. Several were quickly recaptured and the remainder within the day. Mid-afternoon on 16 June 1974, after being informed of several contractors working near the sewerage works, a Royal Scots Dragoon Guards trooper in a 'goon' tower saw five para Royal Engineers approaching him on the catwalk between the compounds and the perimeter fence. Suspicious, because he had not been told about them, he instructed them to wait while he contacted the Operations Room. A sergeant and a Troop then arrived and after establishing that the 'Royal Engineers' were actually IRA escapers, he relieved them of three wooden pistols and batons and handed them over to the prison authorities. On 15 October, Republican internees in Long Kesh Compound 2, protesting at poor food, mutinied and attacked four prison officers. When the governor saw that the prisoners were arming themselves with furniture legs, he requested military support. As 350 soldiers arrived to distribute the prisoners to undamaged Republican compounds, reports circulated among the troops that the kennels had been destroyed and the dogs burnt. The disturbance, which lasted several hours, spread. Nevertheless by the following morning, order had been restored but at the cost of injuries to soldiers, prison officers and prisoners, and compounds wrecked. Some soldiers felt that the Republicans had

164

damaged their compounds at an unfortunate time of the year – autumn with the promise of rain, gales, frost and chilly days and nights – and should suffer the consequences, nevertheless HQ 36 Engineer Regiment arrived for seven weeks to help supervise rebuilding the prison. The unrest had spread to Magilligan Prison and to Armagh Women's Prison where the governor and three women prison officers were held captive before mediation by clergymen.

In March 1975, ten IRA escaped from Newry Courthouse while on trial for attempting to escape from Long Kesh and then, on 25 September 1983, in the largest break-out from a British prison, in which two prison officers were shot, thirty-eight prisoners hijacked a meals lorry and smashed their way to freedom. Nineteen were soon recaptured, but the remainder crossed the border. Ireland also had its share of escapes. Nineteen IRA escaped from Portlaoise Jail in Dublin on 18 August 1972 by blowing up the gates with gelignite and a hijacked helicopter was used to free three terrorists from Mountjoy Prison exercise yard in Dublin, including Seamus Twomey, then the IRA Chief of Staff. He was recaptured in December 1977.

The arrival of 6 (Sphinx) Battery at HMP Long Kesh in March 1977 set the routine for Royal Armoured Corps, Royal Engineers and Royals Signals squadrons, Royal Artillery batteries and Royal Pioneer Corps (RPC) companies providing two to four month roulement Prison Guard Forces. From 16 August to 15 December 1977, a Troop of 42 Survey Regiment RE reinforced the existing Guard Force from 518 Company RPC at HMP Magilligan to move UVF prisoners to Long Kesh by helicopters. It brought the total force to four officers and sixty-eight men. The prison then held 260 Special Category and 140 men convicted of other offences.

The Blanket Protest escalated in 1978 when convicted prisoners refused to slop out waste from their cells and then spiralled when the prison authorities ordered 300 protesting prisoners not to use the washrooms and toilets unless they were wearing prison-issued clothing. The IRA prisoners refused to oblige and covered their cell walls with excrement in the 'Dirty Protest'. In October 1980, the Republican leadership demanded the re-instatement of Special Category status and raised the stakes by persuading seven prisoners to go on hunger strike, a traditional IRA tactic. Mrs Thatcher agreed that prisoners could wear civilian clothes provided that prison rules were obeyed, however the leadership refused the offer and the hunger strike dragged on until it ended in mid-December after fifty-three days. The prisoners gained nothing.

In January 1981, the Prison Service tried to resolve the 'Dirty Protest' until, on 1 March, a well organized second hunger strike grew into a political showdown between the Republican leadership and Mrs Thatcher. Even when the election of Bobby Sands to Westminster generated international interest, the stand-off continued. In spite of intense political pressure, Thatcher remained resilient throughout the hunger strike and stated that:

> We are not prepared to consider special category status for certain groups of people serving sentences for crime. Crime is crime is crime, it is not political.

This led to some foresighted Provisionals realizing their aspirations of ejecting the 'occupying' British Army from Ireland was just that – an aspiration. It was only after ten prisoners, including Sands who was the first, had starved to death that the strike ended on 3 October with the government agreeing to five key demands. With an effective Republican publicity machine engineered by Danny Morrison attracting significant international support, the protest had far reaching consequences and led to Provisional Sinn Fein becoming a mainstream political party.

Following his release from Long Kesh after being convicted of firearms offences, the Provisionals Camp Adjutant, Patrick Magee, joined a Belfast ASU led by Anthony Sloan that had access to an M-60 General Purpose Machine Gun. On 9 April 1980, the ASU killed a constable and wounded two others during an ambush on a RUC patrol on Stewartstown Road. When intelligence reports emerged of a weapons cache at 369, Antrim Road, Belfast, the SAS Belfast Troop was briefed to storm the house. While three SAS secured the rear, five arrived at the front in a car. As Captain Herbert Westmacott, the Troop Commander, approached the address, as a white cloth was being waved from the house, a window was smashed in the neighbouring No. 371 and an M-60 gunner opened fire killing him. His four colleagues returned fire and withdrew. At the rear, the SAS captured Magee while he was preparing a Transit van for the escape of the ASU. Army patrols laid siege to the house until a priest mediated the surrender of the ASU. The SAS would later claim that they had been given the wrong address, however it later emerged the Provisionals were waiting to ambush an Army patrol responding to reports of the cache. Two months later, Magee was one of eight IRA who broke out of Crumlin Road Prison by locking up a prison officer in a cell and then seized clothing from other officers and several solicitors held hostage. The escapers then forced the duty officer at the inner gate to open the inner gate, however when an officer at the middle gate recognized one of the escapers and pressed the alarm, the prisoners sprinted to two cars waiting in the car park, just as an unmarked RUC car pulled up across the street from Crumlin Road Courthouse. Seeing the commotion, the police officers opened fire but were unable to prevent the prisoners escaping. Two days later, Magee was sentenced to life imprisonment *in absentia* with a recommended term of thirty years. Eleven days later, crowds attending the Wolfe Tone commemoration in Bodenstown prevented Gardai and troops arresting Magee. Later arrested in Dublin in January 1982, he was sentenced to ten years' imprisonment for the Crumlin escape under extra-jurisdictional legislation with Great Britain.

On 20 October 1982, after Westminster had published the *Northern Ireland – A Framework for Devolution* in April, Provisional Sinn Fein captured ten seats but its members then refused to sit. At the 1981 Sinn Fein Annual Convention, the fiery Republican Danny Morrison spokesman famously asked, 'Who here really believes we can win the war through the ballot box? But will anyone here object if, with a ballot paper in one hand and an Armalite in this hand, we take power in Ireland?' When the 'ballot and Armalite' strategy to contest elections was agreed, Gerry Adams adopted the political route.

The RUC was steadily imposing law enforcement, although Republican areas remained No Go. Although the force had been suspicious of the SAS, it was prepared to allow its Department E4A and Headquarters Mobile Support Unit to be trained by the Regiment to form a police version of 14 Intelligence Company and the Ulster Squadron in surveillance and direct action. During the dark and rainy night of 11 November, three Provisionals, Sean Burns, Gervase McKerr and Eugene Toman, who had been under surveillance for several months were killed when they allegedly breached a RUC VCP on the Tullygally Road in Craigavon. Since all were unarmed, the officers involved were debriefed by Special Branch and then investigated by detectives several days later. Two weeks later, when two men 'stumbled' on an IRA cache at a farm at Derrymacash near Lurgan, Michael Tighe was shot dead by the Support Unit. Unfortunately, torrential rain disturbed the collection of forensic evidence and Republican propagandists claimed that the pair had found the cache by accident until the claim was rather undermined in 2006 when the survivor, Martin McCauley, was arrested in Columbia accused of teaching dissident guerrillas in the use of explosives.

On 6 December, INLA exploded a devastating bomb in the Droppin' Well disco in Ballykelly killing seventeen people, including eleven soldiers from 1 Cheshires. Six days later, two INLA, including Seamus Grew, were shot by the RUC at a VCP near Mullacravie but their intended main target, Dominic McGlinchey, was not in the car. Grew was widely suspected of terrorism in mid-Ulster as early as 1973. After detectives had investigated the incidents and the Northern Ireland Director of Public Prosecutions recommended the prosecution of the RUC involved in the last shooting, Constable John Robinson claimed in court in March 1984 that he been instructed to lie about the shooting in order to protect a Special Branch informer. When it emerged that other police witnesses had altered their accounts and Robinson was then found not guilty, the resulting Republican and media outcry led Chief Constable John Harmon to seek an independent investigation of the alleged shoot-to-kill policy. The arrival of Deputy Chief Constable John Stalker from the Greater Manchester Police in May was not exactly welcome and shortly before his report was to be published, on 5 June 1986 he was mysteriously suspended over allegations of associations with English criminals. Even though he was cleared in mid-August, the inquiry was taken over by Colin Sampson of the West Yorkshire Police but their conclusions have not been made public. In *The Times* dated 9 February 1988, Stalker commented that, 'I never did find evidence of a shoot-to-kill policy as such ... But there was a clear understanding on the part of the men whose job it was to pull the trigger that that was what was expected of them'. In June 1990, the Inquiry informally concluded that there was no evidence of a shoot-to-kill policy. In his autobiography, Stalker, by now a minor celebrity, criticized the investigation concluding that 'some RUC detectives were amateur and inefficient at even the most basic of murder investigation routines; or that they had been deliberately inept.' Not surprisingly, the RUC was furious and, accusing Stalker of misleading inaccuracies, insisted that the investigating detective superintendent had presented his findings in the approved format. Stalker was also reminded that Security Forces left the scenes of incidents quickly to prevent retaliation and was criticized for having gone outside his remit when he re-investigated the murder of three

RUC when their Land Rover was mined near Oxford Island, Lurgan on 27 October, just three weeks before the Tullygally Road shooting. The investigation set the scene for other English police officers to examine the activities of the Security Forces.

1983 saw the first of several Loyalist and Republican 'supergrass' trials in which some witnesses were granted immunity in return for evidence. When Gerry Adams was elected to Westminster as Sinn Fein member for West Belfast in June, a ban on him entering Great Britain was lifted and he found himself being given some official protection. In March 1984, when he and three colleagues and a military policeman were wounded when the UFF ambushed his car and three Loyalists were convicted, Adams later claimed that the Army had prior knowledge of the attack. The attempt to assassinate Prime Minister Thatcher and her Cabinet at the Grand Hotel saw the Provisionals reminding her, 'Today, we were unlucky, but remember, we have to be unlucky once – you will have to be lucky always.' The attack reinforced Thatcher's view that there could be no negotiation with them. In November 1985, London and Dublin signed the Anglo-Irish Agreement acknowledging that 'any change in the status of Northern Ireland would only come about with the consent of the people of Northern Ireland'. When the Agreement gave Dublin a consultative role in security, political, cross-border and legal affairs in the North, not for the first time, the Unionists were incensed and mounted a long campaign to discredit the Agreement, as they had done in 1974. A factor that emerged from the talks was that Dublin had a clearer understanding of the role of the UDR and several recommendations emerged to improve its image among Nationalists including the removal of powers to arrest, restricting operations to supporting the RUC and a police officer to accompany patrols.

During another split within Provisional Sinn Fein, Rory O'Brady and several IRA veterans, protesting at Adams's proposal for Sinn Fein to sit in Dublin but not Westminster and Stormont, formed Republican Sinn Fein. It had a small military wing known as the Continuity IRA, whose creation was supported by Tom Maguire, who had legitimized the Provisionals in 1969. He described the Continuity Executive as the 'lawful Executive of the Irish Republican Army'. In July, a month after Thatcher had declared, after an aircraft hijacking to Beirut, that terrorists should be starved of the 'oxygen of publicity', the festering confrontation between the government and the BBC exploded when the corporation was banned from broadcasting the documentary *Real Lives: At The Edge of the*

169

Union. It examined political extremism in Northern Ireland through the eyes of two local political leaders, Martin McGuiness and Gregory Campbell of the UUP. When the BBC governors and senior executives clashed, with the former deciding that it should not be broadcast, BBC journalists went on strike for a day. Although the documentary was broadcast with minor tweaks, BBC rules were tightened to ensure that existing procedures on delicate current affairs projects should apply across the board.

By 1986, the Provisional Army Council had assessed that the terrorism was nowhere near to driving the Army from Northern Ireland and therefore an escalation of operations was deemed necessary. Modelled on and named after the Communist 1968 Tet Offensive in the Vietnam War, the Council decided on a strategy of 'liberating' the counties of Armagh, Fermanagh and Tyrone with the intention of provoking Westminster into introducing counterproductive measures, including internment, and thereby persuade the British public that the defence of Northern Ireland was pointless. It was fashionable at the time to regard the Tet Offensive as a Viet Cong victory, however we now know that it was a serious setback. Martin McGuiness took over Northern Command and a hardline Republican businessman living south of the South Armagh border was appointed Director of Operations. The Southern Command Quartermaster General was organizing the dispersal of several weapon consignments smuggled from Libya. In expectation of the delivery of Soviet SA-7 surface-to-air missiles, theoretical training was carried out. Libya was regarded by the West as a pariah state supporting revolutionary groups with training camps, finance and equipment. WPC Yvonne Fletcher had been shot by a gunman inside the Libyan Embassy in London and, in April 1986, after being blockaded by the 6th US Fleet, Tripoli was attacked by US F-111s using USAF Fairford in the United Kingdom, during which Colonel Gaddafi lost a young daughter.

The Gardai had become suspicious that the Provisionals were re-arming when a sizeable cache of modern weapons was found on a beach near Malin Head in Co. Donegal.

By now, the Armed Forces had settled down to contain the terrorists and the excesses of the opposing paramilitaries with patrols, searches and intelligence operations. Casualties were still being taken but not to the same degree as during the 1970s. Two soldiers were killed in 1985 and four in 1986.

For most soldiers, darkness was an ally. Night time in Belfast for Private Shaun Metcalfe, 1 QLR, was almost magical – quiet, eerie, no cars and no people but hiding the dark side of sectarian and 'punishment' shootings, muggings and drunks. It was 1987. Metcalfe was with a patrol returning to RUC Springfield Road when a figure was seen in a shop doorway. Believing the figure was setting up a remote controlled device, the patrol quietly closed to within about ten metres of the shop and then the patrol commander signalled Metcalfe to check out the figure. Unslinging his Federal Riot Gun, as Metcalfe inched forward, he saw the figure stealing the trainers from a drunk lying on the ground and quietly advised the thief that he would shoot if he moved a muscle. The RUC then arrested both men. At about 11 a.m. on 7 April, Metcalfe was in a five-man 'brick' forming a cordon covering waste ground near a primary school in Beechmount Avenue in West Belfast. After a month in the Province, the Battalion had already lost one killed and three wounded. The 'brick' settled down to a period of extended observation, time slowly ticking by and then, at about 8 p.m. – Crack! Thump! Crack! Thump and whine! Metcalfe turned around and saw that a corporal who had been talking to his Section Commander near two Pigs had crumpled to the ground and that an elderly man was shepherding two small girls into cover. Metcalfe found cover in a garden and scratched his hands on rose thorns. When he was asked to hand over his First Field Dressing to help the wounded corporal, he was reluctant to do so because kit was in short supply from yet more defence cuts and he was applying the doctrine of 'don't lose it or else!' Instead, another corporal stuffed the wounded man's beret into the wound until an ambulance collected him. By the time Metcalfe's brick was approaching Clownery Street and Beechmount Parade, the gunman was gone and onlookers had appeared. The Section Commander then realized that he had also been wounded in the thigh and was evacuated. Sensing that the soldiers were tense, the onlookers kept away – no objects thrown, no insults – and the 'brick' returned to Flax Street Mill in Pigs, each soldier left to his own thoughts and, after a long day, a welcome evening meal. The Section Commander was treated for a deep wound from a ricochet while the corporal had part of his lower leg amputated because the bullet had wrecked muscle and reconstruction was impossible. The Provisionals claimed responsibility for the shooting.

At about 2 a.m. a month later, Metcalfe was part of a quick reaction force that left North Howard Street Mill in an Armoured

Land Rover in response to shots fired at RUC Springfield Road and the Broadway OP, which was on top of a block of flats that overlooked the Falls Road, Royal Victoria Hospital, Beechmount and the West link Motorway. As other patrols converged on the area, Metcalfe was waiting for orders when he saw empty bullet cases on the ground and realized that he had found the point from where the shots had been fired. Fearing a booby trap, his Section Commander radioed for a 'Groundhog' – a tracker dog – which followed a scent into the Royal Victoria Hospital grounds where it went cold.

During the July Loyalist marching season, two platoons left North Howard Street Mill with 9 Platoon following as shadow protection. As they patrolled through the Lower Falls, they were diverted to the Falls Road/Grosvenor Road junction to investigate images from a CCTV camera which showed people carrying crates into Dunville Park, apparently unaware of the presence of an Army patrol. Another platoon was patrolling several streets away and probably diverted IRA spotters known as 'dickers'. Outside the park, an RUC officer ordered that the two platoons should be unarmed and after surrounding the park, they then charged into the park where they confronted by about twenty youths and girls being chased by 9 Platoon. Metcalfe selected a youth, decked him, spun him onto his stomach, deftly cuffed him with a plastic cable tie from his belt and, dragging him to his feet, guided his shocked captive to a Land Rover that already had several arrested youths sitting in the back. He noted an overpowering odour of petrol. Metcalfe returned to the fray and, by the time he had made his third arrest, the exhausted youths were handing themselves in. Searching the park, the soldiers found stashes of milk bottles filled with petrol, some ready 'to go' with rags hanging from the mouths, and cans filled with petrol. Metcalfe had no sympathy for the arrested youths because the petrol bombs were intended to inflict serious injuries on Army and police patrols and other people. Indeed, he felt sick at the mindless violence the youths regarded as 'normal'.

Co. Tyrone has a long history of resistance to the English. Even when the IRA split in 1970, the East Tyrone Brigade was not particularly affected, nevertheless their leader, Kevin Mallon, had been appointed Director of Operations after Keenan was arrested in 1979. Since 1970, the Brigade had taken on the Security Forces, occupied communities for short periods and murdered and intimidated UDR and RUC. In many respects, East Tyrone outshone the South Armagh

Brigade. In 1976, RUC Kinawley had been badly damaged when an IED left in a horsebox overnight exploded and in July 1983, four 6 UDR soldiers were killed when a mine exploded underneath their vehicle at Drumquin. By the mid-1980s when Mallon had been discredited after a series of bungled kidnappings of businessmen and the disappearance of the iconic racehorse Shergar, Jim Lynagh took over as the leading light – ruthless, wild, hardline, one of the few Monaghan men to serve time in Long Kesh. Generally critical of Adams's leadership and the content of the Green Book, he had trained in Libya, had murdered the former Stormont speaker Sir Norman Stronge and had survived an 'own goal' in 1974. After the attacks had prompted the Royal Engineers to review the defences of eighty-five RUC stations and thirty-five required immediate improvements, 33 Field Squadron and the roulement 20 Field Squadron upgraded the defences in Operation Niccola between August 1985 and June 1986. 42 Field Squadron arrived from West Germany in July 1986 and, in Operation Jole 2 over the next four months, repaired several damaged RUC stations, including Enniskillen and Belcoo. During the same period, 30 Field Squadron shielded twenty-one Army bases with large mortar cages. Several civilian contractors helping with the work were intimidated by murder threats.

However, it was not all one way. In 1981, after an informant had supplied information and 14 Intelligence Company carried out surveillance, three SAS detachments surrounded a cache of weapons near Coalisland. When a car with three Provisionals stopped nearby and two passengers then approached the cache, they were challenged. A short gun battle broke out during which one passenger was killed and the other was fatally wounded. The driver drove the car through the SAS cordon and when it was later found abandoned, it was evident that he had been wounded. In mid-October 1984, acting from a tip-off that the Provisionals intended to murder an off-duty 8 UDR soldier going to work in a haulage yard near Dungannon, three SAS detachments surrounded the suspected ambush. When a van hijacked by the Provisionals arrived and the SAS tried to stop it, the driver brushed their attempts aside and a gun battle broke out during which a terrorist and a bystander were shot dead. A SAS covert car pursued the van but lost it. Six weeks later in a dark Fermanagh lane, two cars filled with SAS trapped a van known to be about to collect a bomb. Unfortunately, one car halted opposite an ASU preparing the bomb behind a hedge and, as the SAS crew bailed out under fire,

Sergeant Alistair Slater was killed in the exchange of fire. When the SAS fired a flare, the Provisionals broke contact, two crossing the border and the third drowning as he crossed a river.

Lynagh believed the Tet Offensive unworkable because it did not take into account that the British Army was not a conscript force, as the US and South Vietnamese had been in 1968. Although the Army Council had rejected his proposal that a Flying Column based in Ireland should raid Ulster but agreed he could attack RUC and UDR bases. RUC Ballygawley was blown up with the loss of two constables and The Birches RUC station near Portadown was damaged when a JCB bucket loaded with explosive was driven through the perimeter fence and the defences were raked with small arms. Lynagh distrusted Northern Command because he believed it was haemorrhaging information and since there had been no SAS ambushes of the East Tyrone Brigade for some time, it was with some confidence that in the spring of 1987 Lynagh selected eight experienced IRA to attack RUC Loughgall. Gerard O'Callaghan had just served twelve years and Patrick Kelly was thought to have killed two RUC officers. Nevertheless, the planning was poor – no recces and no route clearance, for instance using sheep dogs to flush out OPs and ambushes, as were common in South Armagh. Lynagh was right to distrust Northern Command because the Army had good intelligence of the date, plan and weapons allocated for the proposed attack.

During 8 May 1987, several SAS slipped into RUC Loughall while the remainder of the Troop burrowed into a thin belt of trees and shrubbery along the road opposite the building. During the afternoon, Lynagh's men hijacked a blue Hiace van in Dungannon and stole a JCB from a farm and then, just after 7 p.m., Declan Arthurs, after the not inconsiderable feat of driving the JCB with a 200lbs bomb in its bucket for nine miles along country roads, approached the perimeter fence. One of two men with him then lit the fuse and, covered by five Provisionals firing from the van, Arthurs smashed through the fence and drove the JCB against the building where the bomb exploded, collapsing the walls and roof. Meanwhile the SAS in the tree line had riddled the Hiace and killed six terrorists. The surviving terrorists ran into the SAS cut off group. In the middle of the incident a car driven by Anthony Hughes, a mechanic, and his brother, Oliver, was caught in the crossfire. Unfortunately, both were wearing blue overalls similar to those worn by the ASU and, as Anthony frantically reversed their car, he was killed. His widow later received compensation from the British Government.

Loughgall was an intelligence coup and a classic ambush in which all eight of Lynagh's men were killed. Of the three Heckler and Koch rifles, a FN, two FNC rifles, a Ruger revolver and a shotgun captured, forensics linked some to seven murders and twelve attempted murders in mid-Ulster. One weapon had been stolen from a Reserve RUC constable, killed two years earlier. Much was made by Republican propagandists that the SAS had fired 800 rounds compared with the 70 rounds fired by the terrorists. A major British Army principle of ambushes is that the enemy do not survive. A ninth man, who should have been on the operation, left for England soon afterwards. Suspecting yet another breach of security, the Provisionals abducted Colette O'Neill in 1989 in the belief that she was an informer until she was rescued by the RUC. On 30 October, French Customs intercepted the scruffy trawler MV *Eksund* off the French coast on the pretext that it was suspected of carrying drugs. When the ship was searched in Bordeaux and 120 tons of arms, ammunition and equipment, including RPG-7 grenade launchers, surface-to-air missiles and Semtex was found, the skipper, John Hopkins spent two days of spinning yarns and then admitted that for three years he had been smuggling arms for the Provisionals from Libya to the isolated beach of Clogher Strand in Co. Kerry. To what extent the French authorities knew about the *Eksund* remains something of a mystery, however it is worth bearing in mind that the Provisional IRA was riddled with informants top to bottom. Indeed, a delivery earlier in the year had been postponed when the IRA learnt that the Irish Army knew about it. Nevertheless, the consignment was sufficient to convince Westminster and Dublin that the Provisionals could rely on sufficient logistic support from their Libyan quartermasters to conduct their version of the communist Long War. Although Mrs Thatcher was adamant that there would be no discussions with the IRA, political negotiations were inevitable. The increased threat saw 3 Infantry Brigade being reformed at Drumadd Barracks, Armagh in June 1988, again with specific responsibility for the border.

Enniskillen had seen its fair share of trouble since 26 August 1972 when two 4 UDR, Privates Alfred Johnston and James Eames, were killed by a RCIED car bomb as their patrol approached Cherrymount. In November 1982, Constable Garry Ewing and Helen Woodhouse, a civilian, were killed by a bomb attached to

175

Ewing's car parked outside the Lakeland Forum Leisure Centre and then, in May 1984, another car bomb outside the centre killed the off-duty Corporal Thomas Agar and Lance Corporals Robert Huggins and Peter Gallimore, all 1 RRF. In January 1987, Constable Ivan Crawford was killed when a RCIED in a litter bin exploded while he was on foot patrol in Omagh High Street.

Knowing that Remembrance Sunday, to commemorate Irish losses during the first day of the Battle of the Somme and since, was an important family day, three ASUs from Co. Monaghan, Donegal and East Tyrone combined to attack the Enniskillen parade. During the evening of 7 November, a member smuggled a 50lbs time bomb into St Michael's Reading Room and placed it against the three-story gable wall that backed onto a favourite viewing platform of the ceremony. As the parade assembled around the Cenotaph, at 10.43 a.m. the device exploded collapsing the wall and launching javelins of glass and rubble into the crowd. Videoed images captured by the local businessman, Raymond McCartney, and beamed throughout the world within hours, showing desperate attempts to reach the casualties buried under several feet of rubble, did the Provisionals serious damage. Eleven people were killed, all civilians except for one RUC Reserve officer. Three were married couples aged seventy years and over. One young man was orphaned. Sixty-three were injured. At the same time, a 200lbs RCIED planted by the Provisionals at Tullyhommon Poppy Day ceremony, near Pettigoe, failed to explode. There were no military representatives at the parade, only the Boys' and Girls' Brigades and veterans. A car bomb outside the Belfast British Legion was defused. Next day, the dignity of Gordon Wilson, remembering his student nurse daughter Marie, had a profound effect across the world and was in sharp contrast to the brutality of the incident. He later became a Senator in the Irish Parliament.

It is inconceivable that the Northern Command leadership and Sinn Fein had little or no knowledge of the Poppy Day bombs and, although Gerry Adams apologized for the bomb on Remembrance Day 1997, the Provisionals never really recovered from its ruthlessness.

During the nine months after Enniskillen, the damage that the Security Forces had caused to the Provisionals was clearly demonstrated. Its ranks of inexperienced terrorists killed eighteen people who had little or no connection with anyone or anything. In March 1988, a young Protestant woman was killed near Belleek in an ambush by the remnants of the East Tyrone Brigade in mistake for her UDR brother. On the 16th, when the three Provisionals killed in Gibraltar were being buried in Milltown Cemetery, the renegade Loyalist Michael Stone threw a Soviet grenade and opened fire on the mourners with a Browning and Magnum 357, killing three people, including Volunteer Kevin Brady, who was one of two men who tried to disarm him, and injuring fifty. Chased to the M1, he was arrested by the RUC after being cornered. Three days later, several infamous Falls Road black taxis were leading the funeral cortege of Brady slowly along Andersonstown Road towards the cemetery when a Volkswagen Passat headed straight towards the procession. Millions watched on television as the car swept past a Sinn Fein steward and scattered mourners as it mounted a pavement before turning into a small side road. Realizing the road was blocked, the driver reversed but was trapped by a black taxi. As mourners and stewards wrestled to open the doors, the passenger climbed part of the way out of his window and fired a shot in the air with a Browning. With the Stone incident fresh in their memory and cries of 'He's got a gun!' the crowd scattered and, then assuming the car to contain Loyalist gunmen, it surged back to attack it with a wheel-brace and a stepladder snatched from a photographer. The two occupants were hauled out through the windows and, after being punched and kicked, were dragged to the Casement Park sports ground where they were again beaten up, stripped to their underpants and socks and searched. Their car was set alight. There the television coverage stopped. However, overhead, a Lynx helicopter beamed CCTV images to HQ 39 Infantry Brigade showing both men being bundled into a black taxi, its driver waving his fist in the air with apparent glee. Driving 200 yards to a wall, the two were then thrown over it onto waste ground at Penny Lane in Andersonstown where two gunmen waited with guns brought by another black taxi. One man was quickly shot and the other fought back until he was executed. The Lynx then tracked one gunman in a red Sierra to a workshop. While the pilot was radioing for a patrol, the doors of the workshop opened and two red Sierras emerged and in a well-executed plan split in opposite directions. Unfortunately the pilot followed the wrong car. A lasting image of the incident, which lasted no more than fifteen minutes, was the distress of the Redemptionist Father Alec Reid kneeling beside the near naked bodies administering the last rites. For several years Reid had acted as interface between the Provisional leadership and the British. When a 1 Royal Scots Armoured Land Rover arrived at Penny Lane, Reid arose from his knees while the corporal in command checked the pulses of the bodies. After the fire brigade had extinguished the burning Passat, an armoured plate was found in the backrest of the driver's seat, indicating that it had been driven by a soldier. Later in the day, the IRA issued a statement:

> The Belfast Brigade IRA claims responsibility for the execution in Andersonstown this afternoon of two SAS members, who launched an attack on the funeral cortege of our comrade Volunteer Kevin Brady. The SAS unit was initially apprehended by the people lining the route of the cortege in the belief that armed Loyalists were attacking them, and they were removed from the immediate vicinity of the funeral procession by them. At this point our Volunteers forcibly removed the two men from the crowd and, after clearly ascertaining their identities from equipment and documentation, we executed them.

While the IRA believed they had murdered two SAS in retaliation for the killing of the three IRA in Gibraltar, in fact, the two men were Corporals Woods and David Howes of 233 Signals Squadron. A military document found during the Provisional search read 'Herford', a town in north-west Germany where 4th Armoured Division was based. The searchers read this to be 'Hereford' where the SAS was based. The mistake was the death sentence, not that the IRA took prisoners. Corporal Wood, who had fired warning shots with his Browning, was shot and then stabbed several times. Two men were later convicted of their murders. Why the two corporals should end up in Andersonstown is a mystery, particularly on a day of extreme sensitivity in Nationalist estates when Security Forces' patrols were ordered to be discreet. Denying that the corporals were on surveillance, the Army admitted them to be technicians who regularly visited Army bases in West Belfast and confirmed it was not unusual for soldiers in civilian clothes to be armed. Prime Minister Thatcher was at RAF Northolt when the bodies were flown to England and denounced the murders as 'an act of appalling savagery'. Gerry Adams MP commented that the provocation to the mourners was such that there was no chance to rescue the two soldiers. 'I did my best to restore calm,' he claimed, 'What were they doing there?'

Although the murders were condemned, worse was to follow when Provisional operational inexperience in the East Tyrone Brigade led to a bomb exploding in a school bus near Lisnaskea. It was intended to kill its part-time UDR driver. Instead, it injured several children. In June, a Green Howards corporal, four Royal Signals and a Royal Army Ordnance Corps lance corporal, who had all just completed a charity run in Lisburn, were killed when a large Semtex device moulded into a cone shape to maximize its power exploded under their minibus parked in Market Square. Two civilians and a soldier were killed by a booby trap bomb in the Falls Road swimming pool and a landmine intended for a senior Catholic judge killed the Hanna family near the Killen PVCP in July. During the late evening of 20 August, a coach carrying members of 1 LI returning from leave to Lisanelly Barracks, Omagh from Aldergrove Airport was speeding along the road from the Ballygawley roundabout to Omagh. The stretch was infamous for ambushes. The bus had just passed a telegraph pole when a 200lbs HME bomb planted by the brothers Martin and Gerald Harte, and Brian Mullen, exploded, killing eight Light Infantrymen and wounding twenty-eight others. The very seriously injured were ferried to Dungannon Hospital to be stabilized before being flown to the Royal Victoria Infirmary. The incident led to helicopters being used to ferry troops to and from bases in East Tyrone. Ten days later, informant intelligence suggested that the Harte brothers and Mullen intended to ambush a coalman, who was a part-time UDR soldier, but it was not known when, where or how. When they were seen by 14 Intelligence Company retrieving weapons from a cache, the SAS developed a plan to provoke an attack. Next morning an SAS soldier, masquerading as the coalman, drove the UDR soldier's Leyland coal lorry to an ambush site near Drumnakilly, punctured a tyre and telephoned for help. Covered by eight colleagues, he waited and then, six hours later, the three Provisionals drove past in a stolen car and, returning in another car, as they opened fire at the soldier diving for cover behind a gate, the SAS ambush was sprung and the three gunmen died in a hail of bullets. As usual, Republican propagandists claimed the men were innocent and accused the Security Forces of retaliation after the Ballygawley ambush. An inconclusive formal investigation was unable to explain why the three died in a hail of 236 bullets. The answer is simple. Ambushes are designed to kill.

179

The 'Loughgall Martyrs' became heroes of Nationalist folklore with a poem describing them as 'brave volunteers' while the SAS were 'butchers' accused of using disproportionate force and not offering the eight the opportunity to surrender. Thousands escorted their corteges, the biggest Republican funerals in Northern Ireland since the 1981 hunger strikes. Adams commented that while the British could buy off Ireland, which he described as the pro-British, it could never defeat the likes of the Martyrs. As so often with the movement with whom he is associated, he forgets that Lynagh's men had killed, maimed and damaged.

In another of its bizarre conclusions over Northern Ireland, in 2001 the European Court of Human Rights ruled that the eight terrorists had their human rights violated under Article 2 (Right to Life) because a formal investigation had not been conducted into the deaths. The song *Drumnakilly Ambush* glorified an ASU who had slaughtered eight soldiers, injured twenty-eight and planned to murder a ninth.

The iconic East Tyrone Brigade had been destroyed and with the Tet Offensive proving disastrous and Colonel Gadaffi distancing himself after Enniskillen, the Provisional leadership realized that terrorism was counterproductive and negotiations were inevitable. One estimate suggests that the East Tyrone Brigade lost fifty-three Volunteers killed in the Troubles – the highest of any brigade area, of which twenty-eight were killed between 1987 and 1992.

In October 1990, Desmond Grew, brother to Seamus Grew killed in the third 1982 shoot-to-kill incident, and Martin McCaughey, were shot near Loughgall and in the following June, three more IRA died at Coagh when they were attacked en route to ambush Protestant contractors. For the soldiers patrolling the streets and lanes at risk from attack and bombs, and unable to hit back, the ambushes were welcome news.

Chapter 13

The IRA Campaign in Europe

As the Provisionals came under increasing pressure in Ulster, as part of the Long War strategy, the Army Council appointed a Director of Overseas Operations with instructions to open a third front in Europe. In 1980, *Republican News* published this rationale for attacking British troops:

> Between tours all of them are either stationed in Britain or overseas and here they can rest from the dirty work they are doing...they think they can forget about Ireland until the next tour, but we intend to keep Ireland on their minds so that it haunts them and they want to do something about not going back...Overseas attacks also have a prestige value and internationalize the war in Ireland... we have kept Ireland in the world headlines.

The first incidents attributed to the IRA were several letter bombs in 1973 probably sent by a lone Volunteer. In developing its European campaign in the late 1970s, the Provisionals exploited the relatively open borders, selected safe houses and identified caches in West Germany, the Netherlands, France and Belgium. Opportunities to attack British soldiers existed in Europe that were unavailable in England. As was the practice with NATO forces serving in West Germany, British Service personnel owning cars had special licence plates identifying them to be British. In short, British military personnel and their families were relatively soft targets. However, the Council appear not to have appreciated that European governments had been working together to address international and domestic terrorism, for instance in West Germany, the urban guerilla Bader Meinhoff and communist Red Army Faction, both of which had declared war on the state. Unlike in Northern Ireland where the intelligence agencies competed, in West Germany, the Federal Criminal Bureau led and so far as the British were concerned, they were assisted by the RMP Special Investigation Branch, British police forces and the British Services Security Organization in a relationship that monitored communist intelligence services. Irish sympathizers in universities were closely watched. A seeping disease that briefly emerged was Black Power. Following the discovery that several weapons were missing from the armoury of a unit about to deploy to Northern Ireland, the British military and German security authorities deduced from information received, that a locker in a railway station was a possible cache. A surveillance operation netted several soldiers involved in stealing the weapons to sell them to a German with IRA contacts. Since such subversion could destabilize units, as was evident in US units in Vietnam, the subversion was rooted out and the embryonic Black Power swiftly executed. The terrorism threat led to the British increasing the security of their military facilities with armed patrols.

In 1969, the 60,000 British soldiers of the BAOR and their families based in West Germany were part of the NATO defence of central Europe against the Group of Soviet Forces in East Germany. Most units were gathered in sturdy pre-Second World War barracks. A few bases, including HQ BAOR, RAF (Germany) and HQ Northern Army Group in Rheindalen, were open to the public. Some married quarters were inside barracks. Most were in blocks of flats or houses integrated into German estates. Schools and retail outlets were often outside perimeter fences. The deployments to Northern Ireland had placed considerable pressures on BAOR maintaining its operational commitments, particularly when the Royal Armoured Corps, Royal Artillery and Royal Engineers provided roulement infantry and Prison Guard Forces.

By 1979, ASUs were being sent to Europe on about six month deployments with the order – kill as many British soldiers as possible. Generally self-sufficient in weaponry and supplied with stolen and false documents, points of entry included travelling from Dublin to Cherbourg by ferry and, taking advantage of relaxed border controls, driving to safe houses in the Limburg province in the Netherlands close to the border with Germany. The country was an ideal sanctuary because English was common, the Dutch had a liberal outlook and were not bothered by urban guerrilla groups. More importantly, the border towns in the region were frequently visited by the British and the bases in the Lower Rhine Valley, such as Rheindahlen and Düsseldorf, were about a thirty minutes' drive from the border. Those deeper into West Germany, such as Osnabrück, Bielefeld and Münster, were about a ninety minute drive.

The second campaign opened in 1978 when a bomb left in Rheindahlen was defused. In early July 1979, a bomb damaged the British Consulate in Antwerp and then, on the 29th, another bomb wrecked a bandstand in the Grand Square in Brussels just after the 1 DERR Band had finished a rehearsal to celebrate a millennium of Belgian history. Eight tourists were injured. The IRA claimed responsibility in a phone call to the mayor.

On 16 February 1980, a couple shot Colonel Mark Coe, of the Royal Engineers, as he was parking his car in his married quarters garage in Bielefeld. The most senior officer killed during Operation Banner, he left a widow and six children and appears to have been a speculative target. The following year in March, a 1 Devon and Dorsets' corporal running in woods outside Belfast Barracks in Osnabrück, was badly wounded by a gunman, nevertheless, he displayed considerable resilience and reached a German military hospital. The Battalion had completed its fifth tour in Northern Ireland in May 1979, four of them in Belfast since July 1970, and had noted that the shootings and bombings of previous tours were less frequent. A few incidents in 1981 were in response to the Hunger Strike and two attacks by a coalition of INLA and the German Red cells.

There was a gap of eight years until 23 March 1987, and the beginning of the 'Tet Offensive', when a 300lbs device exploded outside the main Officers' Mess in Rheindahlen, injuring twenty-seven West German Army officers and their wives at a farewell party, and four British Mess staff, most wounded by flying glass. Casualties would have been heavier had not heavy curtains been drawn. The previously unknown National Democratic Front for the Liberation of West Germany claimed responsibility until the IRA issued a statement that, 'Our unit's brief was to inflict a devastating blow but was ordered to be careful to avoid civilian casualties.' Fourteen months later early on 1 May 1988 in Roermond, the picturesque Dutch border town, gunmen shot at four off-duty RAF Regiment airmen from RAF Brüggen, sleeping in a car near a club after a night out, and killed the driver, Senior Aircraftsman (SAC) Ian Shinner. Half an hour later, SACs John Baxter and John Miller, both RAF Regiment from RAF Lahrbruck, were killed when a bomb exploded underneath Baxter's car in the Dutch border town of Nieuw-Bergen. Three other airmen were wounded. The IRA claimed responsibility for both incidents. A suspicious crate in a block of flats occupied by British families in Weeze was declared safe. A military spokesmen suggested that the motivation for attacks was probably because protective security in West Germany was tighter than in the Netherlands. He also commented that since many serviceman had enlisted in the 1970s, most were alert to the IRA threat.

The potent symbol of the British presence in the Mediterranean since the mid-1700s, it seems that Colonel Gaddafi chose Gibraltar for an attack as his price for the arms shipments, in revenge for the expulsions of Libyan diplomats after the murder of WPC Fletcher and British assistance to the F-111 raids on Tripoli in 1986. The resident Battalion was 1 Royal Anglians which had completed its fifth tour in Northern Ireland, twice as the resident Battalion in Londonderry.

During the first months of 1988, an ASU was placed under surveillance by MI5 after members had flown to Malaga. When in February, a known female Republican was noted taking undue interest in the Changing of the Guard by the Royal Anglians outside the Governor's Residence; this was assumed to be the target. On 3 March, after being briefed at the Ministry of Defence for Operation Flavius, an SAS Special Projects unit was deployed to Gibraltar. The Spanish authorities were then advised that an ASU, identified as Daniel McCann, Sean Savage and Mairead Farrell, were flying back to Malaga. McCann had served two years for possession of explosives, Farrell had done fourteen years for causing explosions and was a thoroughly committed Republican and Savage was described as an expert bomb-maker. It was assumed that a bomb would be delivered by car.

In Gibraltar, Commissioner of Police Joseph Canapa, his Acting Deputy Mr Colombo, and Special Branch Detective Chief Inspector Ullger, Security Service liaison officers, the senior military adviser, namely the senior SAS officer, the Special Project commander and an ATO formed an advisory group. Rules of Engagement were agreed that should military intervention be required to arrest or protect life, it would be authorized by the senior police officer and be proportionate. Opening fire without warning was agreed if there were reasonable grounds to believe that the ASU was committing or was about to commit an action which would endanger their and others' lives and there was no other way to prevent this. Warnings had to be a clear direction to surrender and that fire would be opened if it was not obeyed. This principle was enshrined in the Yellow Card, although executing its requirement during the heat of the moment was different, as several soldiers found out to their cost. It was assumed the bomb would be ferried across the border probably on the 7th. Meanwhile, the SAS rehearsed approaching suspects and instructing them to lie on the ground until the police made the arrests. The underpinning aim of the operation was to protect life by foiling the attack and arresting the terrorists with minimum force. Arrangements were made to evacuate the area around Ince's Hall to a radius of 200 metres on 7 and 8 March and traffic diversions planned. When the Joint Operations Centre opened at 8 a.m. on 6 March, Commissioner Canapa instructed his officers to begin surveillance at border crossing points and to prepare to arrest. MI5 surveillance and two man SAS attack teams also deployed. A detective constable sent to the Spanish immigration post, which was separate from the crossing point, watched the border from the computer room, however the Spanish border police showed him only the passports of cars containing two men and a woman, which later drew some criticism, however a senior police officer said this was necessary because of the international delicacy of the operation. At about 12.30 p.m., the MI5 surveillance team reported they had a white Renault car parked in a space near the Assembly Area under observation because the driver, thought to be Savage, had fiddled with something between the seats and then had locked the car before walking towards Southport Gate. At 2 p.m., he was seen at the rear of John Mackintosh Hall and recognized to be the driver. He had also adopted anti-surveillance techniques.

At about 2.30 p.m., McCann and Farrell were noted crossing the border on foot and were followed to the Assembly Area where they met Savage and spent some time staring at the car. Since it was assumed that they were calculating the maximum effect of a bomb, the Joint Operations Room discussed arresting them as they walked through Southport Gate. It was then thought that the trio might be on a recce. Commissioner Canapa's request for positive identification was confirmed by 3.25 p.m., by which time the suspects had returned to the Renault. Control was briefly handed to the SAS to await further verification. Meanwhile the ATO had returned from examining the Renault and concluded that it was a 'suspect car bomb' and thought to be probably radio activated, largely on the basis of an old aerial on a relatively new car. It was known the

Provisionals had recently developed a sophisticated remote control device. After receiving this report, Canapa decided the suspects should be arrested on suspicion of conspiracy to murder and, at 3.40 p.m., signed operational control to the SAS. He then instructed Mr Colombo to assemble all police vehicles and to recall the duty police car immediately. However, it was trapped by traffic in Smith Dorrien Avenue and so the driver activated its siren and beacons and pulled out to overtake the queue. The day was sunny and the area busy with people and traffic.

At the junction of Smith Dorrien Avenue and Winston Churchill Avenue, the three suspects crossed the road and exchanged newspapers. As one of the SAS teams emerged from Landport Tunnel, when Savage left McCann and Farrell and walked towards the tunnel, he brushed the shoulder of one of the SAS. In the knowledge that other SAS were in a position to arrest Savage, both then closed on McCann and Farrell, walking along Winston Churchill Avenue at a brisk pace. They were adjacent to the Shell petrol station when the duty police car siren sounded. McCann looked over his left shoulder toward the sound and apparently realized that the two men behind him were a threat. Four police officers in the vicinity heard the SAS give McCann a warning but when his hand moved across the front of his body, one SAS soldier thought that he was about to detonate the bomb and opened fire, hitting McCann in the back from a distance of three metres. Farrell, on the left of McCann, half turned and when she reached for her handbag which was under her left arm, the soldier also shot her at close range and again fired at McCann. The second soldier, directly behind Farrell, also saw her reach for her handbag and fearing that she was going for the button to activate the bomb, shot Farrell, switched to McCann, who he believed was about to detonate a device, and then shot Farrell a second time. As the police car passed the Shell garage and the senior police officer inside saw two persons lying on the pavement, the driver passed around the Sundial Roundabout and parked opposite the garage, the siren still sounding. The three police officers vaulted the central barrier, and were approached by two men in civilian clothes carrying Brownings and wearing the sandy beret and winged cap badge of the SAS. Meanwhile, the second SAS pair had followed Savage towards the Landport Tunnel with the intention of arresting him. Behind Savage was a woman, who, unknown to the two SAS, was part of MI5 surveillance. Eight feet from the tunnel, as the police siren sounded, followed by the crackle of gunfire behind them, one soldier drew his

186

pistol and shouted at Savage to stop, but as he spun round and his arm went towards his right hip, a soldier pushed the woman from the line of fire and opened fire, aiming for the centre of his body and then his head, and kept firing until Savage lay motionless on the ground. Both soldiers then put on their berets to identify themselves to the police.

By 4.05 p.m., the senior military commander had confirmed that the suspects had been shot and handed control back to Commissioner Canapa. The ATO cleared the Renault and the police began to collect evidence. No weapons or detonating devices were found on the bodies, however a key ring with two keys and a Spanish car registration tag tumbled out of Farrell's handbag. The information was passed to the Spanish police and later that night they found in a red Ford Fiesta in La Linea another set of car keys and a rental agreement indicating that the car had been rented on 6 March by Katharine Smith. This was the name on the passport found inside Farrell's handbag. On 8 March, a Fiesta with a 64kg Semtex bomb and 200 rounds of ammunition with two timers timed for the Changing the Guard concealed in the spare wheel was found.

The Gibraltar Inquest began on 6 September 1988 attended by Army and British Government representatives. The families of the three Provisionals were represented by Patrick Finucane, a lawyer who regularly defended Republicans. In front of a jury, witnesses described the nature of the IRA plot and events leading up to the shootings. Military witnesses denied that there had been a plan to execute the suspects. Pathologists described how the IRA died with one describing the shooting of Savage sixteen times as 'a frenzied attack'. Forensic explosive experts largely agreed that the IRA had developed a sophisticated remote control high frequency device requiring shorter aerials and more accurate line-of-sight targeting. When the jury returned verdicts of lawful killing by a majority of nine to two, the inevitable civil actions that were commenced against the Ministry of Defence for the loss and damage suffered by the estates of the deceased was eventually withdrawn in May 1991. However, the ambush was referred to the European Court of Human Rights and it again found that the United Kingdom had breached Article 2 (Right to Life) by ten votes to nine and the Government was ordered to pay the applicants £38,700 within three months. Claims for damages and costs were dismissed because there was no doubt that the three had been intending to commit terrorism.

Between 1980 and 1996, the British, Belgian, Dutch and German authorities believed that seven ASUs rotated in Europe with probably two active between 1989 and 1990. Early in 1989, an ASU consisting of Donna Maguire, Gerard Harte, Sean Hick, Paul Hughes and Leonard Hardy moved into a safe house near Maastricht. Educated in a convent, a hard-edged Republican from Newry who knew Mairead Farrell, Maguire was apparently trained by Desmond Grew, who was killed by the SAS in 1990. It was not until the summer that they are thought to have begun operations. On 19 June, a civilian employee surprised two men planting twelve devices at the perimeter near a barrack block at Quebec Barracks in Osnabrück. The barracks housed HQ 12 Armoured Brigade. Although serious damage was caused, no one was injured. On 2 July, a bomb attached to his car killed Corporal Steven Smith, of 1 RTR, outside his married quarters in Hanover. He was the third RTR killed in Operation Banner. After six months in Europe, at the end of July, Maguire and Hardy boarded a ferry in Cherbourg but were arrested at Rosslare in Ireland, allegedly in possession of bomb-making equipment and photographs of British military installations in Germany. Two days later after receiving information from the Gardai, the French authorities arrested an ASU in Paris including Pat Murray, Donncha O'Kane and Pauline Drumm and charged them with explosives offences. The Federal Criminal Bureau was now beginning to suspect that the British had credible intelligence on the Provisionals, for instance, knowledge of those responsible for the murder of Corporal Smith, and a proposal to shoot down a Harrier at an RAF base close to the Dutch border with a missile. In September, the Federal authorities issued extradition warrants against the three arrested in Paris and Maguire for terrorism in West Germany by using the international agreement that if the prosecution linked an individual to an organization claiming an attack, it is admissible as evidence.

On 13 July, part of the perimeter fence surrounding Glamorgan Barracks, Duisburg, which housed 6 Squadron RCT, was cut, and two 20lbs bombs badly damaged an accommodation block, wounded nine of the fifty sleeping soldiers and shattered windows of nearby factories. A West German police car intercepted the getaway car about 600 yards from the barracks but came under automatic fire that sprayed buildings but caused no injuries. A month later, Regimental Sergeant Major Richard Heakin, of 1 Royal Welch Fusiliers, was betrayed by his British Forces Germany number plates and shot dead by a gunman at some traffic lights on the outskirts of Ostend on his way to catch the ferry to England. Several weeks later, an incendiary device taped under the saddle of a bicycle lent against the Roy Barracks, Dortmund, perimeter fence injured five Royal Engineers of 14 Topographic Squadron and a German civilian. The barracks housed 3 Map and Chart Depot and since the device detonated near the Sergeants' Mess, it is presumed the timing was to catch SNCOs going for lunch.

Late on 3 September, a car stopped alongside two British soldiers in the British married quarter complex in the village of Gremmendorf and the driver asked directions in English, to nearby Münster. When the soldiers replied, an occupant in the back opened fire with an AK-47, critically wounding one and seriously wounding the other. The IRA claimed responsibility:

> While the undemocratic partition of Ireland is maintained by British military might, the IRA reserves the right to strike at the British Government and British Army wherever they seek respite from their war against the Irish people.

Earlier in the week, a British soldier in Hanover had found a bomb underneath his car set to explode when the door was opened. Mrs Heidi Hazell, the German wife of a British Army staff sergeant, was reversing her car near married quarters in the suburb of Massen in Unna when she was murdered by a gunman wearing a British combat jacket and carrying an AK-47. The IRA claimed that she was working in Dortmund garrison. She was the second wife to be murdered during Operation Banner. Once again, the number plates of her car betrayed her. The British Forces number plates were then replaced – as they had been painfully obvious for years. On 26 October, RAF Corporal Maheshumer (Mick) Islania was in civilian clothes, filling up at a garage near RAF Wildenrath when gunmen armed with AK-47s appeared from some nearby bushes and, in a wild burst, killed him and his 6 month old daughter who was in the back seat of his car. She was the third child of a Service family to be murdered by the IRA.

Meanwhile in Dublin in 1990, Maguire had been acquitted of the explosive charges while Hardy was sentenced to five years. When the West German warrants seeking her arrest in connection with the attack on Quebec Barracks and the murder of Corporal Smith failed, she returned to the Netherlands. On 27 May in Roermond, gunmen murdered two Australian lawyers touring Europe, Stephen Melrose and Nick Spanos, in the belief that they were off-duty soldiers because they were driving a car with British plates. Moral and financial support from Australia dried up. On 1 June, Major Michael Dillon-Lee, of 32 Heavy Regiment RA, was shot outside his married quarter in Dortmund in front of his wife. The murder of the two Australians added to the disastrous publicity surrounding the 'Tet Offensive' in Northern Ireland.

At the same time in New York, the US Ambassador to London protested to the mayor of New York that a street corner should be named after Joseph Doherty. He was part of the M-60 gang that had murdered Captain Westmacott and had escaped to the United States in 1983.

Later in the month, a Belgian farmer and his two sons, both of whom had served in the Belgian Army, heard shots from a wood on the border not far from the autobahn connecting Antwerp with Rotterdam. Thinking it was poachers, they investigated and found a couple claiming to be lovers. While the father and one son were talking to them, the second son had found a cache of four weapons when a second man suddenly appeared from the trees but ran off. The family immediately alerted the Belgian police, who arrested the couple and named the woman as Donna Maguire. The Dutch arrested the man who had ran away and another man in a car. A second cache contained four more weapons and several bombs made with Semtex. After some confusion over identities, the three man were named as Gerard Harte, Sean Hick and Paul Hughes, who was using the alias Michael Collins. The ASU had blundered by test-firing cached weapons.

When the Belgians extradited the four to the Netherlands where, in December, they were charged with the murders in Roermond of the three RAF Regiment and the two Australians, Maguire entered an international legal process that removed her from circulation for a record six years on remand. She had the distinction of being branded 'the most dangerous woman in Europe'. In March 1991, Harte was convicted of the murder of the Australians and sentenced to eighteen years. The remaining three were extradited to Germany accused of the murder of Major Dillon-Lee and attempted murder in the Quebec Barracks bombing. Forensics proved the rifle used to murder Major Dillon-Lee had been used to kill Corporal Islania and his child. In August 1992, Murray, O'Kane and Drumm were extradited from France to Germany to answer charges relating to the murder of Corporal Smith and were acquitted. At their trial in Düsseldorf in

June 1994, the prosecution linked Maguire, Harte and Hick to a terrorist organization, however their defence argued that their political opinions were being used against their human rights and they were acquitted. The presiding judge commented, 'They are members of the IRA and trained as IRA volunteers'. Harte and Hick returned to Dublin while Maguire was remanded in custody on charges relating to the Quebec Barracks bombing and in July 1995 was convicted in Celle for attempted murder and gathering information on British bases in Germany with intent to sabotage, and was sentenced to nine years. Since she had already spent six years on remand, she was released. Court officials emphasized that the changing political climate in Northern Ireland was also a factor.

On her return to Ireland, Maguire married Hardy. In 2000, she clashed with the Provisional leadership when her brother Malachy was subjected to a typically vicious IRA punishment beating with iron bars and was shot in both wrists and ankles. In August 2005, the long arm of European extradition snared Hardy while he was on a family holiday in Torremolinos when the Spanish police arrested him in connection with the 1989 bombing of Quebec Barracks. Extradited to Germany, he was convicted and sentenced to six years for attempted murder. It later emerged that he never went to prison and left the court with his wife.

The last attack on the British Army in Germany took place during the evening of 28 June 1996 when two Mark 10 mortar bombs were fired from a van parked outside Quebec Barracks. It was accommodating troops on leave from Bosnia. One bomb hit a tree and exploded inside the perimeter not far from its target, the fuel point. The second bomb failed to explode. German and British investigators feared that the IRA was planning more terrorist attacks, however these diminished when the Peace Process gathered pace in Ulster. Nevertheless, the German authorities issued an extradition warrant against Roisin McAliskey on the grounds of fingerprint and witness evidence that she took part in the attack. The daughter of Bernadette McAliskey and four months pregnant, the warrant was denied on health grounds by Home Secretary Jack Straw after a long international campaign by her mother. In May 2007, the Germans again issued an extradition warrant and, when she was arrested in Coalisland, Martin McGuiness complained that many would see it as 'petty and vindictive', this at a time when Sinn Fein were maintaining their demand for a Bloody Sunday inquiry. The warrant was rejected in November.

191

Chapter 14

Containment
1990 to 1994

Troop levels in Northern Ireland remained at about 10,500 divided into six Resident Battalions and four Roulement Battalions. Of the 102 Regulars killed during the decade, fifty-two had been killed in six bombings in Northern Ireland and three bombings in England. Between 1976 and 1987, Army patrols had killed just nine armed terrorists and it was not unusual for battalions to complete a tour without firing a shot. The SAS had been in Northern Ireland eleven years and, until the Conservative Party met in Brighton in 1984, had shot nine IRA, with none killed between December 1978 and December 1983. But, when the IRA escalated their operations, a determination to contain Republican extremism saw a change in the rules of engagement, from arrest to offensive Ops, resulting in thirty-five terrorists killed until 1990. A large number of soldiers who enlisted in the late 1960s had spent their careers alternating between postings and Northern Ireland. To the public in Great Britain, Northern Ireland had become a sideshow.

By 1990, the Army had undergone significant changes, not the least of which was NATO, mainly US, terminology. In 1982, the 200 year old 'Brigade Major' was replaced by 'Chief of Staff' and the 'General Staff Officer Grade 3 (Intelligence)' (GSO 3 (Int) to 'Staff Officer Grade 3 (G2)' (SO3 G2). Brigade HQs had also taken some responsibility for decision-making from commanding officers under the concept of Mission Command to the extent that, by the late 1980s, this often amounted to nominating the number of men required for permanent OPs and patrols. This was a departure from the early days when unit commanders had the flexibility to deploy their men as they saw fit. The 'multiple' consisted of two 'bricks' or more, giving mutual support in the event that part of the 'multiple' was attacked. The initiative remained to move quickly and deny the terrorists space to manoeuvre. Framework Operations encompassed routine patrolling, support of the RUC, searches, VCPs and manning the network of permanent and temporary OPs. Purpose-built high standing Mars OPs fitted with computer terminals, camera stands and improved protection replaced the breeze blocks and corrugated iron OPs. Battalions usually had a strengthened Operational Company deployable for specific operations, such as swamping areas without warning to disrupt terrorism, protecting military operations such as convoy route protection, and supporting SAS and RUC operations. The snub-nosed automatic 5.56mm SA-80 rifle had replaced the loyal semi-automatic SLR and '58 pattern webbing had been exchanged for the heavier '90 Infantry Equipment, body armour and helmets, the US flak jackets, sweaters and combat jackets of the 1970s now a distant memory. Although GPMGs were still in evidence, a 'brick' carried a 5.56mm Light Support Weapon and lightweight Remote Controlled Devices (RCD) to detect RCIEDS. When the warning tone sounded, the soldiers took cover because movement could block the signal. When some paramilitaries agreed not to place bombs in hospitals, patrols passing through the grounds switched off their RCDs to minimize interference with medical equipment. However, in November 1991 in an attack that damaged the credibility of the Provisionals, a hospital porter took advantage of this agreement to deposit a 20lbs Semtex bomb in a fire tunnel of the military wing of Musgrave Park Hospital that killed Company Sergeant Major Phil Cross RAMC and Driver Craig Pantry, seriously injured eight and caused extensive damage. Saxon APCs had replaced the battle weary Saracens and Pigs. The military strategy remained the same – to reassure the public by containing terrorism with attrition.

The longer that Operation Banner lasted, the more sophisticated intelligence gathering became, but war is a dirty business and most intelligence operations were being played out in the shadows of conventional operations. The naïve describe this as dirty tricks – the unethical, duplicitous or illegal use of mechanisms designed to destroy or diminish the effectiveness of opponents. In order to reduce intelligence operations being compromised, HQ Northern Ireland took greater responsibility from Brigade Intelligence Sections which were consequently reduced in size. 12 Intelligence and Security Company was renamed the Force Intelligence Unit and enlarged to include Operation Crucible Data Base Management, Weapons Intelligence and the SMIU liaison function. With the Soviet Union collapsing, MI5 took more interest in Irish terrorism and advised Mrs Thatcher that if there had been tighter control of police and military intelligence, then the emerging allegations of loose alliances with Loyalist organizations and the necessity for the Stalker investigation could have been avoided. In reality, the extremists had been assembling files on each other from local knowledge, the press and other sources for decades, admittedly not always accurate. Thatcher seems to have been unmoved by the comments, possibly because MI5 had a credibility problem by failing to signal the Trotskyist nature of the Provisionals. The FRU had developed into a powerful force with a good understanding of the culture and aspirations of the terrorists. It and Special Branch had so thoroughly penetrated Northern Command that its Internal Security Department was kept busy plugging the haemorrhaging of information. The methods of interrogations of suspected collaborators, using torture and brutality that lasted several days before a last postcard, and then execution by shooting, their bound and hooded bodies often unceremoniously dumped on some minor road or waste ground, often attached to an IED, put the 1971 accusations of Army interrogation in the shade and yet Amnesty International and *The Sunday Times* editors remained largely silent. Informant handling remained dangerous but it was also open to envy. Through its liaison officer, MI5 knew that the FRU had recruited a senior UDA.

Brian Nelson was born in the Shankill in 1946 and after serving four years in the Black Watch became deeply involved in sectarian violence and had become a respected leader in the Ulster Protestant Volunteer Force. A 42 Commando patrol had rescued a partially sighted Catholic after he had been randomly selected by Nelson and several Loyalists to be tortured in revenge for the murder of the three Army sergeants in Lisburn in March 1973. Sentenced to seven years, Nelson was free by 1977 and used his employment as a carpet-fitter to travel around Belfast collecting information for UDA intelligence. Recruited by the FRU in about 1979, he was also sent to West Germany to work with Army counter-intelligence targeting Irish enclaves until, in 1982, he returned to Belfast and is said to have warned the FRU about the 1984 UFF assassination attempt on Gerry Adams. In 1985, he returned to Germany as a bricklayer. When MI5 asked to meet Nelson, the FRU had no reason to suspect their motives and after a meeting in London he returned to Belfast where, as the UDA intelligence coordinator, he was implicated in the murders of several Catholics claimed by the UFF between 1987 and 1990, including that of Pat Finucane in February 1989. Finucane was a lawyer who had successfully defended Republican offenders. The murder of the parents of the Dungannon IRA commander in their house, displayed military precision except that he was absent from the house, planting a bomb in the town. Nelson is said to have divulged that the UDA intended to latch a limpet mine on the roof of Adams's car in August 1988 while he was travelling to a constituency surgery. By now, the British Government had realized the value of Adams in the search for negotiation.

With the nature of the Loyalist attacks worrying HQ Northern Ireland because they threatened the stuttering steps toward political agreement, in mid-1989, the Brigade Intelligence Sections visited every Army base, sangar, watchtower and permanent OP carrying out a detailed audit of the 'bingo lists' and photo montages but, before a conclusion was reached, on 25 August, the Rathfriland poultry farmer Loughlin Maginn was murdered by four UFF because the UDA believed him to be an IRA liaison officer. When doubts emerged that he was, four days later, in an attempt to prove the accuracy of their targeting, the UDA claimed that he had figured on Security Forces intelligence files. Then on 11 September, when the UDA leaked a montage and the UDR were suspected as the source, Sinn Fein demanded the disbandment of the Regiment alleging proven collusion between the Army and Loyalist paramilitaries. RUC Chief Constable Hugh Annesley, just three months into his appointment, was in a dilemma and accepted the advice of MI5 to demand an inquiry by a mainland police officer to clear the RUC of any complicity in the allegations. This resulted in the recently-appointed Deputy Chief Constable John Stevens of the Cambridgeshire Constabulary being selected to investigate. The containment of terrorism still high intensity, Stalker's investigation a fresh memory, and yet another English police officer about to arrive, Annesley instructed the GOC, Lieutenant General Sir John Waters, and Special Branch, that Stevens should be denied access to Army intelligence operations on the principle of need to know. It was a fateful instruction.

Stevens arrived in September and working in near total isolation quickly had twenty-eight UDR soldiers arrested. Four were later awarded damages for wrongful arrest and six were charged for possession of a firearm and ammunition. His refusal to give Nelson immunity and his probes into Army intelligence operations were rather undermined when the RUC Carrickfergus office, in which his team had stored their files, caught fire in January 1990. The RUC concluded that it was an accident until, in 2003, a former RUC Assistant Chief Constable implicated the FRU. When a witness close to the UDA leadership turned out to be an MI5 informant and Stevens insisted he should be interviewed, arrangements were made that he should not be prosecuted. UDA resentment about the inquiry emerged on 10 February when an RUC patrol came under fire in the Shankill and then later in the month, BBC *Panorama* joined the circus by highlighting that several UDR had been convicted of serious offences; nothing new here. On 9 April, four 3 UDR were killed when a 1,000lbs RCIED landmine wrecked two Land Rovers near Downpatrick in a crater measuring 50 feet long, 40 feet wide and 15 feet deep.

The Stevens Report issued on 17 May was a stinging criticism of the Security Forces and concluded that there had been collusion between Loyalist paramilitaries and a small number of UDR, but it was neither widespread nor institutionalized and the RUC was not involved. When the recommendations led to RUC detectives being given access to their vetting records, many UDR found themselves under investigation. Meanwhile, the Brigade Intelligence Sections concluded that photo montages were a vital intelligence resource, as they had been since the early 1970s, however with the furore surrounding the Report, not surprisingly, at first HQ Northern Ireland disagreed until instructions were issued that they should be locked in frames and be treated as classified documents. Gone were the days when patrols carried montages as an important intelligence aide. The shallow political and media storm that surrounded the Stevens Report forgot that, since 1969, 422 soldiers, 181 UDR, 266 police officers and 1,549 civilians had been killed in a part of the United Kingdom that was only an hour's flight from London. Nine soldiers were killed between the day that Stevens arrived and the day he published his report. Three 3 Para soldiers were killed when their Land Rover was destroyed by a landmine near Mayorbridge, Co. Down in November 1989 and two 1 KOSB died in a bomb, gun and grenade attack on the Derryadd PVCP in Co. Fermanagh in December. In early May 1990, in a HQ 3 Infantry Brigade operation to entice the South Armagh Brigade by using a 1 LI section as a 'tethered goat', 2 Scots Guards laid sixteen ambushes covering the road between Cullyhanna and Silverbridge. But locals reported the troop activity and on 3 May, an ambush near Cullyhanna was raked by two 12.7mm heavy machine guns in rocks near an abandoned building and Lance Sergeant Graham Stewart was fatally wounded. This show of formidable force proved that the South Armagh Brigade could rely on good information. When Private Colin McCullough, a part-time member of 11 UDR and former Royal Irish Ranger, was shot thirteen times in September as he sat in his car with his fiancée in Lurgan, the murder sparked several tit-for-tat murders, some claimed by the Protestant Action Force, which was widely regarded to be the UFF. McCullough's family suffered years of taunting by Republican sympathizers. To the infantry, the removal by death, imprisonment or inactivity of one IRA was still one less to cause casualties.

During the year, the Provisional Army Council authorized proxy bomb attacks using drivers associated with the Security Forces. During the early hours of 24 October, Patsy Gillespie, a Catholic father of three children living in a city in which unemployment was high, was seized from his Londonderry home and forced into a car packed with a 1,000lbs RCIED. Gillespie was a cook employed by the Army and regarded as a collaborator. It was the second time he had been selected as a proxy bomber. Instructed to drive to the Buncranna Road PCVP at Coshquin, the bomb killed Gillespie and a lance corporal and four soldiers from 1 King's. Although many Irish, including those from Ireland, had served in the Province, no Irish units had done so except the 5th Inniskilling Dragoon Guards which arrived on a four month roulement tour in April 1981. It was followed eight years later by the 1st Royal Irish Rangers (R Irish Rangers) who took over as the Roulement Battalion in Lisnaskea and then by the 2nd Battalion in Co. Fermanagh in 1990. Both Battalions recruited from throughout Ireland and had a significant number of Catholics. In a coordinated attack on the same day as the Coshquin attack, the Provisionals kidnapped the two sons of former UDR soldier James McEvoy and told him to deliver a bomb to the Newry PVCP, which was manned by 2 R Irish Rangers, and tell the soldiers they had forty minutes to get clear. At the PVCP, after McEvoy told Ranger Cyril Smith that there was a bomb in his car, Smith ran to warn his colleagues but the bomb exploded, killing him and wounding thirteen others. Smith was posthumously awarded the Queen's Gallantry Medal. In another attack on Lisanelly Barracks, Omagh, the driver was strapped into his car, however the bomb failed to explode. In response to the surge in terrorism, 2 LI, on its twelfth deployment since September 1969, arrived as reinforcement in Operation Derivable and was withdrawn in December when the Provisionals declared their first Christmas ceasefire for fifteen years. Proxy bombs targeted the Rosslea PCVP on 21 December and wrecked the Magherafelt UDR barracks in early February 1991. Even though the brutality of the proxy bombs caused public outrage, it was several months before Northern Command admitted the tactic to be counter productive. Prior to the Coshquin bomb, the Army and the Derry IRA began an experiment to soften their images, which led to increased trust in the community and an easing of the military profile in Londonderry.

By the beginning of the third decade of the troubles, the undermining of Provisionals in Northern Ireland led the Army Council to again transfer the focus of its operations to England in the belief that another campaign would lead to negotiations for the liberation for all Ireland. The previous bombings had produced little except English resilience, however it was well known that the defence of the mainland was uncoordinated and that the economy was vulnerable to disruption and chaos. It is inconceivable that Provisional Sinn Fein negotiators were not fully aware of the strategy.

The English ASUs opened their sixth blitz on 22 September 1989 at 8.27 a.m. when a 15lbs time bomb exploded in the Royal Marines School of Music recreational centre changing room in Deal and destroyed the centre, levelled the adjacent three storey accommodation building and damaged nearby civilian homes. Most of the Royal Marines were rehearsing for a performance at Strasbourg to celebrate the fortieth anniversary of the Council of Europe, however ten were killed in the accommodation building. Kent Ambulance Services discontinued industrial strike action to treat the wounded and those trapped in the rubble. One Royal Marine died on 18 October. When the Provisionals claimed responsibility, declaring that it was part of their campaign to liberate Northern Ireland, many were shocked not only that another band had been targeted but that the security of the barracks was partly provided by an unarmed private security firm, as a cost saving measure imposed by the Ministry of Defence. A week later, the School marched through Deal with gaps in the ranks marking those killed and wounded. A memorial bandstand was later erected at Walmer Green in memory of those who 'only ever wanted to play music'.

During May 1990, Sergeant Charles Chapman, of the Queen's

Regiment, and a colleague had locked up the Army Recruiting Office in Wembley and then checked their Sherpa van, which was parked outside an electronics retailer, for devices. Checking their vehicles was standard practice by military personnel. But when Chapman turned on the ignition, a small bomb exploded, killing him and wounding his colleague.

In June, Private William Davis, of 1 RRW, was shot dead at Lichfield Railway Station while returning from leave and then in July, a large bomb rocked the City of London. Sir Ian Gow MP, no friend of the IRA, died when a bomb exploded under his car in Eastbourne and in September, gunmen seriously wounded Air Chief Marshal Sir Peter Terry in the face by firing through windows in his Staffordshire home. They also injured his wife and caused considerable distress to their daughter. Terry had been Governor of Gibraltar during the SAS attack in 1988.

The Provisional Army Council then instructed the English ASUs to concentrate on bombings and sent two experienced men from Belfast to coordinate an attack on No. 10 Downing Street, a project first conceived before Mrs Thatcher had resigned as Prime Minister in November. During the snowy morning of 7 February 1991, a London ASU, unnoticed by patrolling police officers, parked a Transit van in Whitehall. Inside were three Mark 10 mortars, loaded with projectiles filled with a mix of nitrobenzine and ammonium nitrate. At about 10.45 a.m., the projectiles straddled Downing Street during the weekly Cabinet meeting and smashed several windows in the garden. To some extent, the attack was predictable because, in 1988, an Anti-Terrorist Branch raid on an IRA safe house in London had unearthed details for making mortars, however such was the uncoordinated nature of the national defence, in spite of the wealth of military experience gained in Northern Ireland, that the find was not investigated, as it would have been across the water. Provisional IRA confidence of their ability to operate in England, with relative impunity, grew, and two weeks later bombs in litter bins at three London railway terminals that killed one person and injured fifty-nine reminded the public that the IRA was a force that could bring disruption to the national infrastructure.

In March, when threats were made against an Army motor rally in the Aldershot area, E (Home Service Force) Company, 2 Wessex (V) protected several checkpoints, it being one of the very few times that the Territorial Army was operationally issued with live rounds in the United Kingdom in peacetime. The HSF was raised in 1982 to guard national key points against Soviet attack and consisted largely of former Regular and Reserve Armed Forces, many of whom had served in Cyprus, Aden, Borneo, the Falklands and Northern Ireland. Later in the year during the Gulf War, E Company guarded Marchwood Military Port from terrorist attack and was again issued with live ammunition.

In April 1992, the Provisionals changed tactics by attacking the British economy and reputation of London as a major city with two massive lorry-bombs that shredded the Commercial Union and Baltic Exchange tower blocks and killed three people, injured ninety-nine and caused significant economic damage, quite apart from the incalculable disruption of business and lost records. Some other bomb warnings were telephoned to NHS hospitals, most of which were clearly ill-prepared to deal with such calls.

As the Soviet Union and Warsaw Pact disintegrated, in 1990, not only did the IRA lose its ideological impetus, Secretary of State for Defence Tom King announced a cost-saving exercise being mirrored by most NATO nations, optimistically known as the Peace Dividend and announced Options for Change to cut naval and military manpower by approximately 18 per cent. The BAOR was rebranded British Forces Germany and the Infantry was reduced from fifty-five to thirty-eight battalions. Some regiments experienced their second amalgamation within three decades. Service support, such as the RCT, was assembled into the Royal Logistic Corps, while the Adjutant General's Corps was formed from the RAOC and the remaining small Corps. The WRAC was disbanded and women enlisted, as men did, direct into chosen units and, by June 1993, were authorized to carry weapons. Several defence contracts were cancelled. Saddam Hussein then upset the applecart by invading Kuwait, and once again the Armed Forces were overstretched as military operations commenced in the Middle East.

Fortunately the suggestions in the 1989 Bennett Report that since the UDR had fulfilled its original purpose, and was unlikely to be free of Loyalist subversion, should be disbanded were rejected and, on 1 July 1992, under Options for Change, the Royal Irish Rangers merged with the UDR to form the Royal Irish Regiment, a title that had been lost in 1922. The Regular 1st Battalion became the air landing battalion of 16 Air Assault Brigade while the 2nd Battalion (TA) was the Regimental Reserve based in Northern Ireland with a global deployment role at short notice and the 6,000 UDR formed into the 1st to 6th (Home Service Force) Battalions. Sergeant Robert

Irvine, full time 9 UDR and former RUC, murdered in October at his sister's home in Rasharkin in front of his wife, one of his two children – a daughter – and his sister, was the Regiment's first fatality.

In May 1992, a soldier from 3 Para stepped on a mine near the village of Cappagh and lost both legs. A suspect device was then reported in Coalisland several hours later and, while the Army and RUC were cordoning parts of the town, a platoon was stoned by some youths. The paras followed them into a bar to arrest them and some damage was caused. 3 Para had been involved in several incidents since arriving in March and had been targeted by Nationalists whipping up complaints with the ubiquitous Father Denis Faul claiming that the Parachute Regiment should not be in Northern Ireland, anyway. When Brigadier Tom Langland, who commanded 3 Infantry Brigade, departed to his next posting, this was seen by Faul and others to be associated with the incident. Five days later, there was more trouble in Coalisland when a 1 KOSB patrol was attacked by a mob of youths and a SA-80 and GPMG were stolen and two soldiers hospitalized. If there is an unforgivable military sin, it is the loss of a personal weapon and although the rifle was quickly recovered, the machine gun was not. When reinforcements from 3 Para arrived to help the search, a patrol was attacked by youths outside the Rossmoyne Bar and in another mêlée, the landlord and two others were shot and four others injured. The matter was raised in Dublin and even though the machine gun was not recovered, the re-introduction of 3 Para into the town so soon after 12 May was seen as ill-judged. Nothing was said about the amputee.

After training with the Irish Guards, a strong Blues and Royals Troop reinforced 1 RRF in Fermanagh and at first were based in the hyper-modern base at Rosscor Bridge for several weeks. Four men then joined the Intelligence Section and six were sent to the Operations Company at St Angelo, which was commanded by a dangerous sport enthusiast. The CSM had just spent five years in the SAS, which meant that some of the operations were liable to be unconventional. The remainder was split between two multiples covering west Fermanagh, with those joining the multiple at the former RUC Kesh finding the accommodation a Blues and Royals' officer described as 'disgusting portakabins with twelve men sharing six bunks and twelve drawers'. That it rained almost every day did not help. The men worked a system of twenty-four hours on patrol,

202

covering twenty kilometres, visiting at night people associated with the Security Forces, deploying VCPs and showing a presence, and then twelve hours in base grabbing some sleep and preparing kit for the next patrol. As always, patrols had their adventures. A 'brick' dropped at night by helicopter leapt fifteen feet into the darkness, as opposed to the expected six inches. One patrol was attacked by a badger and another unknowingly crept past a donkey one dark night until it let loose a series of eee-orrs. A shot fired at another patrol was not met with moving 'hard, fast and aggressively' as the pre-deployment training required, but by the patrol commander, believing it was an accidental discharge, spinning around and asking 'Who was that, then?'

In June, BBC *Panorama* suggested that Brian Nelson had been involved in ten murders, attempted murders or conspiracies to murder, and that the FRU had failed to pass the information to the RUC. Stevens began his second inquiry in 1993. As the net closed around him, Nelson shared information with him in the hope that he would be granted immunity, however the Director of Public Prosecutions pressed hard and despite mitigation from a senior Army intelligence officer that his information had saved about 200 lives, in September Nelson was sentenced to ten years in prison in England on five counts of conspiracy to murder, one possession of firearms with intent and eleven counts of possession of Security Forces' documents. Stevens, his experience in Northern Ireland limited to a few weeks, concluded that Nelson had saved two lives. It was another nail in the Army's influence in intelligence gathering and so it was that MI5 took control of intelligence in Northern Ireland. Since the police had primacy, Special Branch led counterintelligence operations. Increased bureaucracy, enforced through the need to know principle, led to the collapse of inter-agency relationships that had existed for two decades. The new regime was quickly exposed when the relocation and development of new identities for several supergrasses was mismanaged and those responsible failed to work with the Department of Social Security, as had been practised by the RUC.

Shortly before being released from prison in Dublin, Patrick Magee was served with an extradition warrant to return to Northern Ireland to serve his sentence for the murder of Captain Westmacott. Jumping bail, he fled to England and joined a north-east ASU where, on 7 June, he and Michael O'Brien were stopped on the A64 between York and Tadcaster by two police officers. When they became suspicious and called for back-up, Magee shot Special Constable Glenn

Goodman dead and wounded PC Kelly four times. The two Irishmen were followed to Burton Salmon where they opened fire on pursuing police cars until members of the public arrived, and they managed to escape. Trapped four days later in a culvert, during a massive manhunt, they were found to be in possession of two handguns and a sawn-off AK-47 rifle.

In March 1993, Magee was sentenced to life for the murder of Goodman and the attempted murder of three police officers. On 9 September 1994, he and five other prisoners, including Danny McNamee, the radio control expert from Crossmaglen, escaped from HM Prison Whitemoor by scaling the prison walls using knotted sheets and shooting a prison officer with one of two revolvers smuggled into the prison. All five were captured within minutes. During the trial for the escape, lawyers argued that an *Evening Standard* article, describing Magee and two defendants as 'terrorists', was contrary to an order made at the start preventing disclosure of their background and convictions and the judge had no alternative but to dismiss the case. Objecting to the glass screens that separated prisoners from visitors in Belmarsh Prison, Magee staged a 'dirty protest' for two years and refused to see his wife and five children, prompting Sinn Fein to accuse the British government of maintaining a regime that 'is damaging physically and psychologically'. In 1998, Magee was repatriated to Ireland to serve the remainder of his sentence in Portlaoise Prison with Liam Quinn and the Balcombe Street Gang and was released the following year under the terms of the Good Friday Agreement. The Criminal Cases Review Commission overturned McNamee's conviction because the fingerprints of another IRA bomber were also on the circuits, a fact not raised at his trial, and he was also released under the Good Friday Agreement. The Commission pointedly did not suggest that McNamee was innocent of the conspiracy charge. Although re-arrested in 2000 on an outstanding extradition warrant, Magee did not return to Northern Ireland until a Royal Prerogative allowed him to do so without fear of prosecution.

On Saturday 23 October 1993, when the Provisionals heard that several senior UFF were scheduled to meet in a room above Frizzel's Fish and Chip Shop on the Shankill Road, two inexperienced Provisionals, Thomas Begley and Sean Kelly dressed as deliverymen, entered the crowded shop late in the afternoon. Underneath the napkin on their tray was a bomb, which exploded prematurely before a warning could be given. As the building collapsed and customers were crushed in the rubble, ten people were killed, including Begley and John Frizzell and his daughter. Fifty-seven were injured. The Loyalist meeting, which included the UFF leader, Johnny 'Mad Dog' Adair, did not take place. Although the bombing was widely condemned, the UFF retaliated over the next week by murdering twelve Catholics, including six, and a Protestant, in the attack on the Rising Star bar in Greysteel in which a gunman had shouted 'Trick or treat!' before opening fire. Thirteen people were injured. With twenty-seven deaths, October 1993 was the worst month for casualties since 1978. During the funeral of Begley, at which Gerry Adams was criticized for being a pall bearer, a 9/12th Lancers Troop was posted outside his house to prevent Loyalists interfering with the cortège. Trooper Andrew Clarke was in a Land Rover when he suddenly opened fire, wounding Eddie Copeland from the Ardoyne. Clarke was sentenced at Belfast Crown Court in February 1995 to ten years for the attempted murder of Copeland and his colleagues were criticized for not disarming him. They had no idea that he was about to open fire with an automatic rifle. Why Clarke should do so remains something of a mystery; he had, however, seen the carnage of the Shankill bomb. In December 1996, Copeland received £60,000 for injuries received in a Loyalist car bomb and three years later was awarded £27,500 compensation for injuries received when Clarke opened fire. In 2001, he was refused bail on charges of kidnapping, false imprisonment, assault and threatening to kill.

If there was one element of Operation Banner in which the Provisionals scored a significant psychological victory, it was the South Armagh Sniper. When, in March 1990, the damaged helmet of a Light Infantry soldier was examined, it was thought that a Barrett was responsible and so was born the myth of the South Armagh Sniper. The M82 Barrett Light semi-automatic heavy sniper rifle was accurate up to 2,000 yards when stabilized and was a truly powerful weapon that fired the same ammunition as the M2 .50 Browning machine gun from an eleven round magazine; however it weighed 32lbs. After smuggling probably two upgraded Barretts from the US, the Provisionals appeared to have carried out eight snipes at decreasing ranges, all of which ended in misses and then, on 28 August 1992, the Borucki OP reported a known player loitering outside the Northern Bank in Crossmaglen. However, the information arrived too late for a 2 LI patrol passing the bank and Private Paul Turner, aged 18 years, was killed by a .50-inch bullet. It seems likely the loiterer was helping the gunman to adjust his sights. The Battalion was on its fourteenth tour since 1969. Lance Corporal Lawrence Dickson, of 1 Royal Scots, was killed in Forkhill on 17 March 1993 by a 7.62mm bullet while pursuing a man apparently running from a patrol on Bog Road, Forkhill. Private John Randall, 1 DERR and aged 19 years, was killed crossing a field near the Tullyvallen River not far from Newtownhamilton on 26 June when a .50-inch bullet damaged his Light Support Weapon and drove lethal debris into his body. This Barrett was later seized in Belfast. Lance Corporal Kevin Pullen, also 1 DERR, was killed on Carran Road, Crossmaglen on 17 July soon after checking a known player at a VCP. Reserve Constable Brian Woods was then shot dead on 2 November at Newry. A month later, Lance Bombardier Paul Garrett was killed in Keady. Even though the Sniper missed the large target of HMS *Cygnet* in Carlingford Lough, albeit at long range, a competent sniper was clearly at large, but systematic surveillance in South Armagh of several high profile terrorists had little impact. On 30 December, a week after charges, laid against Lance Corporal Elkington and Marine Callaghan of 45 Commando, were dropped for the murder of Sinn Fein councillor Fergal Caraher and the attempted murder of his brother, Michael, at a VCP outside the Lite 'N Easy Pub in Cullyhanna because a third Royal Marine had been hit by their car, the 6 foot 6 inch Grenadier Guardsman Daniel Blinco, aged 22 years, was shot dead outside Murtagh's Bar in Crossmaglen.

The locals were not slow to taunt patrols that the gunman had been given the nicknames of Goldfinger or Terminator in the bars of Crossmaglen. Editorial gullibility enhanced the myth with claims that he had been trained in America. A poem entitled *The Armagh Sniper* and the erection of 'Sniper at Work' road signs in Crossmaglen and such places as the Silverbridge Crossroads, raised the psychological bar. The snipings led to the greater use of helicopters and operations focused on hunting for the Barrett. When intelligence indicated that the sniper was active, Operation Poacher was activated, instructing that military and police patrols take hard cover from probable firing positions to the south. Body armour weighing 32lbs and costing £4,000 was issued to PCVPs and patrols. Heavy and awkward, troops found it difficult to move aggressively and fast. Although anxious every time they left their bases, soldiers had a sneaking admiration for the skill of the Sniper. While military snipers spend weeks learning the art of stalking and sniping, the South Armagh Sniper was a terrorist with few opportunities to train and zero the weapon and at risk of compromise, betrayal and perhaps death every time he squeezed the trigger. Every operation had to be meticulously planned with approach routes cleared to a position concealed from the watchtowers so that when the sniper arrived at the firing point, he was sufficiently cool and calm to peer through the scope, select the target, fire a shot and withdraw quickly along protected routes. The risk increased when the sniper reduced the range to 250 metres, because of the lack of success, and came within range of patrol Light Support Weapons and the likelihood of being spotted by a helicopter.

Provisional operations in England began to be characterized by switching targets, disposing of bomb-making equipment and weapons in caches throughout England until required, and using English-based sympathizers to assist experts sent from Northern Ireland. Few were bound to the strictures of the Green Book and while most had connections with Irish Republicanism, some were reliable, others were less so under operational conditions. During the attack on the Longford Gas Terminal at Warrington on the night of 26 February 1993 by a Nottinghamshire ASU, PC Mark Stoker was alert enough to note that the driver of a battered Mazda van near the terminal appeared to be drunk. Stoker confirmed that Denis Kinsella was the driver but when his suspicions were aroused by two men in the back, one of them, Pairic MacFhloinn, shot Stoker three times with the pistol at close range. The police officer, however, was able to report the incident. The three Provisionals then hijacked a car and locked the driver in the boot but abandoned it after it ran out of petrol on the M62 when he managed to disconnect the petrol gauge wire. The three were quickly arrested by police. A gas tank was damaged by an explosion next day. Public protests in England and Ireland after two small bombs exploded in Bridge Street, Warrington on 20 March gave London and Dublin impetus to find a solution. The attack is chiefly remembered for the deaths of Tim Parry and Johnathan Ball, aged 12 and 3 years respectively. Five days later, Queen Elizabeth II visited Northern Ireland but, when Irish President Mary Robinson visited Belfast on 18 June and met Gerry Adams, now President of Sinn Fein, the Unionist Belfast City Council barred her from visiting any council property, including City Hall. The Provisionals exploded five Semtex time bombs in London on 4

October causing massive disruption during the early morning rush hour.

For years, the Secret Intelligence Service officer Michael Oatley had maintained links with the Provisional leadership through the Londonderry businessman Brendan Duddy. In November 1991, he was attending a retirement farewell dinner with Duddy when Martin McGuinness arrived to discuss options for negotiations with London. Like Gerry Adams, McGuiness had become a Sinn Fein politician. On the 28th, the *Observer* claimed that Sinn Fein had sent the message, 'The conflict is over but we need your advice on how to bring it to a close. We wish to have an unannounced ceasefire in order to hold dialogue leading to peace.' With Prime Minister Major insisting that he would not engage in diplomacy that would lead to a united Ireland, on 15 December 1993, he and Taoiseach Albert Reynolds issued the Downing Street Joint Declaration on Peace upholding the right of Northern Ireland to foster a new political framework founded on consent and encompassing arrangements within Northern Ireland, for the whole island and between UK and all Ireland – the Irish Dimension. The parties linked with paramilitaries were invited to negotiate – provided they abandoned violence.

Amid informal and formal meetings between London, Dublin and Provisional Sinn Fein, during which emerging factors were the decommissioning of IRA weapons and heightened security after the 1990 Gulf War, the Provisionals continued to apply pressure to demonstrate that they could attack targets in England at will. From a plan developed in 1993 and, after coded warnings, during the early evening of 9 March 1994, three projectiles fired from an array of Mark 15 Barrackbusters fitted into a stolen Nissan Micra hit the northern runway of Heathrow Airport but failed to explode. Two days later, the Heathrow authorities again evacuated passengers and staff from Terminal Four and closed the southern runway after four projectiles landed but again failed to explode. The two failures led to speculation that the projectiles had been specifically designed not to explode but this does not compute because the warheads were filled with explosive. A third attack three days later again proved just how feeble the protective security of Heathrow was. Coded telephone warnings sent to three news organizations in the early morning led to the closure of the southern runway and when flights were about to resume about ninety minutes later, three projectiles landed near several parked aircraft and a fourth hit the Terminal 4 roof leading to its evacuation. It was reopened after lunch. Two coded warnings of more devices telephoned to Sky News during the early evening led to Heathrow and Gatwick closing. Terminal 4 was again sealed and thousands of passengers moved to secure areas. While the perimeters of both airports were inspected, outbound aircraft were checked and passengers and visitors leaving for car parks, and catching buses and taxis, were ushered inside the terminal buildings. Gatwick Railway Station was closed. At Heathrow, some passengers were confined to their aircraft to prevent overcrowding in the terminals and incoming flights were diverted from Heathrow and Gatwick to Stansted, Luton, Manchester, Bristol, Cardiff and Birmingham. Heathrow eventually reopened at 9.30 p.m. and Gatwick half an hour later.

The attacks took place in a period of intense pressure on the Sinn Fein leadership and seem to have been a demonstration to reassure the Provisional rank and file. Metropolitan Police Commissioner Paul Condon called the 'scares' a cynical attempt to frighten passengers, cause confusion and part of the Provisional strategy to remind the negotiators not to squander opportunities for peace. Stating that there was no prospect of the Army patrolling Heathrow, the police nevertheless asked for mine detectors and thermal imaging equipment after it emerged that the third array of projectiles had been fired, probably by timing devices, from a camouflaged mortar pit in scrubland bordering the south-west perimeter in an area that had previously been searched. Five weeks later, a huge lorry bomb in Bishopsgate struck at the financial centre of London. On the same day, two London taxi drivers, forced to deliver proxy car bombs to Downing Street and New Scotland Yard, shouted warnings and abandoned their cars. The ring of steel of roadblocks, CCTV and identity checks protecting the city were, in some respects, the first steps of a seeping deprivation of basic civil liberties in the United Kingdom, such as freedom from suspicion and freedom of movement. The Provisional Army Council then moved its centre of operations to the north-east when a north-east ASU attacked three Esso gas holders at Gateshead and demonstrated that it could access a key point without interruption and could strike anywhere in England. The one organization trained to protect key points, the HSF, had been disbanded the previous year.

In 1994, Northern Ireland had the usual sectarian bombings, shootings and punishment beatings and attacks. Constable William Beacom was killed and two officers were injured in February when their Land Rover was hit by a RPG-7 projectile in the Markets area of Belfast. RUC Beragh was badly damaged by mortars, as was the village from overshoots. In March, a Mark 15 'Barrackbuster' 150lbs gas container projectile, fired from a tube in a tractor bucket, in a farmyard 150 yards from RUC Crossmaglen, damaged the tail of a Lynx helicopter as it was landing with supplies. A three day ceasefire called by the IRA for 6 April in recognition of the visit by Prime Minister Major ended with attacks on military and police patrols at Aughnacloy and in Belfast. The only British soldier to be killed in action during the year was 27 year old Lance Corporal David Wilson, of the Royal Logistic Corps, when the Keady PVCP on the road to Castleblaney was blasted by a bomb on 14 May. On 9 August, Corporal Trelford Withers, a part-time soldier with 8 (Home Service Force) Royal Irish Regiment, shot in his shop at Crossgar, was the last member of the Royal Irish Regiment to be killed during Operation Banner.

At a special Sinn Fein convention Adams suggested that the Downing Street Declaration offered opportunities to resolve the conflict in Ireland and a week later, on 1 September 1993, Provisional Sinn Fein announced the cessation of military operations to allow the political process to find a solution. Three weeks later, the ban on Sinn Fein broadcasting on public service radio stations, imposed in October 1988, was lifted and several border roads were re-opened. Five days later, the Combined Loyalist Military Command representing Loyalist paramilitary groups also declared a ceasefire.

Chapter 15

Phase Six: The End
1994 – 2007

On 28 November 1994, Dublin and London issued a communiqué agreeing to a twin-track process on decommissioning and all-party negotiations by the end of February 1996, but deadlock followed as the Provisional Sinn Fein refused to consider disarming because they had not surrendered and there was no commitment for the Army to disarm. When, in February 1995, London and Dublin launched the Frameworks for Accountable Government, proposing a single-chamber assembly elected by proportional representation, and Agreement addressing North/South institutions, Unionist politicians denounced them as routes to unification with Ireland. President Clinton undertook to establish independent observers on decommissioning and appointed the former Senator George Mitchell to lead this body. Two days later, Clinton paid the first of three visits to Northern Ireland but when he then invited Gerry Adams to the St Patrick's Day White House reception, it infuriated Prime Minister Major because he believed that Adams would be seen on the Washington circuit as the plucky resistance fighter who had spent most of his adult life either hiding from British patrols or in prison. The Queen paid her second visit to Belfast and was followed by Prince Charles on a two-day visit to Ireland, the first official visit by a member of the Royal Family since 1922. Inward investment began to re-appear.

Apart from South Armagh, internal security in Northern Ireland was progressively relaxed with soldiers wearing berets and discarding flak jackets. Daylight patrols in Belfast ended on 17 January 1995 and were followed six weeks later by the withdrawal of patrols in east Belfast and the city centre. Three weeks later all patrols in

Belfast were suspended. There was one entirely predictable flash-point – the Loyalist marching season. Within a day of landing at Aldergrove, a Life Guards detachment attached to Right Flank, 1 Scots Guards, was occupying a chilly, soaking trench because the Battalion Intelligence Section believed two bombs were being smuggled across the border. Several days later, before the Orange Order parade on 11 July, the Scots Guards deployed to Drumcree Church where Royal Engineers had dug a 7-foot ditch protected by

DRUMCREE CHURCH

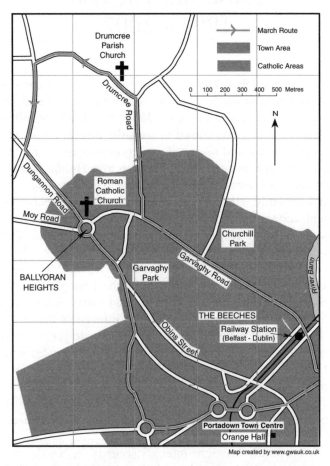

Map created by www.gwauk.co.uk

barbed wire, then a 25-foot gap and more barbed wire entangle-ments behind which stood 1,000 RUC and several hundred soldiers. For the first two days, the parade was a relaxed carnival of hot dog stands and bands entertaining the 10,000 Loyalists, until the atmosphere changed when thousands arrived from Belfast, bringing the total to about 25,000 people, all angry at the weakness of their leaders defending their cause. A Life Guard described the scene as being reminiscent of the film *Zulu* as, for the next eight hours until dawn the next day, protesters charged the fence and hurled bottles, stones, rocks and fireworks at the barricades. Eventually on 11 July, 500 members of the Orange Order were permitted to march along the Catholic Garvaghy Road but without bands; a decision that was greeted with ill-feeling among the residents.

When rogue elements and paramilitaries from both factions moved into the drugs trade, several murders were claimed by Direct Action Against Drugs (DAAD), a pseudonym used by the IRA. In December, the RUC released figures showing that in the fourteen months since the ceasefire, there had been 148 Republican and seventy-five Loyalist 'punishment' beatings compared with eight Republicans and thirteen Loyalist beatings before the ceasefire. South of the border in early April, the Gardai arrested four men from Northern Ireland near Balbriggan, Co. Dublin, in possession of twenty handguns, six rifles and 2,500 rounds of ammunition. In the same month, RUC officers found forty weapons and hundreds of rounds in a UVF cache near Holywood, Co. Down, and more material in the town after the arrest of three men. Between 1985 and 1993, the Garda and the Irish Army had seized over 800 firearms, including 12.7mm heavy machine guns, and 300,000 rounds of ammunition.

On 22 January 1996, Senator Mitchell established the rules for the peace negotiations:

1. Negotiate to resolve political issues.
2. Agree total disarmament of all paramilitary organizations.
3. Agree that disarmament must be verified by an independent commission.
4. Paramilitary leadership to oppose the use of, and threatening, force to influence the outcome of all-party negotiations.
5. Agree to abide by the terms of any agreement reached and to resort to democratic and peaceful methods to alter aspects of that outcome with which they may disagree.
6. Stop 'punishment' killings and beatings to take effective steps to prevent such actions.

Known as the Mitchell Principles, they were welcomed by Sinn Fein and rejected by the Reverend Paisley's Democratic Unionist Party

(DUP), which held the Loyalist majority. However Adams had a problem. Unlike a democracy in which armed forces are answerable to the executive, he was in the hands of an undemocratic military council that answered to no one. The Loyalists were in the hands of their history. In February, Provisional Sinn Fein ended its ceasefire by accusing Prime Minister Major and the Unionists of squandering an opportunity to end the troubles by refusing to negotiate with them, a view not rejected by Taoiseach Reynolds. Major's problem was that he had lost his Parliamentary majority and, although dependent on the Unionists, he had intended to meet Sinn Fein at Downing Street for the first time. Nevertheless within the hour, the Provisionals exploded a massive lorry bomb that wrecked offices in Canary Wharf and killed two and injured 100. Again, it is inconceivable that the Sinn Fein negotiators were not aware of the plot. Negotiations recommenced. The blitz in London ceased a week later when Edward O'Brien 'scored an own goal' on a bus in Aldwych, injuring eight others.

London and Dublin set 10 June for all-party talks to discuss the Mitchell Principles, however continued terrorism in Northern Ireland led to Sinn Fein being barred, a decision that was reinforced when Gardai Detective Constable Jerry McCabe was murdered during an IRA post office robbery in Co. Limerick. Four days later, the Northern Ireland Assembly met for the first time – minus Sinn Fein. Next day, the Provisionals emphasized their anger by exploding a bomb in the Arndale Centre in Manchester that injured over 200 people and caused damages costing over £150 million. Adams's suggestion that the attack was not linked to the conflict in Ireland was derided as nonsense. When the Gardai then found a Provisional bomb factory a week later, Dublin ended all contact with Sinn Fein, thereby isolating Adams, who was now under pressure from opponents of the ceasefire from within the Republican movement.

When a car bomb injured seventeen people in Enniskillen in July, it was claimed by the dissident Continuity IRA. Provisional commitment to the peace process was tested on 7 October when two 800lbs bombs, embarrassingly smuggled into Thiepval Barracks, Lisburn in two Volvos by a Northern Command dissident unit spearheading the resumption of terrorism, injured thirty-one people. Warrant Officer One James Bradwell of the REME died of horrific wounds four days later. The second device was designed to catch medics treating the wounded from the first bomb. The devices coincided with the start of the Conservative Party conference in Bournemouth and were the first attacks against the Security Forces since the ceasefire on 31 August 1994. In November, the Provisionals held a tense extraordinary Convention in which Gerry Adams was heavily criticized for signing up to the ceasefire and then near the end, his close friend Brian Keenan, who had been released from prison two years earlier, switched sides, thus allowing Adams to emerge badly bruised but with his political aspirations intact.

The ceasefire had permitted the Security Forces to analyse the South Armagh Sniper. Between May 1990 and 26 June 1993, there had been twelve attacks resulting in nine Security Forces killed, seven of them in 1993, and one wounded. One Barrett had been seized in Belfast and a second was at large in South Armagh. 14 Intelligence Company surveillance operations on selected Provisionals in the general area of Crossmaglen, had been underway since November. A hard fact of military life is that sometimes the enemy must be tempted with the 'tethered goat' strategy.

In mid-January 1997 in Crossmaglen, a Mazda 323 became of interest because it had been identified in the area of some sniper attacks. When it was then associated with a suspect terrorist base at a farm on Cregganduff Road, it was fitted with a surveillance device. In early February, information was emerging that the Provisionals were planning an attack using the car but what, where and when remained unknown. At about 6.25 p.m. on 12 February, a 3 RHA patrol was manning the Green Road PVCP south of Bessbrook Mill. The Regiment was on its sixth deployment since September 1969. Just as Lance Bombardier Stephen Restorick was returning her driving licence to Lorraine McElroy, a .50-inch bullet fired from the direction of Green Lane smashed his SA-80 and hurled scraps of metal into his body. Slightly injured and in shock, Lorraine comforted the dying gunner until he was taken to hospital where he later died. Because she failed to condone the killing and also sent a wreath to the soldier's funeral, such was the intimidation against Lorraine, a cousin of Donna Maguire, that she was forced to leave her home.

The shooting came as something of a surprise because of the 14 Intelligence Company operation. Although the SAS Troop was angry that it had been refused permission to carry out a close target recce on the car on the 12th and believed it should have been more intently targeted, the evidence connecting the Mazda to the shooting was circumstantial. Nevertheless on the day of the shooting, it had been tracked from Cullyhanna to Bessbrook where it had remained static

215

for about an hour. When the SAS covertly filmed the car in the Cregganduff Road farm early on the 14th and images showed a gun port had been carved in the boot, intelligence concluded that it had probably been involved in the shooting. Constable Ronnie Galway then almost lost his leg on 29 March when a .50-inch bullet was fired from a house in which a family was being held hostage, just as he left RUC Forkhill with 1 Welsh Guards on their first patrol. Orders were issued to intercept the Mazda and arrest the occupants but such were the restraints on the Security Forces in the mid-1990s that the following criteria were applied: 1. The arrest must be away from houses. 2. Take place when the car was stationary. and 3. while it was under surveillance. These proved difficult and then on 10 April, the jigsaw fell into place and eight SAS stormed the farm in a Transit and during a short scuffle arrested four Provisionals, including Michael Caraher. Next day, search teams found the Barrett and an AK-47 concealed in a secret compartment of a pig trailer. The Barrett was identified as having been used only during the murder of Lance Bombardier Restorick and wounding of Constable Galway. The sniper team was sentenced to a total of 640 years.

The entire operation was a far cry from the 1980s of Loughgall and Gibraltar when the IRA knew that if they encountered the SAS, it was usually fatal. As the myth of the South Armagh Sniper unravelled, the truth was banal. Two ASUs were involved and although two Barretts had been used, so had a 7.62mm rifle. The Mazda had been used as a firing platform with the sniper firing through the gun port. The use of a car meant that the sniper team could leave the scene quickly without depositing major forensic traces.

When the *Sunday Times* suggested that Lance Bombardier Restorick had been sacrificed to protect 'a spy', an investigation by the Police Ombudsman proved the claim to be unfounded. Although Restorick was the last soldier to be killed as a direct result of enemy action on Operation Banner, two others were killed after him. A month later, Private Andrew Richardson of 3 LI was one of two soldiers in the rear of two armoured Land Rovers patrolling in Belfast. Soon after the patrol commander had been warned that the rear one was to be ambushed with a RPG-7, a car pulled in between the two Rovers and slowed down. The commander of the second Rover instructed his driver to overtake the car but, in avoiding the weaving car, the driver hit the central reservation at a roundabout and the Rover flipped over several times, killing Richardson who was riding top cover. Two years later Private Gary Fenton, of 1st

Royal Gloucestershire, Berkshire and Wiltshire Regiment was run over when he tried to stop a tanker, believed to be smuggling fuel, breaching a VCP near Crossmaglen and crossing the border. The deaths of both these soldiers occurred in the middle of the Peace Process.

As Tony Blair swept to power in June 1997, Sinn Fein increased its vote and sent Gerry Adams and Martin McGuiness to Westminster. Six days later, a coalition that included Fianna Fail won the Irish General Election. Just over three weeks later, Westminster and Dublin gave Sinn Fein five weeks to call an unequivocal ceasefire and rejoin the talks. The Loyalists rejected the North Report of the Independent Review of Parades and Marches, published in January, as erosion of their right of assembly but agreed to reroute seven marches in 1997. When the Provisional Army Council agreed to a ceasefire with Secretary of State for Northern Ireland, Mo Mowlam, on 20 July, Sinn Fein accepted the Mitchell Principles and also admitted to internal ideological disagreements over the ceasefire. The shallowness of the influence claimed by Sinn Fein emerged when factions supporting Adams in Northern Command supported the Mitchell Principles while dissidents in Southern Command led by Quartermaster-General Michael McKevitt and his common-law wife and fellow Executive member, Bernadette Sands-McKevitt, widow of Bobby Sands, rejected them. Styling themselves the Real IRA, the dissidents also aimed to achieve a united Ireland by driving the British from Northern Ireland. The nomenclature had entered common usage when dissidents manning an illegal roadblock near Jonesborough told motorists, 'We're from the IRA, the real IRA'. As became a feature of the Real IRA, the inaccuracy of warning about a car bomb in Banbridge on 1 August led to the RUC having insufficient time to clear the danger zone and thirty-five people were injured. With the Provisionals no longer at war, the Real IRA, the Continuity IRA and INLA then collaborated in a grouping generally known as the Dissident IRA, with a terrorist campaign largely confined to Co. Armagh beginning with a van bomb attack on RUC Markethill in September.

By early 1998, the talks were beginning to show results, particularly as London and Dublin agreed to bar Sinn Fein and the Unionists if progress was not made. After the inevitable procrastination, at 5.36 p.m. on Good Friday 10 April 1998, Mitchell declared: 'I am pleased to announce that the two governments and the political parties in

217

Northern Ireland have reached agreement.' It later emerged that President Clinton had lent on the party leaders to agree that:

The future of Northern Ireland be democratically determined.

The people could choose to identify themselves as Irish or British, or both, and would not be affected by the status of Northern Ireland.

An Assembly, an Executive and a cross-border Ministerial Council would develop cross-border cooperation.

Ireland would abolish Article 2 and 3 of its Constitutional territorial claim to Northern Ireland. This was overwhelmingly agreed by a referendum in the South.

Normalization of security measures by the closure of British Army bases and decommissioning of paramilitary weapons.

Lord Patten to recommend reforms to the RUC.

Prisoner of war releases are a facet of modern peace talks but, with Northern Ireland, most were convicted criminals. Those sentenced to five years or more became eligible for release after serving a third of their sentence and those serving life were to complete terms comparable to a prisoner not sentenced to terrorist-related crimes minus one-third. The Dissident IRA and the Loyalist Red Hand Defenders and Orange Volunteers were ineligible because they had not agreed to the ceasefire. The public in England, subjected to thirty years of violence, and the families of killed and wounded Service personnel had a hard time accepting the early releases of criminals. The Security Forces believed some would return to paramilitary activities, because they knew nothing else.

By 30 June, 426 prisoners had been freed, many of them high profile terrorists, including the killers of Lance Bombardier Restorick. Guardsmen Wright and Fisher and Trooper Clarke were released amid hypocritical hysterical protests by the US and Irish Governments and widespread unrest in Nationalist estates. Private Clegg was not released. Dignified in her grieving, Rita, the mother of Stephen Restorick commented:

It is so painful to see these people released from prison after doing very short sentences after doing horrible crimes, whether it is shooting somebody or placing a bomb…At the moment we, as victims' families, are being asked to give everything. We are seeing people found guilty of our loved ones' murders walk free. It is time the paramilitaries gave that little bit towards decommissioning.

A referendum in Northern Ireland on the Agreement was agreed, nevertheless difficulties would arise over the next nine years during which the Army, still about 10,000 strong, was largely a bystander. 321 EOD was kept busy defusing grenades known as pipe bombs. Some hardline Nationalist areas were still No Go areas to RUC patrols. During the annual Orange Order disturbances at Drumcree Church, Constable Frank O'Reilly was hit on the head by a homemade grenade claimed by the splinter Red Hand Defenders and died on 5 September. He was the last RUC officer to die. The first RUC officer to be killed, Constable Victor Arbuckle, had also been killed by Loyalists.

Meanwhile the Dissident IRA combined to carry out the worst atrocity of The Troubles. The Continuity IRA selected Omagh Courthouse as the target, INLA stole a Vauxhall Cavalier in Carrickmancross in Co. Monaghan and fitted it with false Northern Ireland number plates and the Real IRA provided the personnel, bomb and the codeword. Early during the afternoon of 15 August, two Real IRA, unable to park the Cavalier outside the Courthouse, dumped it 400 metres away outside a draper's shop on Market Street. When the RUC analysed the codeword warnings from Ulster Television and the Coleraine Samaritans, of a bomb at the Courthouse, the RUC evacuated the street, straight towards the car. When the Cavalier exploded, twenty-eight people were killed, including a woman expecting twins and several Spanish tourists on a day trip from Co. Donegal. Two hundred and twenty people were injured. It was an atrocity which Prime Minister Blair described as an 'appalling act of savagery and evil'. In apologizing on 14 December, the Real IRA released a statement admitting 'minimal involvement' and when its spokesman suggested that two MI5 agents were responsible, the claim severely damaged the credibility of the IRA. Such was the outrage that the Dissident IRA declared a ceasefire. The bombing remains controversial. RUC Chief Constable Flanagan was forced to remind Nuala O'Loan, the newly instituted Police Ombudsman, that his officers had guided the public toward the bomb because they had received inaccurate information. The search for the bombers continues, with suspects arrested and released and others being sued by relatives of the victims. An inquiry in BBC Panorama suggesting that mobile phone intercepts collected by the Government Communications Headquarters were not passed to the RUC appear unfounded. Not for the first time in Northern Ireland, the Corporation investigations were weak.

Despite the ceasefire, which had seen Army patrols reduced by about a third, the Republican factions still had the capability to resume their campaign. In order for battalions to maintain a high level of readiness, an internal security virtual reality simulator known as Invertron was introduced at the Ballykinler Training Centre. Facing a large screen showing hardline Nationalist enclaves in Belfast, the Directing Staff could simulate urban street noises and gunfire and introduce riots and ambushes, in order to test command and control systems.

The Assembly started confidently enough but was suspended because of Unionist anger at the refusal of the Provisionals to decommission their weapons openly, and the level of sectarian feuding. As the twenty-first century emerged and politicians struggled to reach agreement amid sectarian pressures, in June 2000, tension in the narrow streets of the Ardoyne exploded when Catholics took every opportunity to gain more space by attacking Protestants living in their neighbouring neat streets of 1930s suburban houses and 1960s builds. In December, a Protestant taxi driver was murdered as he waited for a bogus fare which led to the UFF retaliating by shooting a Catholic. Tension between Catholic parents from the Holy Cross Girls Primary School with the Glybryn residents then erupted in June 2001.

While Protestants were erecting decorations for the Loyalist marching season, a car raced out of the Ardoyne and rammed the ladder being used by a man nailing a flag to a lamp post and was followed by a gang who stabbed the man with screwdrivers. When a riot developed with petrol and blast bombs, stones and missiles hurtling between the two groups, the Belfast Resident Battalion, 1 Argyll and Sutherland Highlanders reinforced by the 1 Royal Irish Regiment Operations Company was sent to the area. The Irish soldiers who lived locally recognized that some 'concerned parents' were Provisional, UDA and UFF suspects yet to sire children. The Irish battalion, on its second roulement tour, was commanded by the charismatic Lieutenant Colonel Tim Collins and based in Dungannon. For riot control, gone were steel helmets and flak jackets over Heavy Duty sweaters and in were cotton combat dress, body armour, shin and arm protective pads, a fireproof face mask and helmets and 6 feet long clear shields. Dressing and squeezing into Saxons was exhausting before the soldiers even arrived at the disturbance. The basic riot unit was now built around the 'brick' with one man equipped with a fire extinguisher behind his three colleagues ready to douse flames. When HQ Northern Ireland ordered that masks were not to be worn unless there was rioting, Collins refused to obey, in order to protect the identity of his soldiers. As the international media gathered to witness the confrontation, the RUC arranged for the terrified Catholic schoolgirls to pass through another school to the Holy Cross. On 20 June, the RUC fired new L21 plastic baton rounds. Intimidation stopped when term ended nine days later but resumed on 3 September at the beginning of term with troops giving the children clear passage. Next day, fifteen blast and 250 petrol bombs were thrown and forty-one RUC and two soldiers were injured. In retaliation, Loyalists, claiming to represent the Red Hand Defenders, caused an immediate panic when a blast bomb was thrown at the children and their parents. The disturbances continued almost daily until 23 November when Father Aiden Troy and the Reverend Stewart Heaney brokered an agreement.

Simmering faction fighting between the Provisionals and Real IRA exploded into terrorism when the Real IRA reneged on their ceasefire and attacked England. On 1 June 2000, the 32lbs Semtex bomb that caused some damage to Hammersmith Bridge was the largest high-explosive device planted on the British mainland. Fortunately, only the detonator went off saving possibly hundreds of lives. In August, bomb disposal officers performed two controlled explosions on a device on the train line near Ealing Broadway underground station. A month later, the Real IRA had the audacity to fire a RPG-7 projectile across the River Thames at the Secret Intelligence Service headquarters in Vauxhall Cross causing some damage. And then, in March 2001 a small car bomb, exploding outside the BBC Television Centre in West London, possibly in retaliation for BBC *Panorama* investigating the Omagh bombing. In mid-April and early May, the second of two small incendiary devices exploding at the same spot outside the Hyde Postal Depot in Hendon injured a passer-by. A car bomb at Ealing Broadway in August 2001 injured seven people when conflicting warning telephone calls led to confusion. The bombing ceased after Michael McKevitt was arrested when MI5 and the FBI infiltrated the Real IRA. The 2001 Drumcree Orange

Parade passed off without incident but 11 July saw the beginning of two days of serious disturbances in Belfast during which thirty-one RUC were injured and water cannon was used. There was a suspicion that Sinn Fein may have orchestrated the violence. On 10 August, the *Irish Times* reported that Loyalists had used 134 pipe bombs since the New Year, of which fifty had exploded.

Following the publication of Lord Patten's Report on policing in August, the courageous RUC disappeared into the sands of history and was rebranded the Police Service of Northern Ireland (PSNI) on 4 November and the first intake of 350 recruits equally distributed between Protestants and Catholics. The force was commanded by Chief Constable Hugh Orde, an Englishman who had formerly served in the Metropolitan Police and had been part of Stevens's investigation team. The RUC, which had lost 199 Regulars and 103 Reserves since 1969, some kidnapped or murdered while off duty, was awarded a thoroughly deserved George Cross for its gallantry and commitment. The PSNI remained largely unacceptable to Sinn Fein until 2005 when the majority expressed confidence in its policing and in tackling robbery, racketeering, intimidation and drug dealing. Undermining the grip of paramilitary organizations was tough, particularly in South Armagh. In May 2007, concern about reverse discrimination in a part of the United Kingdom that had a Protestant majority emerged when it was announced that over 700 recruits had been rejected because they were not Catholic.

In March 2002, the IRA was suspected of a break-in at Castlereagh Police HQ and even though they redeemed themselves in April by announcing that a second consignment of weapons had been put beyond use, there was still widespread disbelief among Loyalists. On 4 October, as part of an investigation into Republican intelligence gathering, the PSNI raided Sinn Fein's offices at Stormont, which inevitably resulted in the collapse of trust between the Republicans and other delegations. The Unionists remained unconvinced that Sinn Fein could be trusted. One of three officials arrested was Denis Donaldson, the Sinn Fein's Head of Administration.

Meanwhile, allegations of Security Forces' collusion with Loyalists simmered.

In March 1998, the UN had accused the RUC of systematic intimidation of lawyers representing paramilitary suspects and called for an inquiry into the murder of Pat Finucane. Allegations raised by British-Irish Rights Watch and a BBC documentary claiming that the UFF relied on information from the Security Forces led to John

Stevens, now Deputy Commissioner of the Metropolitan Police, launching his third inquiry, this time focusing on the murder of Finucane. Stevens was helped by a former Intelligence Corps sergeant using the pseudonym 'Martin Ingram' who had served with the FRU and left the Army in the early 1990s, after about ten years, to marry his Irish fiancée, who had strong Nationalist connections. In 1999, 'Ingram' was the source of several articles in the *Sunday Times* alleging collusion and although his level of knowledge was low, in November 2000, Stevens intimidated another former FRU with threats of arrest if he revealed 'Ingram's' identity. In June 2002, BBC *Panorama* investigated the FRU and repeated that the Security Forces had collaborated with Loyalist paramilitaries in the murder of Finucane. In his third report issued in April 2003, Stevens concluded that there had been collusion, a failure to keep records, an absence of accountability and the withholding of intelligence. In 2004 in his book *Stakeknife*, when 'Ingram' identified a senior member of the Internal Security Department to be an informant, the media frenzy endangered the life of Freddie Scappaticci by alleging that he was an informer. When 'Ingram' wrote that he hoped to see a free, democratic and united Ireland and wondered why his Army colleagues had not also come forward, the answer could be that unlike him, they had not forgotten that the most important person that they serve is the soldier in the front line.

When the Cory Report was published in April 2004 on the persistent allegations that the Security Forces had colluded with Loyalists in the murder of Patrick Finucane, it accused the FRU of 'acts of collusion' and questioned the honesty of a senior Army officer when he presented his evidence at the Nelson trial, it was clear that that the Sinn Fein propaganda targeting the FRU had, to some extent, succeeded. That officer and other members of the FRU then found themselves scrutinized by the Public Prosecution Service (Northern Ireland) until June 2007 when it announced that: 'There was insufficient evidence to establish that any member of the FRU had agreed with Brian Nelson or any other person that Patrick Finucane should be murdered or had knowledge at the relevant time that the murder was to take place.' Lord Stevens was also criticized by lawyers for pursuing his allegations over a thirteen-year period against soldiers working in dangerous conditions and subjected to hostile media scrutiny while serving their country. For such a senior police officer to publish his conclusions of a criminal investigation before it was heard in court, the lawyers suggested, was without precedent. Yet again a senior mainland police officer with no experience of conditions in Northern Ireland had failed to prove that the Security Forces had behaved injudiciously. Stevens achieved little except to muddy the waters at a critical time.

In September 2004, talks at Leeds Castle led to Sinn Fein agreeing to a Protestant clergyman and a Catholic priest witnessing a decommissioning session, but this still fell short of Unionist demands until December when the DUP agreed to photographs being circulated but Sinn Fein rejected this on the grounds that Unionists might use them to humiliate Republicans. The Reverend Paisley countered – no photographs, no deal. Blair and Ahern announced a final settlement package and Sinn Fein agreed that complete decommissioning was acceptable. The accusation by Dublin and Westminster that the IRA had masterminded the robbery of £26.5m from a Northern Bank branch in Belfast in December 2004 led to Sinn Fein withdrawing from decommissioning in February 2005 and accusing the PSNI and the British of staging the robbery. The murder of Robert McCartney in January 2005 outside a Belfast pub after an argument with several IRA sparked an unexpected display of anger in the Nationalist Short Strand and led to his five sisters accusing Sinn Fein of covering up the crime. While Gerry Adams condemned the murder, he stopped short of handing the suspects over to the PSNI, claiming that those responsible 'ran contrary to Republican ideals' – which was news to most – and then offered to execute them, an offer rejected by the sisters. To some extent, this offer from Adams the politician was the first step in dismantling his credibility. In spite of several attempts, the failure of PSNI to discover those behind the Omagh bomb, the murder of McCartney and the robbery, has rather exposed Chief Constable Orde.

The Irish Minister for Justice, Michael McDowell, then alleged that Adams and Martin McGuiness were members of the Provisional Army Council. McGuiness who, four months earlier, had told the Bloody Sunday Inquiry that he was an IRA commander in the 1970s, rejected the allegation as political manoeuvring. The isolation of Adams gathered pace when President George Bush withdrew his invitation to the White House St Patrick's Day celebration and met the McCartney sisters instead. Out manoeuvred, discredited and isolated, Adams had no other choice but accept the inevitable and, in April, he launched his General Election campaign on the platform that the climate was right for Republicans to embrace democracy. On 28 July, the Provisional General Army Council published a statement:

> The leadership has formally ordered an end to the armed
> campaign. This will take effect from 4 p.m. this afternoon. All
> IRA units have been ordered to dump arms. All Volunteers have
> been instructed to assist the development of purely political and
> democratic programmes through exclusively peaceful means.

Between July and September 2005, the Provisionals are thought to
have decommissioned 1,000 rifles, three tons of Semtex, about
twenty-five medium machine guns, seven surface-to-air missiles,
seven flame throwers, twenty RPGs and about 100 grenades, figures
that compared favourably with Security Forces' statistics. The
faction stated that this contribution to the Peace Process was an
alternative method of ending British rule in Northern Ireland. It
rather forgot that the Republican struggle was entirely legitimate
although the manner in which it had been conducted since 1970 was
undemocratic. In January 2006, legislation that would have
permitted those 'on the run', accused of paramilitary crimes before
1998, being freed by a special tribunal on licence was rejected,
including by Sinn Fein. In April, Denis Donaldson, one of three Sinn
Fein administrators arrested at Stormont, was murdered outside a
remote cottage in Co. Donegal several hours before Prime Ministers
Blair and Ahern unveiled their blueprint for reviving the Stormont
Assembly. Expelled from Sinn Fein a year earlier, he had admitted
passing information to the British for twenty years. The IRA denied
involvement. When Stormont finally assembled, after the threat of
salaries being withdrawn, the presence of David Ervine with the
Unionist grouping caused uproar from Sinn Fein. Formerly UVF and
a Long Kesh prisoner, he had amused himself by using his knowledge
of Gaelic to disrupt IRA parades. He had brokered the 1994 Loyalist
paramilitary ceasefire.

The Decommissioning Commission suggesting, in October, that
Provisionals no longer had the capacity to mount a sustained
campaign, led to Blair claiming that the 'campaign is over' and after
the St Andrews Talks discussing transitional arrangements to the
Assembly, Sinn Fein agreed to support the PSNI and the criminal
justice system. When, on 7 March 2005, Northern Ireland elected
the Assembly, the DUP emerged as the largest party with Sinn Fein
second and then on the 26th, the unbelievable happened when
devolved government was returned to Stormont and the Reverend

225

Paisley and Gerry Adams sat side-by-side to confirm the return of power-sharing on 8 May. Demands by Sinn Fein that the Army, the constitutional military force, should disarm, had been rejected outright, nevertheless the Ministry of Defence planned to reduce troop levels from 10,000 to 5,000 by 31 July 2007, the date that Operation Banner would be terminated. The Civil Service presence would be reduced to 3,000. The proviso remained that levels could change to meet the operational requirements of reinforcing the garrison and PSNI with 321 EOD and military support to the civil community under Operation Helvetic, in the same manner as provided by the Armed Forces in Great Britain.

The roulement Northern Ireland Battalion 1 was withdrawn on 16 January 2006 leaving Northern Ireland Battalion 2 in South Armagh, its coverage reduced with troops withdrawing from Forkhill, Newtownhamilton, Crossmaglen, Newtownbutler, Middletown, Keady and Maydown. By 31 March, troop levels were down to about 8,500 with no troops in Kinawley and Rosslea. The watchtowers at Creevekeeran, Drumackavall, Sugarloaf, Croslieve, Camlough Mountain and Jonesborough in South Armagh and on top of the Divis Flats and the Masonic Base in Londonderry, were dismantled. Grosvenor Barracks in Enniskillen and Mahon Barracks in Portadown were handed back and 3 Squadron, RAF Regiment left for RAF Wittering. The Omagh resident battalion at Lisanelly Barracks was not replaced. HQ 8 Infantry Brigade at Shackleton Barracks, Ballykelly, was disbanded and handed over to HQ 39 Infantry Brigade on 1 September. HQ Northern Ireland became an administrative function. 15 Signal Regiment at Thiepval Barracks was reduced to two Independent Signals Squadrons. On 1 October 2006, three Royal Irish Regiment Home Service Force battalions paraded for the final time before the Queen at a commemorative event at the Balmoral Showground, Belfast, to mark the end of operational duties of the UDR in Northern Ireland after thirty-six years of service. At the parade, the Queen presented the Conspicuous Gallantry Cross to Corporal Claire Withers, daughter of Corporal Withers, the last part-time soldier to be murdered in 1994, representing the UDR and the Regiment, for thirty-six years of continuous active service during which it lost 197 serving men and four women and sixty-one former UDR. One hundred and sixty-two men were murdered at home or at work, amounting to 79 per cent of their total casualty list. Six were killed by Loyalists. UDR and Royal Irish Regiment soldiers can wear the Cross on their 1962 General Service

Medal.

From 1 April to 31 July 2007, Drumadd Barracks, Armagh, Lisanelly Barracks, and Moscow Barracks were closed and the OP at PSNI Rosemount, Londonderry was dismantled. At the end of June, Lieutenant James Phipps, a Platoon Commander with 2 Princess of Wales Royal Regiment led the evacuation from Bessbrook Mill. The bases at Harmony House in Lisburn and the Masonic Base in Londonderry were closed and the remaining military structures in PSNI stations dismantled. HQ Northern Ireland was further reduced to fit the needs of the garrison. On 31 July, the remaining three Home Service Force Battalions were disbanded, as was the Northern Ireland Training Regiment. 6 Regiment, RMP and Northern Ireland Combat Service Support Regiment were both reduced to approximately one third of their strength. And then, Captain Paul Walkley, a Stafford posted as a Duty Operations Officer, HQ 39 Infantry Brigade, radioed:

'Charlie, Charlie One, this is Zero. Operation Banner is terminated. All call signs acknowledge. Over.'

Chapter 16

Conclusions

On 1 August 2007, 38 (Irish) Brigade replaced 39 Infantry Brigade as a non-deployable brigade with its headquarters in Lisburn until a week later, HQ Northern Ireland and 38 Brigade combined to create the single transitional HQ 38 Brigade with regional functions, under the command of HQ 2 Division in Edinburgh and supported by Operation Helvetic to enable the PSNI to receive military support in the event of extreme public disorder or an environmental crisis.

In 1942 a British film, depicting a force of Germans posing as Royal Engineers occupying a small east coast village in preparation for invasion, was quaintly titled *How Went the Day?* The same question can be asked of the approximately 300,000 Armed Forces who served in Northern Ireland.

For the third time in English history, the Armed Forces defeated a threat to England's back door; a French invasion in 1690, which resulted in the Battle of the Boyne, a second French landing in 1798 to support Irish dissidents and a third between 1970 and 1996 when Irish Republican radicals were determined to create a Marxist state in Ireland. Arriving to support the civil community, the soldiers were confronted by insurgency which, once freed of restraints imposed by Stormont, they destroyed. They then faced terrorism directed at England and the Armed Forces. Throughout, restraint and discipline remained solid, as did their capability to win in the Falklands, peace keep in the former Yugoslavia, intervene in Sierra Leone, support operations in the Gulf and Afghanistan and maintain the British commitment to NATO. Unexpectedly pitched into a shooting war an hour's flight from Heathrow and other regional airports, the Armed Forces adjusted tactics and developed new equipment. While there was undoubtedly mischief, mistakes and misjudgments by the troops and by politicians but not, it seems, by editors who regularly forced the Security Forces to play uphill throughout with revelations, and then largely ignored Operation Banner, as they tried to do with Iraq and Afghanistan. But there were no emotional televised homecomings, no memorial parades at the end of tours and no fund raising for these men and women who, for thirty-eight years, successfully defended Great Britain against an insidious, subversive and violent threat from across the Irish Sea. Instead, they faded into anxious anonymity, their sacrifices and deeds largely forgotten, to protect themselves and their families from murder and intimidation by Republican extremists who were determined to pursue the Armed Forces Army wherever they were deployed. In effect the soldiers remained at risk at work, at leisure and on leave, throughout their active service. The stress of this lifestyle has not been recognized.

While the bulk of the fighting fell to the Infantry and UDR, the converting of the Royal Armoured Corps, Royal Artillery and Royal Engineers to boots on the grounds was crucial to allow patrolling in the streets, lanes and fields, collecting information and carrying out limited hearts and minds. There is little recognition that many soldiers spent entire tours in that most difficult of environments – fighting in built up areas in which every letterbox was a gun port, every window a firing position for a gunman, every culvert, vehicle and plot of wasteland, a location for a bomb and every person a potential insurgent or terrorist. There was one difference from the classic street fighting – while soldiers patrolled, around them were people going about their normal day and, if they came under fire, they could not take cover in a wrecked house or burrow into a garden. The echoes from the gun battles in the narrow streets were incredibly noisy. Combat support from the Royal Navy, Royal Air Force, Army Air Corps, Royal Engineers and service support in the form of the transport, medics and logistic units was critical, as it always is, and the RMP were vital in re-establishing law enforcement with the RUC.

The intelligence framework was split by feuding and pettiness, with only the Intelligence Corps being crucial in creating intelligence networks and undermining the paramilitary factions to the extent that information about people, plots and plans was haemorrhaging to the very end. The Republican factions were particularly prone to infiltration and penetration and such paranoia was induced in their ranks that every time an operation was mounted, they could not guarantee that they would return home.

It will come as something of a shock to the Fleet Street warriors that offensive operations against terrorists are a necessity. The arrival of the SAS nine years after Operation Banner began, typically full of misplaced confidence, after their exploits in Dhofar. Once settled down to the reality of Northern Ireland, their military expertise, and that of the SBS, was a major contributor to undermining the Republican factions by using the intelligence gained from informants to carry out surveillance and then ambush. The Regiment has been criticized for opening fire before issuing challenges, but very few of those who challenge SAS operations have experienced the tension of lying in wait for hours, if not days, for armed terrorists to appear. One consolation for the infantrymen was that the SAS could do what they had wanted to do for years and that was kill those who had shot, murdered and bombed their colleagues and many innocent people, and were getting away with it because the law favoured the terrorist. The SAS ambushes were no worse than the ambushes, bombings and murder perpetrated by the extremists and by 1980, no longer could those extremists regard the streets, fields and lanes as their own.

Insinuations that the Army overstepped the mark several times are well wide of the mark. The most quoted example is internment. Internment was not a military decision; it was a political one jointly agreed by Westminster and Stormont, and favoured the Security Forces. Nevertheless, the fact is that it had worked before, mostly recently during the Border War, when hardliners had been removed from circulation, and there was no reason why it should not do so again. The problem was that the public relations and psychological warfare operations being undertaken by the Northern Ireland Office, were so feeble that it was outflanked, not only by Fleet Street and the liberal chattering classes just a one hour's flight from London, but also by Sinn Fein who have kept the pot boiling ever since. While internees may well have been locked up without trial, at least they were alive, which was more than could be said for those their colleagues killed. Indeed, an internee is nothing more than a prisoner of war in which there are no front lines.

It is also fashionable to accuse the Army of torture and brutality in interrogation but far less fashionable to accuse the Provisionals of similar offences. Interrogation is a legitimate resource in the pursuit of military information to help commanders draw up plans to defeat the enemy. However the problem was that the Northern Ireland Office folded in the face of clever exploitation by Sinn Fein. The Fleet

Street warriors, who used the same debriefing techniques as military interrogators with impunity, continued to latch on to the mysteries of interrogation and placed the Army under intense international criticism. Consequently the politicians had little option but to instruct that interrogation should cease; a decision that probably lengthened Operation Banner by about twenty years.

When the journalist Peter Taylor wrote in a *Sunday Times* article in 2007 that 'Sinn Fein has hijacked the history of Ulster', he cannot complain because it was his profession that failed to challenge the IRA and allowed the various factions to exploit politicians and editors to its advantage. As early as 1971, Sinn Fein was expert at forcing through its political agenda. Which other terrorist organization had the audacity to ensure that hundreds of convicted terrorists, terrorism being internationally recognized as a crime, should be released en masse as a part of peace deal? But what did the IRA gain from its campaign? Apart from taking its historical place at the negotiation table after a long period of abstaining from Westminster and Stormont, the answer is – not much. Northern Ireland remains a democratic society and is not part of a thirty-two-county Marxist state but it remains pestered by dissidents still refusing to acknowledge the Peace Process. The American-Irish Northern Aid website describing Operation Banner as Britain's Dirty War is an insult.

Controversy surrounds statistics and is likely to do so for many years. The Northern Ireland Conflict, Politics, & Society CAIN website probably gives the most accurate account and statistics. It lists a total of 3,524 deaths of which 2,148 are attributed to Irish Republicans, 1,071 to Loyalists and the remainder to the Security Forces. Of the 47,541 injured, 63 per cent were civilians. Not calculated is the cost of damage. An ironic statistic is that in their pursuit of the Army, Republican terrorists killed 30 per cent more people in internal feuding, which rather suggests that the Republican factions were by no means unified.

About 300,000 former and present members of the Armed Forces are entitled to wear the green and blue ribbon of the General Service Medal 1962 with the single bar 'Northern Ireland'. Those who served a total of 1,000 days are entitled to the Accumulated Service Medal. The Northern Ireland Veterans Association, which has more accurate figures than the Ministry of Defence, lists 763 Service personnel killed in action and 6,116 wounded. Six hundred and thirty-eight were Regular Army, thirteen Royal Marines, four RAF and one Royal Navy. More were killed in 1972 than in the first four

232

years in Afghanistan. Five Regulars did not survive capture. Forty-five Service personnel were killed in England and eight in Germany, Belgium and the Netherlands, of which eleven were Royal Marines and four were RAF. Two Army wives and three children were murdered. The Ministry of Defence has only recently acknowledged that non-battle casualties should be included in the statistics, which will take the fatalities to over 1,000. The Palace Barracks Memorial site suggests that 262 died in incidents associated with vehicles. Others died from natural causes, friendly fire, which were mercifully rare, drowning while crossing rivers on patrol and self-inflicted deaths. The Intelligence Corps, for instance, lists one killed in its Rolls of Honour whereas another ten lost their lives, five in the Mull of Kintyre Chinook crash and five from road accidents and natural causes.

So how went the day? The question was answered by Prime Minister Gordon Brown at the Commemoration to end Operation Banner at St Paul's Cathedral on 10 September 2008 when he said, 'They helped create conditions for the people of Northern Ireland and those committed to the Province's future and today we salute their courage'. Bishop of London Dr Richard Chartres was entirely accurate, 'Operation Banner kept open that vital pass through which a more hopeful future for Ulster could enter'. So to answer the question,

The day went well.

Appendices

APPENDIX A
COMPARISON OF INCIDENTS/TOTAL DEATHS/SECURITY FORCES IN NORTHERN IRELAND CASUALTIES

Year	Shootings	IEDS	Incendiary	Total Deaths	Army	RM	RN	RAF	UDR	R Irish	TA	Non Battle	RUC
1969	73	10		16								7	1
1970	213	170		28								9	2
1971	1,756	1,515		171	43				5			2	11
1972	10,631	1,853											
1973	5,019	1,520		253	56	2			8			6	13
1974	3,208	1,113	270	294	26	2			7		1	6	15
1975	1,803	635	56	260	14				6			3	11
1976	1,908	1,192	236	295	14				15			7	23
1977	1,081	535	608	111	14	1			14		1	1	14
1978	755	633	115	81	12	2			7			6	11
1979	728	564	60	121	38				10		1	3	14
1980	642	400	2	80	8				9		1	4	9
1981	1,142	529	49	113	9	1			13			3	21
1982	547	332	36	110	21				7			4	12
1983	424	367	43	85	5				10		1	4	18
1984	334	248	10	69	9				10		1	1	9
1985	238	215	36	57	2				4			1	23
1986	392	254	21	61	4				8				12
1987	674	384	9	98	3				8			2	16
1988	538	458	8	104	17		1	3	12			2	6
1989	566	420	7	75	9	12		1	2		1	2	8
1990	557	286	33	81	6				8				8
1991	499	368	237	96	4				8			1	12
1992	506	371	126	89	3				1	3	1	1	6
1993	476	289	61	88	5					2		2	2
1994	348	222	115	64						2		2	3

236

Year													
1995	50	2	10	9								7	1
1996	125	25	4	18	1							3	4
1997	225	93	9	21	1							11	1
1998	211	243	20	55	1							2	
1999	125	100	7	8									
2000	302	135	22	19								1	1
2001	355	444	6	16									
2002	350	239	3	11									
2003	229	88	8	10								2	
2004	185	69	28	2									
2005	167	105	9										
2006	69	31	11	3									
2007	47	22		0									
TOTAL	37,498	16,479	2,275	3,523	294	24	1	4	198	7	8	105	285

Sources
1. Shootings – Shots fired by Security Forces; by insurgents/terrorists; paramilitary shootings, such as punishments; shots heard confirmed; and incidents such as armed robberies when shots were fired
2. AIN Malcolm Sutton: *An Index of Deaths from the Conflict in Injured*
3. www.britains-smallwars.com, *Northern Ireland: Lest We Forget.*
4. Police Service of Northern Ireland.
5. Ken Wharton: *A Long, Long War.* Non-Battle – Military non-battle fatalities, including natural causes, road traffic incidents, friendly fire, drowning and self-inflicted.

APPENDIX B
Non-Military Casualties

NON ALIGNED	
Civilians	1799
Prison Services	24
Irish Army	1
Gardai	9
British Police	6
IRISH REPUBLICAN GROUPS	
Irish National Liberation Army (INLA)	37
Irish People's Liberation Organisation (IPLO)	9
IRA	276
IRA Youth Section	15
OIRA	24
Real IRA	2
LOYALIST GROUPS	
Loyalist Volunteer Force	3
Red Hand Commando	2
UDA	75
UVF	57

APPENDIX C
All Fatalities by Location

COUNTY/CITY	FATALITIES
Antrim	207
Armagh	276
Down	243
Fermanagh	112
East Belfast	128
North Belfast	576
West Belfast	623
Tyrone	339
Londonderry	227
The City	123
Republic of Ireland	113
England	125
Europe (Gibraltar, Belgium, Germany)	18

Source: CAIN - Malcolm Sutton

238

APPENDIX D
ASSEMBLY OF OTHER STATISTICS

NON ALIGNED DEATHS	
Civilians	1799
Prison Services	24
Irish Army	1
Gardai	9
British Police	6
IRISH REPUBLICAN GROUPS DEATHS	
Irish National Liberation Army (INLA)	37
Irish People's Liberation Organisation (IPLO)	9
Provisional IRA	276
IRA Youth Section	15
Official IRA	24
Real IRA	2
LOYALIST GROUPS DEATHS	
Loyalist Volunteer Force	3
Red Hand Commando	2
UDA	75
UVF	57
OTHER INFORMATION	
Armed robbery	22,250
Persons imprisoned	19,600
Weapons recovered	14,000

Source: Malcolm Sutton; CAIN Website

APPENDIX E
EXAMPLES OF IRA WEAPON SMUGGLING

DATE	COUNTRY	CONSIGNMENT
1969	USA	About 70 M1 carbines, M3 SMGs and hand guns. 60,000 rounds of ammo acquired for the Border War by Harrison network.
1970	Spain	50 revolvers supplied by Basque ETA.
1969-70		9mm Brownings, 500 grenades, 180,000 rounds bought for defence groups in north. Four acquitted in arms trial.
1970	USA	AR-15 Armalite rifles smuggled to Ireland by Philadelphia sympathizers.
1971	USA	Small arms and ammo seized in Dublin after being landed by ship.
	Czechoslovakia	4.5 tons of mixed stores bought from Prague seized at Schiphol Airport.
1972	Europe	Reported import of RPG-7s.
Early 1970s	USA	M-16s and AR-15s smuggled by Harrison network on *Queen Elizabeth II*.
1973	Libya	*Claudia* intercepted by Irish Naval Service and 250 AK-47 and other materiel seized. Several IRA arrested.
1974	USA	100 rifles seized by US Treasury in plot to smuggle consignment bought at Maryland gun shop. Five jailed in USA.
1977	PLO Al-Fatah	27 x K-47s, 29 x SMGs, 7 x RPG-7, 2 x Bren Guns, grenades, ammo and explosives sent by ship via Cyprus seized at Antwerp. One IRA arrested by Irish police.
1973-78	USA	6 x M-60 GPMGs and about 100 x M-16 rifles stolen from US Army depot by Harrison network.
	USA	Estimated 500,000 5.56mm x .45 mm rounds stolen from USMC Camp Lejeune by Harrison network.
1979	USA	150 guns including 2 x M-60 GPMGs, 15 x M-16s, 14 x M-14s and 1 AK-47 and 60,000 rounds of ammo stolen by Harrison network seized at Dublin.
1981	USA	350 x MAC-10 SMGs and 12 x AK-47s stolen by Harrison network plot foiled in FBI 'sting'. Network broken up.
1982	USA	50 x firearms, ammo and tone frequency switches found by US Customs in truck at Newark, New Jersey. Four IRA jailed in US.
	USA	Five men with 'shopping list' for 200 cases of mixed ammo arrested entering USA from Canada.
1983	USA	Bid to buy explosive foiled by FBI in Wyoming. Man arrested.
1984	USA	*Marita Ann* intercepted by Irish Naval Service and seven tons of arms, ammo and explosives procured by Boston drugs gang seized. Men jailed in USA and Ireland.
1985	USA	FBI foils IRA bid to buy small arms in Colorado. Irishman deported.

August 1985	Libya	10 ton of weapons including 7 x RPG-7s landed by fishing boat *Casmara* at Clogher Strand.
October 1985	Libya	Fishing boat *Kula* (formerly *Casmara*) skippered by Anthony Hopkins landed 10 tons of arms, including 12.7mm machine guns, at Clogher Strand.
1986	Netherlands	40 firearms, including 13 x FAL rifles, 1 x AK-47, 2 x hand grenades, drums of nitrobenzene and 70,000 rounds seized by Dutch police in raid on Amsterdam apartment. Four IRA arrested.
1984-86	Norway	10 x G3 Heckler & Koch G3 rifles seized by Gardai. Part of batch of 100 rifles stolen from Norwegian Reserve base near Oslo in 1984.
1982-86	USA	IRA supporters in Boston jailed in 1990 for trying to smuggle a home-made missile system to Ireland. Member of group also believed to have supplied detonators in 1982-88.
1986	USA	Redeye SAMs, M-60 GPMGs, M-16 rifles, MP-5 SMGs and 11 x bullet-proof vests foiled by FBI 'sting'. Plot to fly cargo by private jet from Boston.
July 1986	Libya	Oil rig supplier *Villa* skippered by Hopkins landed 10 tons of arms at Clogher Strand.
October 1986	Libya	*Villa* skippered by Hopkins landed 80 tons of arms at Clogher Strand, including SAM-7s and Semtex.
November 1987	Libya	Trawler *Eksund* intercepted by French Customs off Brittany and 150 tons, including 1,000 x AK-47's, 20 x SAM-7, RPG-7s and 2 tonnes of Semtex seized. Hopkins and four IRA arrested.
1988	Netherlands	380 gallons of nitrobenzene smuggled from Amsterdam aboard truck seized by Irish police at Kells, Co. Meath. Driver jailed.
1988	USA	Small arms described as 'high-powered rifles' seized by US Customs from Alabama gun dealer. Two jailed.

Sources: CAIN *The Irish War*

241

APPENDIX F
A LIST OF IRA INCIDENTS IN ENGLAND 1867 TO 2001

1867-1985	
1939	Several bombs in London, including House of Commons, Tower of London, Scotland causing fatalities and injuries.
1956 – 1962 (Border War)	IRA Declares war on England. Several bombs in London and Coventry cause fatalities and injuries.
	England. IRA raid cadet armouries.
1971	
1 October	London. Bomb that damaged Post Office Tower claimed by Kilburn IRA.
1972	
22 February	Aldershot, Hants. Official IRA car bomb at 16 Parachute Brigade's Officer Mess kills Army chaplain and 6 civilians.
1973	
8 March	London. Car bombs outside New Scotland Yard and British Forces Broadcasting Service office defused. Two other bombs injure 180. Ten Provisionals arrested at Heathrow.
29 August	Solihull. Two bombs explode. London. Incendiary device in Harrods.
10 September	London. Provisional bombs at King's Cross and Euston Stations injured 21 people.
14 September	London. Bombs in Sloane Square and Chelsea.
20 September	London. Bomb at Chelsea Barracks.
23 September	Birmingham. ATO Captain Robert Wilkinson killed defusing bomb.
4 February	M62. Bomb on coach kills 8 soldiers and 4 civilians.
1974	
12 February	Latimer, Bucks. Bomb at National Defence College injures 10.
17 June	London. Bomb in Westminster Hall injures 11.
26 July	London. Bomb at the Tower of London kills 1 and injures 41.

242

5 October	Guildford. Two pub bombings kill 5 soldiers and a civilian and injures 44.
9 October	London. East Kent bus inspector Basil Dalton kidnapped from the Buckingham Palace Road Coach Station.
11 October	London. Bombs thrown at Victory Club, Seymour Street and Army and Navy Club, St James's Square where 70 former Royal West Africa Frontier Force are at their annual reunion.
18 October	London. Two armed IRA disturbed by two police officers in Semley Place. PC Michael Lloyd has his watch stolen.
22 October	London. Bomb thrown at Brooks Club injures 3.
24 October	Harrow. Bomb in a master's flat at public school explodes.
7 November	Woolwich. Bomb at King's Arms kills a soldier and civilian. Several injuries.
11 November	London. Insurance broker Allan Quartermaine murdered.
14 November	Coventry. IRA own goal in attack on telephone exchange.
21 November	Birmingham. Bombs in two pubs kill 21 and injure 182.
25 November	London. Bombs in three pillar boxes. ASU ignores orders to cease operations.
27 November	London. Two pillar box bombs in Tite Street, Chelsea.
30 November	London. Two bombs thrown into the Talbot Arms, Belgravia.
11 December	London. Bomb thrown into the Naval and Military Club in Piccadilly and Cavalry Club raked with small arms fire.
14 December	London. Churchill Hotel, Portman Square, raked with small arms fire.
17 December	London. Bombs explode in New Compton Street, Soho, Draycott and Museum Telephone Exchanges killing a telephonist.
19 December	London. Car bomb outside Selfridges, Oxford Street.
20 December	Aldershot. Holdall bomb at railway station defused.
21 December	London. Bomb at Harrods.
22 December	London. Bomb thrown into Edward Heath's flat.
1975	
17 January	IRA Ceasefire ended.
19 January	London. Shootings at Carlton Tower and Portman Hotels injures 12.
24 January	London. Teacher in Greenwich is mistaken for an Army brigadier and is shot and wounded.
27 January	London. 7 bombs over a 6 hour period injures 2.
27 January	Manchester. Bomb injures 26.

243

10 February	IRA Ceasefire.
26 February	**London**. PC Tibble murdered by gunman near Baron's Court. ASU scatters. IRA safe houses found in Fairholme Rd flat.
27 August	**Caterham, Surrey.** Bomb in Caterham Arms frequented by Welsh Guards causes casualties.
28 August	**London**. Bomb in Peter Brown's shoe shop Oxford Street injures seven.
29 August	**London**. Bomb in K Shoe Shop, Kensington. ATO Captain Goad posthumously awarded the George Cross.
30 August	**London**. Bomb at the National Westminster Bank, High Holborn.
5 September	**London**. Bomb in London Hilton kills 2 people and injures 63. Last warning by ASU.
15 September	**London**. Letter bombs sent from Dublin. One sent to Lady Pamela Onslow in Notting Hill explodes.
29 September	**London**. Bomb in Oxford St injures 7.
8 October	**London**. Bomber priming Ritz Hotel bomb in Green Park toilets is disturbed and throws it at a bus stop killing 1 and injuries 20.
12 October	**London**. Bomb at Lockett's Restaurant, Westminster, a popular haunt of Tory MPs is defused.
22 October	Guildford Four convicted.
	London. Car bomb designed for Hugh Fraser MP in Camden Hill Square kills Professor Gordon Hamilton-Fairley.
30 October	**London**. Bomb at the Trattoria Fiore, Mount Street injures 17.
3 November	**London**. Car bomb designed for John Gorst MP or Derreck Raynor, Selfridges MD injuries a City lawyer in mistake.
8 November	**London**. Bomb in bag outside Edward Heath's home is defused.
13 November	**London**. Bomb thrown into Scott's Restaurant, Mayfair kills 1 and injuries 15.
19 November	**London**. Bomb at Walton's Restaurant, Chelsea kills 2 and injuries 17.
27 November	**London**. Ross McWhirter murdered at home at Enfield.
6 to 13 December	**London**. ASU opening fire on Scott's Restaurant, Mayfair leads to police pursuit to Balcombe St. ASU take two hostage. Siege ends with arrest of four and conviction of London ASU.
1979	
30 March	**London**. Airey Neave MP killed by INLA car bomb at Palace of Westminster.
1981	
9 May	**Shetlands Islands.** Bomb at oil terminal during Royal visit.
10 October	**London**. Bomb outside Chelsea Barracks kills 2 civilians and injures 23.

244

17 October	**London.** Royal Marines Lt General Pringle badly injured by bomb outside home.
26 October	**London.** ATO killed effusing device in Oxford St.
13 November	**London.** Bomb outside home of Attorney-General Sir Michael Havers.
1982	
20 July	**London.** Hyde Park and Regents Park bombings 4 Household Cavalry and 7 Royal Green Jackets.
1983	
17 December	**London.** Bombing of Harrods attempt to cause mass casualties. Chairman Alec Craddock does not order evacuation and saves 20,000 from death and injury. However 3 police and 3 civilians and 90 injured at staff entrance.
1984	
12 October	**Brighton.** Grand Hotel bombing kills five.
1989	
22 September	**Deal.** Bombs kill 11 Royal Marines and injures 22.
November	**Colchester.** Royal Military Police NCO severely wounded by bomb.
1990	
16 May	**London.** Car bomb in Wembley kills Queen's Regiment recruiting Sergeant Chapman and wounds colleague.
1 June	**Lichfield.** Shooting at railway station kills a soldier.
20 July	**London.** Car bomb damages London Stock Exchange.
30 July	**Eastbourne.** Ian Gow MP killed by a car bomb at home.
10 September	**Staffordshire.** Former Gibraltar Governor Sir Peter Terry and family injured in shooting attack on home.
1991	
7 February	**London.** IRA mortar attack on 10, Downing Street.
18 February	**London.** Bomb at Victoria Station kills 1 and injures 38.
28 February	**London.** Bomb at London Bridge Station injuries 29.
19 December	**St Albans, Herts.** Two IRA killed in 'own goal' when bomb targeted concert given by Blues and Royals Band.
1992	
10 April	**London.** Lorry bomb in the City kills 3 and causes extensive damage.

7 June	**Tadcaster.** Special Constable Goodman killed and PC Kelly wounded by IRA gunmen, who are both later arrested.
25 August	**Shrewsbury.** Three fire bombs damage Shropshire Regimental Museum.
12 October	**London.** Bomb in Sussex Arms, Covent Garden kills 1 and injures 4.
16 November	**London.** Bomb at Canary Wharf spotted by security officers and defused.
3 December	**Manchester.** Two bombs in Manchester injure 65.
1993	
23 October	**Reading.** Bomb found at railway signal post and in the station toilets.
26 February	**Warrington.** After attack on Longford Gas Works, PC Stoker shot and injured. Two IRA arrested next day.
20 March	**Warrington.** Bomb attacks on Bridge Street kill 2 children and injured many others.
24 April	**London.** Lorry bomb at Bishopsgate kills 1 and injures 40. Extent of damage places financial crisis in London insurance market.
2 October	**Three bombs in Hampstead injure 6 and cause damage to shops.**
4 October	**Five bombs in north London injure 4.**
1994	
9 March	**Heathrow Airport.** Mortar bombs land on the northern runway.
11 March	**Heathrow Airport.** Second mortar bombs landing on the southern runway failed to explode.
14 March	**Heathrow Airport.** Third mortar attack on Heathrow.
9 September	**HMP Whitemoor.** Prison officer shot during an IRA escape .
1996	
9 February	**London.** Docklands South Quay bombing kills 2.
15 June	**Manchester.** Bomb in Arndale Centre injures 206. Largest bomb since the Second World War.
15 February	**London.** Bomb in Charing Cross Road telephone box defused.
18 February	**London.** IRA 'own goal' on a bus at Aldwych injures 8.
24 April	**London.** Bomb damages Hammersmith Bridge. Previously been targeted in the S-Campaign.

2000	
1 June	**Real IRA campaign** London. Second bomb damages Hammersmith Bridge.
19 July	London. Controlled explosion at Ealing Broadway Underground closes Victoria and Paddington Stations and halts Underground.
21 September	London. RPG-22 fired at the MI 6 Headquarters.

2001	
21 February	London. Torch bomb outside the Shepherd's Bush TA Centre blinds ACF cadet.
4 March	London. BBC Shepherd's Bush Television Centre bombed.
14 April	London. Bomb at Hendon Royal Mail office causes minor damage.
6 May	London. Second bomb at Hendon sorting office causes slight injuries.
3 August	London. Car bomb in Ealing injures seven people.
3 November	Birmingham. Car bomb in city centre fails to detonate.

Bibliography

Books

Adams, James, Morgan, Robin and Bambridge, Anthony, *Ambush: The War between the SAS and the IRA*, Pan, London, 1988

Barzilay, David, *The British Army in Ulster: Vols 1 (1973), 2 (1975), 3 (1978) and 4 (1981)* , Century Services, Belfast

Birchall, Peter, *The Longest Walk: The World of Bomb Disposal*, Arms and Armour, London, 1997

Collins, Tim, *Rules of Engagement*, BCA, 2005

Connor, Ken, *Ghost Force: The Secret History of the SAS*, Weidenfeld & Nicolson, London, 1998

Dewar, Colonel Michael, *The British Army in Northern Ireland*, Arms and Armour, London 1985 and 1996

Dillon, Martin, *The Dirty War*, Arrow, London 1991
— *The Enemy Within, The IRA's War Against the British*, Doubleday, 1994

Dorrill, Stephen, *MI 6: Fifty Years of Operations*, Fourth Estate, London, 2000

Geraghty, Tony, *The Irish War: The Military History of a Domestic Conflict*, HarperCollins, London, 2000
— *This is the SAS – A Pictorial History*, Arms and Armour, London, 1982

Harnden, Toby, *Bandit Country: The IRA & South Armagh*, Coronet books, 1999

Holroyd, Fred, *War without Honour: True Story of Military Intelligence in Northern Ireland*, Medium, 1989

Ingram, Martin and Harkin, Greg, *Stakeknife: Britain's Secret Agents in Ireland*, The O'Brein Press, Dublin, 2004

Institution of Royal Engineers, *A Short History of the Royal Engineers*, Chatham, 2006

Jackson, General Sir Mike, *Soldier: An Autobiography*, Bantam Press, London, 2007

McDonald, P.G, *Stopping the Clock*, Robert Hale, London, 1977

Macdonald, Peter, *The SAS in Action*, Sidgwick & Jackson, London, 1990

Merse, Peter, *Intelligence Operations Against the IRA in the Netherlands and Federal Republic of Germany*, Extract from *Battleground Western Europe, Intelligence Operations in Germany and the Netherlands in the 20th Century*, Het Spinhuis, 2000

Mockaitis, Thomas, *British Counter-Insurgency in the Post-Imperial Era*, Manchester University Press, Manchester, 1993

Moloney, Ed, *A Secret History of the IRA*, Penguin, London, 2007

Ripley, Tim, *The Security Forces in Northern Ireland*, Osprey, Oxford, 1993

Southby-Tailyour Ewen, *HMS Fearless, The Mighty Lion*, Pen & Sword, Barnsley, 2006

Streatfield, Dominic, *Brainwishing, The Secret History of Mind Control*, Hodder & Stoughton, London 2006

Sutton, Brig John, *The Story of the Royal Army Service Corps and Story of the Royal Corps of Transport 1945-1982*, Leo Cooper, Barnsley, 1982

— *Wait for the Waggon, The Story of the Royal Corps of Transport and its Predecessors 1794-1993*, Leo Cooper, Barnsley, 1998

Thatcher, Margaret, *The Downing Street Years*, HarperCollins, London, 1993

Watson, J.N.P, *Sefton: The Story of a Cavalry Horse*, Souvenir Press, London, 1983

Newspapers and Magazines
Barclay, Capt J.P., *'Harambe' in Fermanagh*, The Household Cavalry Journal, 1993

Guardian, The, *German Bombing Claimed by IRA*, London, 25 March 1987

Independent, The, *Terrorists in Mortar Attack on Barracks*, London, 29 June 1996

New York Times:

3 May 1988 – *IRA Attacks Make Wary Britons even more so*

6 August 1988 – *British Barracks Bombed in West Germany*

20 August 1988 – *Land Mine kills 7 British Soldiers on Bus in Ulster*

9 September 1989 – *IRA Gunman Kills Wife of Briton*

Soldier: Northern Ireland articles:

Life Saving Medical Services – February 1972

Sapper Support – Under Fire – July 1972

RMP in Northern Ireland, 3-16 Oct 83

Tale of the Troubles, September 2007

Tiffoney, Lance Corporal, *A Tour in Northern Ireland with the Scots Guard*, The Household Cavalry Journal 1998

Reports

Ministry of Defence, *Operation BANNER, An Analysis of Military Operations in Northern Ireland* (Army Code 71842), July 2006.

Police Ombudsman for Northern Ireland, *Report into a Complaint from Rita and John Restorick Regarding the Circumstances of the Murder of their son Lance Bombardier Stephen Restorick on 12th February 1997*

Widgery Report, *Report of the Tribual Appointed to Inquire into the Events on Sunday 30th January 1972*, HMSO, 1972

Television Programmes

BBC 2, *The Secret Peacemaker*, 26 March 2008

Websites

www.britains-smallwars.com
General Statistics
Lest We Forget 1969-2002
  Military casualties
  Royal Irish, Royal Ulster and Ulster Special Constabularies and Belfast Harbour
  Police casualties.
Across The Sea to Ireland..
www.operationbanner.com
Operation Banner Deaths – Roll of Honour
www.redcoat.info
Northern Ireland – Officer casualties
www.scottishloyalists.co.uk
Three Scottish Soldiers, March 9 1971
www.ulst.ac.uk
Chronology of the Conflict 1969 – 2001
Deployment of Troops: O'Dochartaigh, Niall, 1997 – The British Army

Index

252

weaponry and clothing, 24, 35, 91, 99, 110, 194, 220-1
see also Royal Marines
British Army, *UNITS*
3 Armoured Division Transport Regiment, 114
3 Infantry Brigade, 46, 58, 67-8, 80, 84, 100, 104, 105, 120, 126, 159, 162, 175, 197-8, 202
5 Infantry Brigade, 66
8 Infantry Brigade, 27, 48, 67, 80, 84, 100, 126, 162, 226
38 (Irish) Brigade, 229
39 Independent Infantry Brigade, 12-13, 47, 48, 66-7, 110, 125-6, 161, 177, 226, 227, 229
5 Airportable Brigade, 34, 46
19 Airportable Brigade, 39, 42-3
24 Airportable Brigade, 20, 27, 34, 37
39 Airportable Brigade, 12, 16, 17, 19, 20, 34
12 Armoured Brigade, 188
16 Parachute Brigade, 20, 37, 39, 139
Life Guards, 66, 75, 212-13
Blues and Royals, 69-70, 147-8, 202-3
Coldstream Guards, 67, 125
Grenadier Guards, 87-90, 93, 119, 206
Irish Guards, 202
Scots Guards, 67, 68, 98, 112, 161, 197-8, 212
Welsh Guards, 64, 66, 111-12, 144, 216
4/7th Dragoon Guards, 156
Queen's Dragoon Guards, 126, 162
Royal Scots Dragoon Guards, 71, 164
5th Inniskilling Dragoon Guards, 198
1 Argyll & Sutherland Highlanders (1A&SH), 58, 68, 80, 119, 125, 162, 220
1 Cheshires (ICR), 168
1 Devon & Dorsets (1D&D), 35, 183

Duke of Edinburgh's Royal Regt (DERR), 183, 206
1 Duke of Wellington's Regt (1DWR), 127
1 Glosters (IGR), 57, 94, 110
1 Gordon Highlanders, 68
1 Green Howards (1GH), 71, 122, 179
1 Hampshire Regt, 20, 21
14/20 Hussars, 45
15/19 Hussars, 126, 163
13/18 Hussars, 126
1 King's Regt, 64, 66, 126, 198
1 King's Own (Royal) Border Regt (1 KORBR), 153-4
1 King's Own Scottish Borderers (1KOSB), 33, 34, 67, 87, 110, 125, 197, 202
16/5 Lancers, 80
9/12 Lancers, 205
17/21 Lancers, 37-8, 56, 80, 125
1 Light Infantry (1LI), 16, 22, 65-6, 70-2, 96, 122, 179, 197-8
2 Light Infantry (2LI), 67, 87-8, 199, 205-6
3 Light Infantry (3LI), 20, 24, 37, 126, 216
94 (Locating) Regt, 36-7
1st Parachute Battn (1 Para), 25, 47-50, 52, 58, 66
2nd Parachute Battn (2 Para), 67, 157-60
3rd Parachute Battn (3 Para), 38, 87, 97-8, 154-5, 197, 202
1 Prince of Wales Yorkshire Light Infantry (1PWO), 16, 18, 19, 66
2 Princess of Wales Royal Regt, 227
1 Queen's Regt, 156, 200
2 Queen's Regt, 16, 34-5, 67, 93-4, 127
3 Queen's Regt, 87, 89-90, 125
1 Queen's Lancashire Regt (1 QLR), 51, 126, 171-2
1 Queen's Own Highlanders, 68, 112, 156, 157-9

Royal Anglian Regt, 66, 162, 184
Royal Armoured Corps, 83, 163, 165, 182, 230
Royal Gloucestershire, Berkshire & Wiltshire Regt, 217
1 Royal Green Jackets (1RGJ), 20, 47, 59, 75, 82, 106, 148, 162
3 Royal Green Jackets (3RGJ), 110-11
Royal Highland Fusiliers (RHF), 73, 74, 102
Royal Irish Rangers (RIRangers), 60, 198, 201
Royal Irish Regt (RIR), 201-2, 210, 220-1, 226-7
Royal Regt of Fusiliers (1RRF), 34, 66, 67, 69, 87, 122, 141, 161, 176, 202
1 Royal Regt of Wales (1RRW), 17-18, 19, 60, 65, 115, 200
1 Royal Scots (1RS), 32-3, 34, 67, 69, 126, 128, 129-30, 162, 178, 206
1 Royal Tank Regt (1RTR), 133
1 Royal Welsh Fusiliers (1 RWF), 161
1 Worcestershire & Sherwood Foresters, 126
Special Air Service (SAS) see Special Air Service (SAS)
Royal Artillery, Regts, Battn and Sqdns (RA), 36-7, 63, 66, 67, 68, 100-1, 125, 126, 165, 190, 206, 230
Royal Horse Artillery (RHA), 114-15, 126, 164, 215
120 Security Section (Lisburn), 32
Army Air Corps (AAC), 80-1, 94, 230
Royal Engineers, 13, 25, 32, 34, 58, 60-1, 67, 68-9, 70, 71, 83, 85-6, 88, 90, 100, 101, 102, 111, 126, 127, 165, 173, 182, 183, 189, 212, 230
Royal Military Police (RMP), 55, 99, 127, 153, 182, 230

Royal Signals, 13, 20, 37, 38, 42-3, 56-7, 57, 106-7, 165, 177-8, 179, 226
Adjutant General's Corps, 201
APC Regiment, 100
Intelligence Corps, 74-5, 99, 103-5, 233
REME, 13, 57, 99, 100, 104, 214
Royal Army Medical Corps (RAMC), 115-16, 194
Royal Army Ordnance Corps (RAOC), 13, 54, 99, 113-14, 179
Explosive Ordnance Detachment (321 EOD), 54-9, 219, 226
Royal Army Veterinary Corps (RAVC), 59
Royal Corps of Transport (RCT), 12, 20, 64, 67, 90, 100-1, 114, 188, 201
Royal Logistics Corps (RLC), 54, 201, 210
Royal Pioneer Corps (RPC), 46, 165
Women's Royal Army Corps (WRAC), 74, 201
Women's Royal Army Corps (WRAC), 181 Provost Coy, 127
Brown, Gordon, 233
Browne, Albert (Loyalist), 110
Bryson, Jim, 111
Bullock, Pte Thomas (4 UDR), 86
Burns, Sean, 167
Burntollet (1969), 15
Bush, George W. (U.S. President), 224
Butcher, Sgt Anthony (ATO), 57-8
Butler, Edward, 142
Cahill, Joe, 28, 41
Callaghan, Mne Andrew (RM), 206
Callaghan, James, offers troops for NI, 17
Calledene, Maj Bernard (ATO), 58
Cameron, Lord, Report on August(1969) unrest, 23-4
Campbell, Gregory (UUP), 170

incidents
  comparison of type and
    resulting casualties, 236-7
  IRA attacks in England (1867-
    2001), 242-7
'Ingram, Martin' (pseudonym),
  alleged 'collusion' articles and
  book, 223
Intelligence, 99, 102-6, 161, 230
  alleged 'dirty tricks', 119-22,
    194
  Brigade and Battalion intelli-
    gence sections, 104-5
  British Services Security
    Organization, 182
  collusion with Loyalists
    suspected, 119-20, 222-4
  The Det, 74-5, 151
  'doomsday book' database, 63-
    4, 75
  Force Intelligence Unit, 194-5
  Force Research Unit (FRU),
    195-7, 223
  Four Square Laundry, 72-4
  Human, Electronic and Signals
    Intelligence, 106-7
  inter-agency relations collapse,
    203
  interrogation techniques, 39-
    41, 53, 76, 91, 231, 232
  IRA local intelligence, 87, 195
  liaison with RUC, 102, 105
  mapping, 64
  Military Reconnaissance Force
    (MRF), 73-4
  Naval Intelligence, 104
  'Northern Ireland: Future
    Terrorist Trends' (Glover),
    154
  photo montages, 197
  source/informant handling,
    104-5, 112, 195-6, 231
  Special Military Intelligence
    Unit (SMIU), 105, 195
  surveillance operations, 161,
    215-16
  Weapons Intelligence, 195
  see also MI5; MI6; Special Air
    Service
International Red Cross, prison
  visits, 163
internment, 13, 14, 39, 41-2, 61,
  92, 109, 110, 113, 122, 124,
  231

Intrepid, HMS, 66
Iraq, invasion of Kuwait (1990),
  201
Ireland
  Civil War (1922-23), 10
  Home Rule politics (19th-
    century to 1920), 5-6
  roots of conflict, 1-5, 10
  War of Independence (1919-
    21), 7-10
  see also Irish Free State (later
    Eire); Republic of Ireland
Irish Army, 19, 83-4, 84, 161,
  213, 239
Irish Citizen Army, 6
Irish Free State (later Eire), 10,
  12
  see also Republic of Ireland
Irish National Liberation Army
  (INLA), 30, 130, 154-5, 168,
  183, 217, 219, 239
Irish Naval Service, 84
Irish Parliamentary Party, 6, 7
Irish Republican Army ([Official]
  IRA), 5, 7, 7-14, 21, 24, 27-9,
  34, 46, 60, 230
  Aldershot bomb (Feb.1972),
    52, 139
  attacks on UDR, 163
  Border Campaign, 79-90
  civilian casualties and, 91
  internal punishments, 36, 213
  internment, 39, 41-2, 61, 122
  Marxist-Leninist philosophy,
    14-15, 232
  numbers killed, 239
  recruitment following
    Compton Report (1971), 42
  response to 'Bloody Sunday',
    51
  S-Plan, 10-11
  Special Convention (Dublin
    1969), 27-8
  split (1970), 28
  'supergrass' trials, 169
  see also Provisional IRA
    (PIRA)
Irish Republican Brotherhood
  (IRB), 5, 6, 8
Irish Republican Socialist Party
  (IRSP), 29-30
Irish Sunday Business Post
  (newspaper), 141
The Irish Times, 65, 222

Powell, Cpl David (17/21 Lancers), 56
Powell, Enoch, 117
Price, Dolores and Marion, 140, 142
Price, Sgt Philip (Welsh Gds), 64
propaganda, 42, 134, 223, 231-2
  see also psychological warfare
Protestant Action Force (PAF), 198
Protestant Action Group (PAG), 117
Protestant Orange marches, 3, 17, 32-3, 34, 212, 212-13, 219, 222
Provisional IRA (PIRA), 27-9, 38, 60, 131, 136, 151, 157, 176-9, 222
  alliances with other radical groups, 134
  armament and weapons, 82, 133, 136, 166, 170, 173, 190, 208-9, 211
  arrests of leaders (1973), 110-12
  attacks in Germany, 181-4, 188-9
  'Bloody Friday' (July 1972), 64-5
  Border Campaign, 79-90
  breaks agreement on hospitals, 194
  campaigns in England, 38, 54, 60, 139-49, 175-6, 199-201, 203-4, 207-9, 214, 242-7
  ceasefires, 118, 144, 210, 214, 225
  civilian casualties and, 91, 143, 144, 197
  Continuity IRA split, 169
  East Tyrone Brigade, 84, 85, 123, 172-80
  fatalities (1969-2001), 239
  Green Book, 130-1, 134-7, 173
  hunger strikes, 166
  indoctrination and training, 134-5, 137
  infiltrated by British Security Forces, 135, 230
  informers, 112, 175, 195, 225
  internal punishments, 36, 195
  Internal Security Department, 195

  internment and, 39, 41-2, 61, 109, 122
  interrogation methods, 134, 155, 195, 231
  juvenile activists, 112
  local intelligence networks, 87, 195, 198
  The Long War strategy, 123, 131-7, 181-91
  Marxist-Leninist philosophy, 130-7, 232
  and Military Intelligence, 73-4
  military structure, 132-3
  negotiations with British, 60-1, 109, 140, 180
  offensives (1971-73), 45-61, 63
  opposed by Irish military and Gardai, 83-4
  psychological effect on of SAS, 156-7
  publicity successes, 133-4
  secret meeting with Protestant clergy (1974), 117-18
  Shankill Rd fish and chip shop bomb, 204-5
  South Armagh Brigade, 86-90, 110, 123, 158-60, 197-9
  South Armagh Sniper, 205-7, 215-16
  'supergrass' trials, 169
  support from Central and South America, 123
  support from NORAID, 30, 133, 232
  testing time for Mrs Thatcher, 162-5
  'Tet' Offensive (late 1980s), 170, 183
  train hijack, 88
  Warrenpoint ambush, 158-9
  women, 102, 132, 140, 147
  see also Irish Republican Army ([Official] IRA)
Provisional Sinn Fein, 28-9, 166, 199, 215, 224
  'ballot paper and Armalite' strategy, 167
  ceasefire ultimatum from London and Dublin (1997), 217
  cessation of military operations announced, 210

267

271